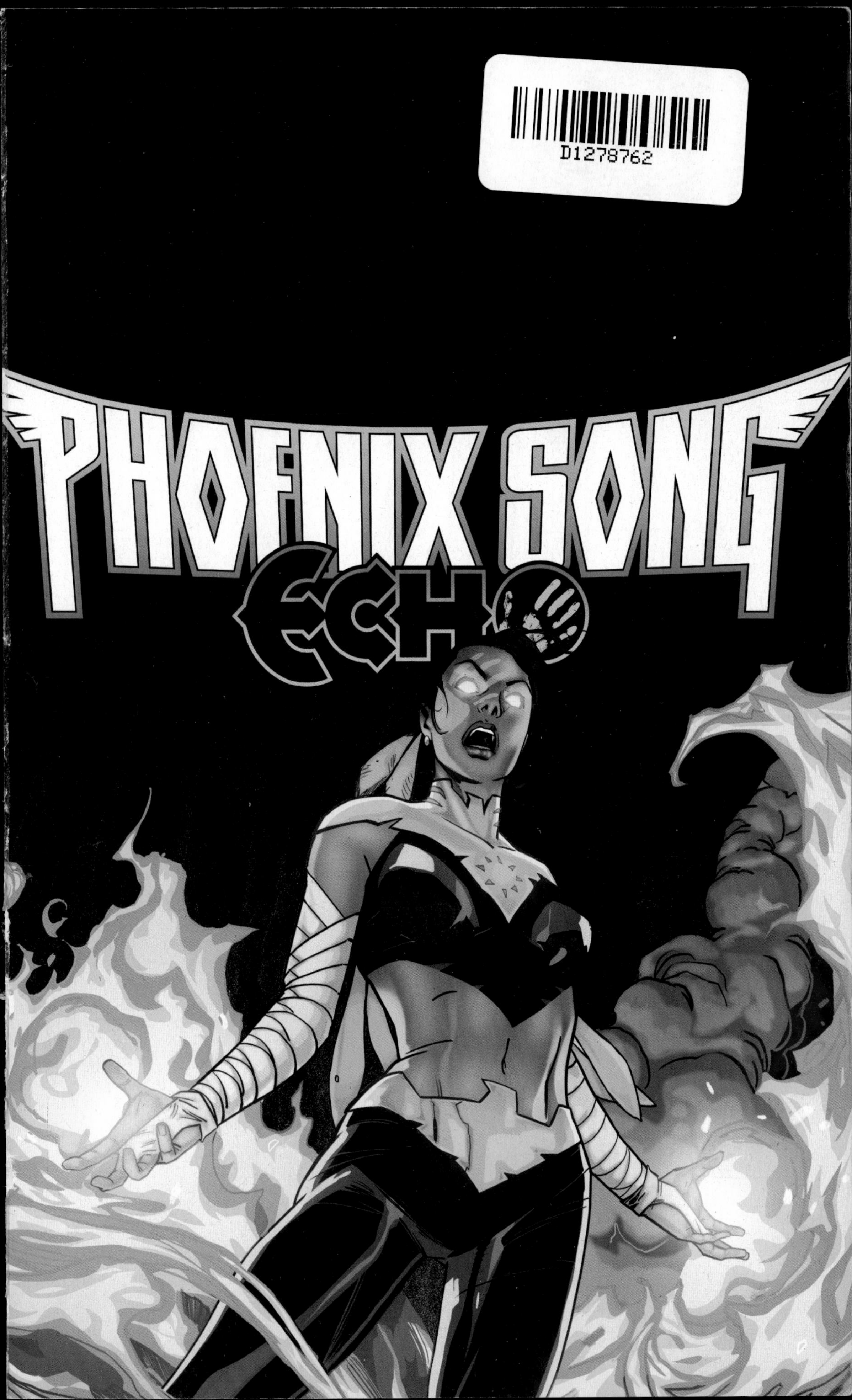
PHOENIX SONG
ECHO

Born deaf, **Maya Lopez**, A.K.A. **Echo**, was an otherwise happy child until the **Kingpin** murdered her father and blamed it on **Daredevil**, raising Maya as his own daughter for years. Maya eventually learned the truth, rejected her adoptive father and joined the ranks of super heroes thanks to the photographic reflexes that make her an unparalleled dancer and hand-to-hand combatant.

PHOENIX SONG: ECHO

COLLECTION EDITOR **JENNIFER GRÜNWALD**
ASSISTANT EDITOR **DANIEL KIRCHHOFFER**
ASSISTANT MANAGING EDITOR **MAIA LOY**
ASSOCIATE MANAGER, TALENT RELATIONS **LISA MONTALBANO**
VP PRODUCTION & SPECIAL PROJECTS **JEFF YOUNGQUIST**
SVP PRINT, SALES & MARKETING **DAVID GABRIEL**
BOOK DESIGNER **STACIE ZUCKER**
EDITOR IN CHIEF **C.B. CEBULSKI**

PHOENIX SONG: ECHO. Contains material originally published in magazine form as PHOENIX SONG: ECHO (2021) #1-5. First printing 2022. ISBN 978-1-302-93026-4. Published by MARVEL WORLDWIDE, INC., a subsidiary of MARVEL ENTERTAINMENT, LLC. OFFICE OF PUBLICATION: 1290 Avenue of the Americas, New York, NY 10104.

Printed in Canada. KEVIN FEIGE, Chief Creative Officer; DAN BUCKLEY, President, Marvel Entertainment; JOE QUESADA, EVP & Creative Director; DAVID BOGART, Associate Publisher & SVP of Talent Affairs; TOM BREVOORT, VP, Executive Editor; NICK LOWE, Executive Editor, VP of Content, Digital Publishing; DAVID GABRIEL, VP of Print & Digital Publishing; MARK ANNUNZIATO, VP of Planning & Forecasting; JEFF YOUNGQUIST, VP of Production & Special Projects; ALEX MORALES, Director of Publishing Operations; DAN EDINGTON, Director of Editorial Operations; RICKEY PURDIN, Director of Talent Relations; JENNIFER GRÜNWALD, Director of Production & Special Projects; SUSAN CRESPI, Production Manager; STAN LEE, Chairman Emeritus. For information regarding advertising in Marvel Comics or on Marvel.com, please contact Vit DeBellis, Custom Solutions & Integrated Advertising Manager, at vdebellis@marvel.com. For Marvel subscription inquiries, please call 888-511-5480. **Manufactured between 2/11/2022 and 3/15/2022 by SOLISCO PRINTERS, SCOTT, QC, CANADA.**

10 9 8 7 6 5 4 3 2 1

Still, she was the backup, the stealth agent...until the **Phoenix Force** came searching for a champion and pitted heroes against one another. It chose Maya as its new host, even though Maya lost her fight against **Namor**. No one really understands why, least of all Maya, but she must have a purpose in this cosmos...

REBECCA ROANHORSE
WRITER

LUCA MARESCA (#1-5) & KYLE CHARLES (#2-4)
ARTISTS

CARLOS LOPEZ (#1-5) & BRYAN VALENZA (#2-4)
COLOR ARTISTS

VC's ARIANA MAHER
LETTERER

CORY SMITH WITH ALEJANDRO SÁNCHEZ (#1), DAVID CURIEL (#2-3) & CARLOS LOPEZ (#4-5)
COVER ARTISTS

JAY BOWEN
LOGO

ANITA OKOYE
ASSISTANT EDITOR

SARAH BRUNSTAD
EDITOR

TOM BREVOORT
EXECUTIVE EDITOR

1

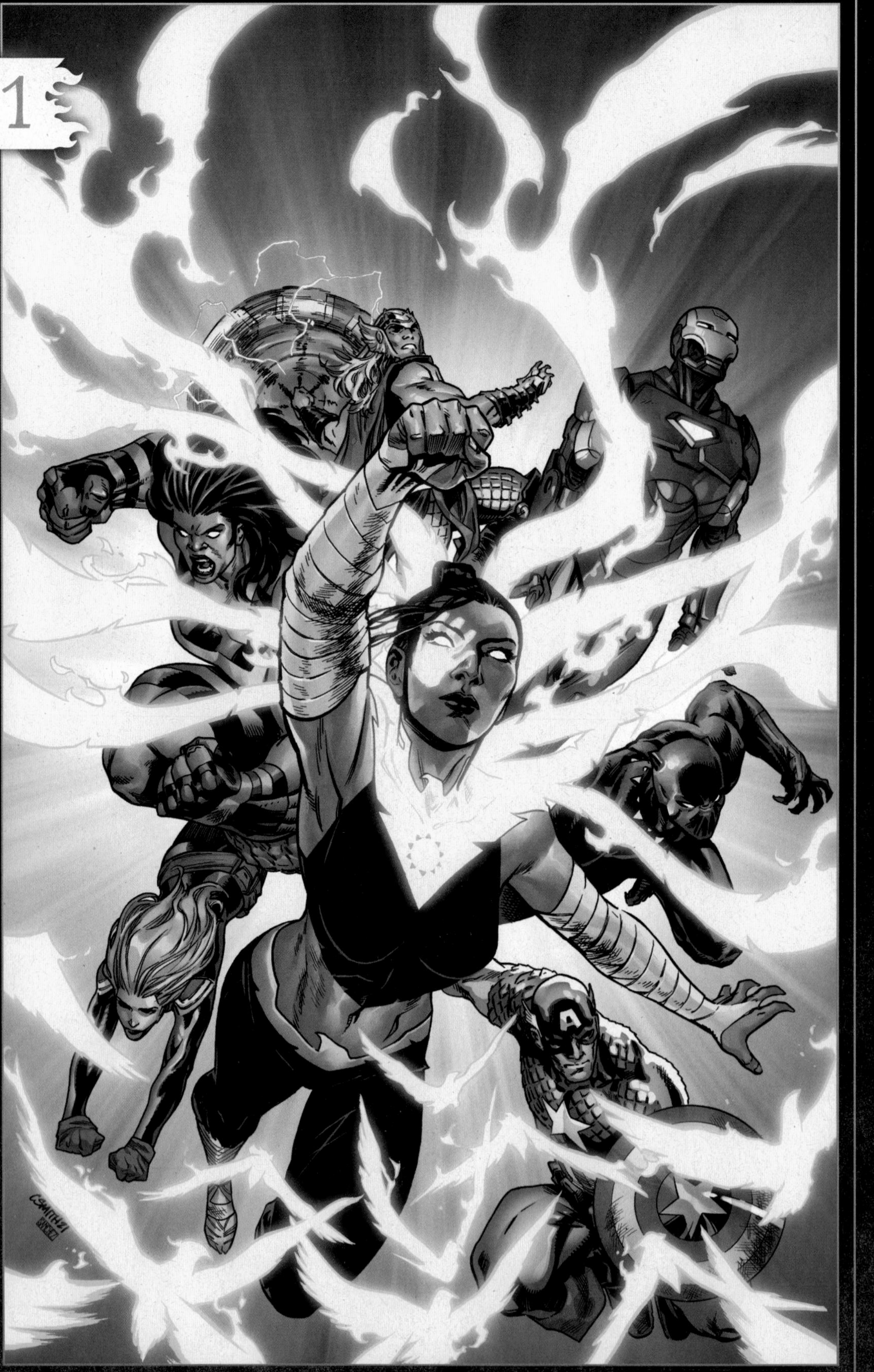

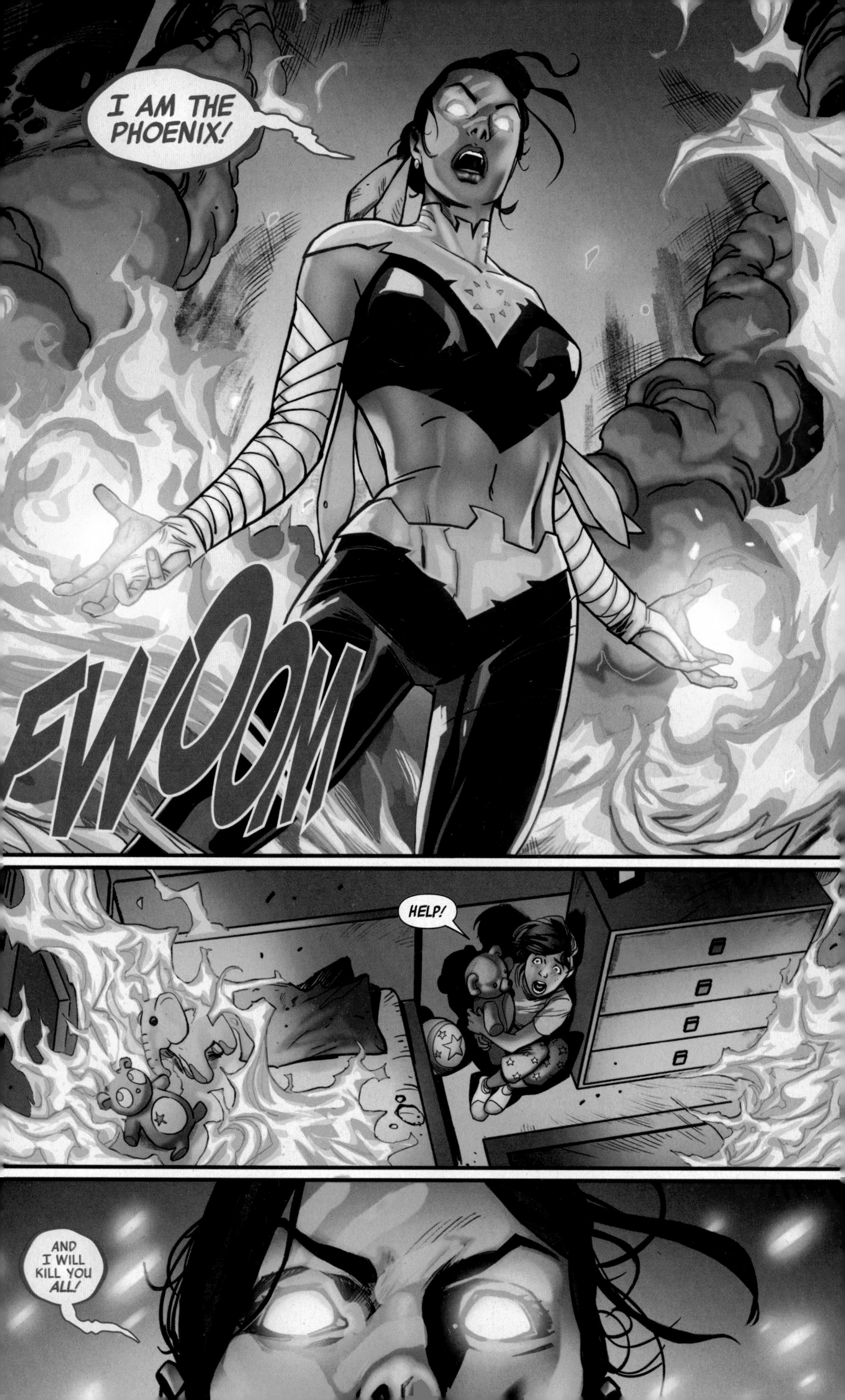
I AM THE PHOENIX!
FWOOM
HELP!
AND I WILL KILL YOU ALL!

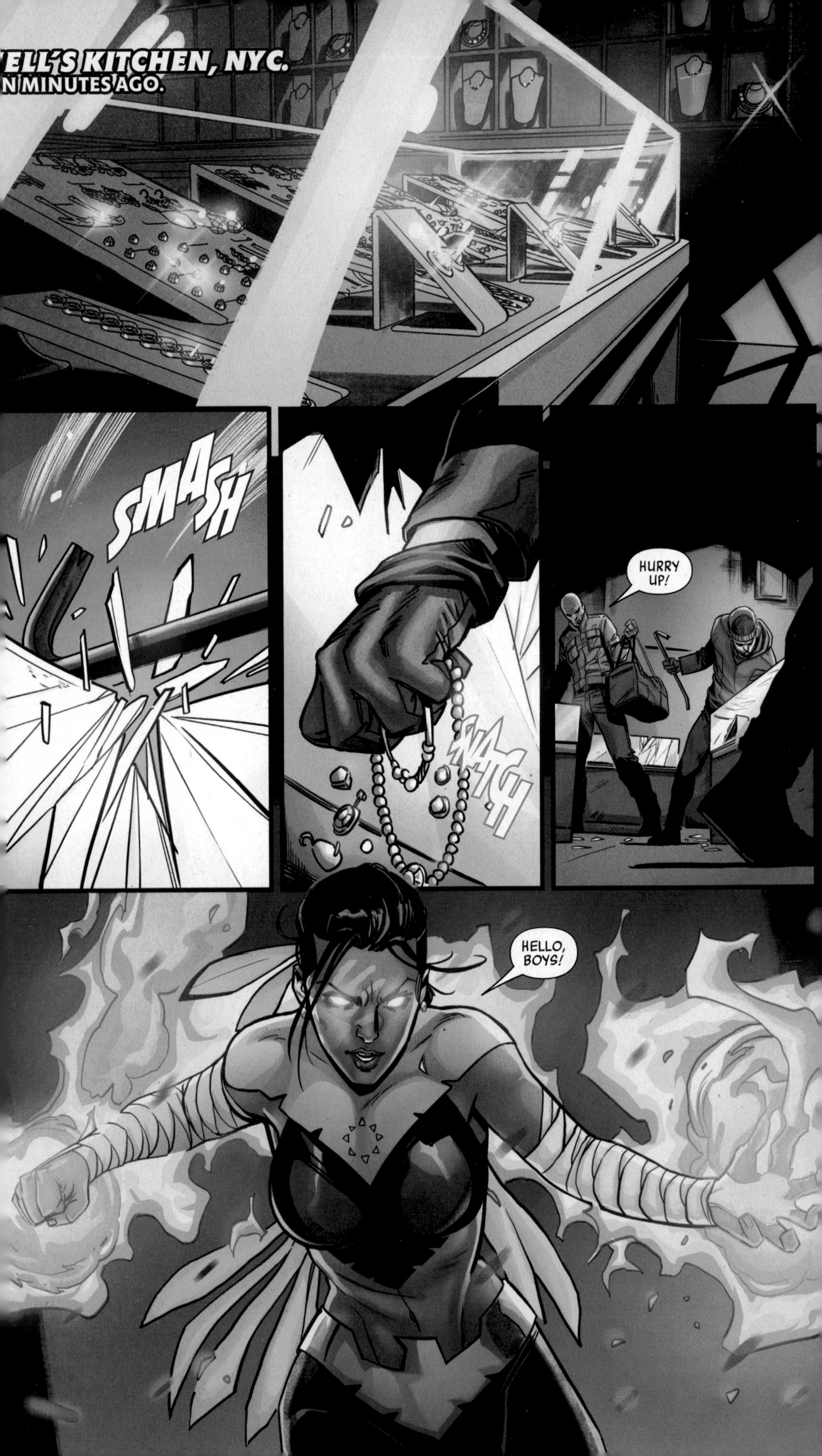
ELL'S KITCHEN, NYC.
N MINUTES AGO.
SMASH
SNATCH
HURRY UP!
HELLO, BOYS!

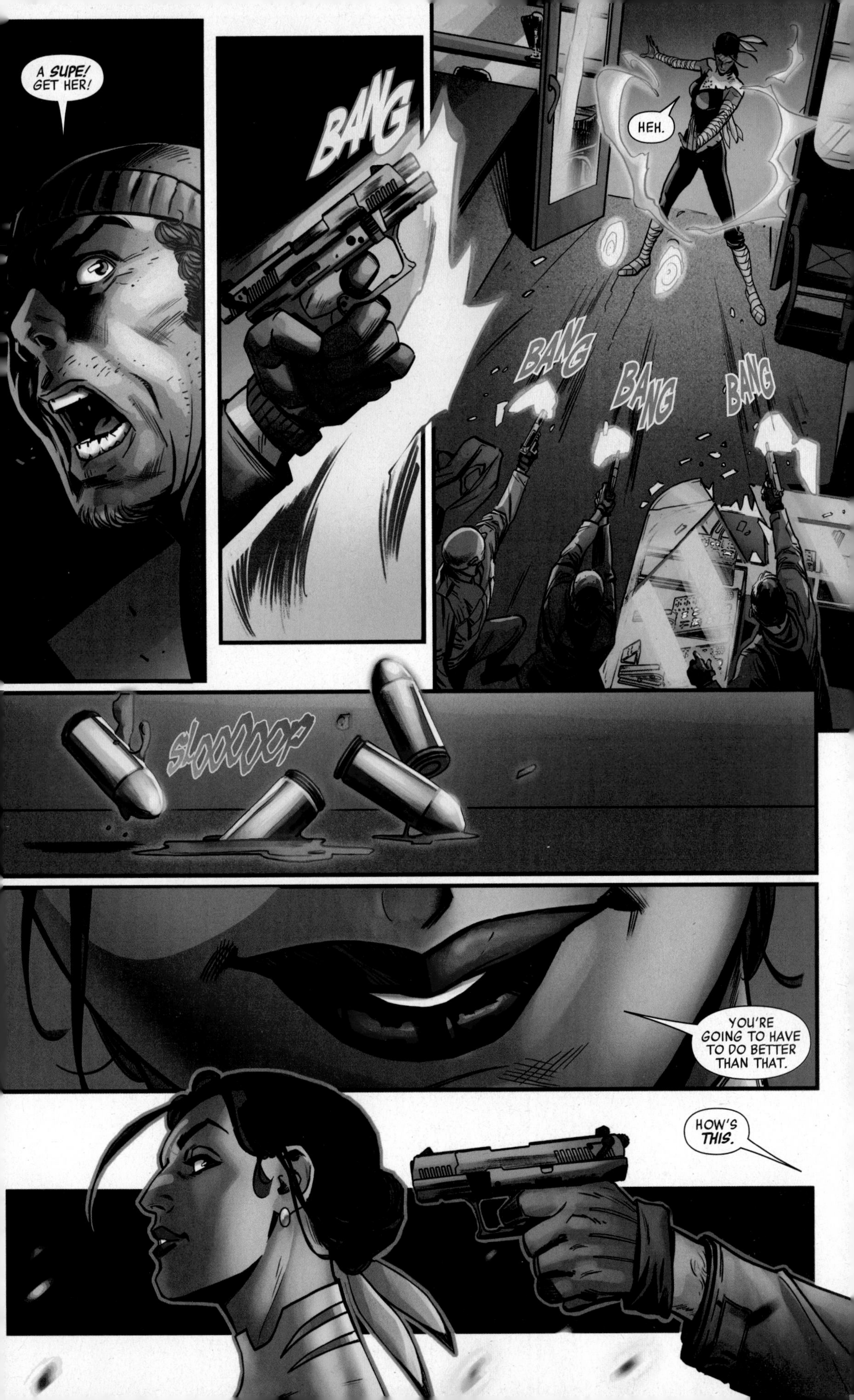
A SUPE! GET HER!
BANG
HEH.
BANG
BANG
BANG
SLOOOOOP
YOU'RE GOING TO HAVE TO DO BETTER THAN THAT.
HOW'S THIS.

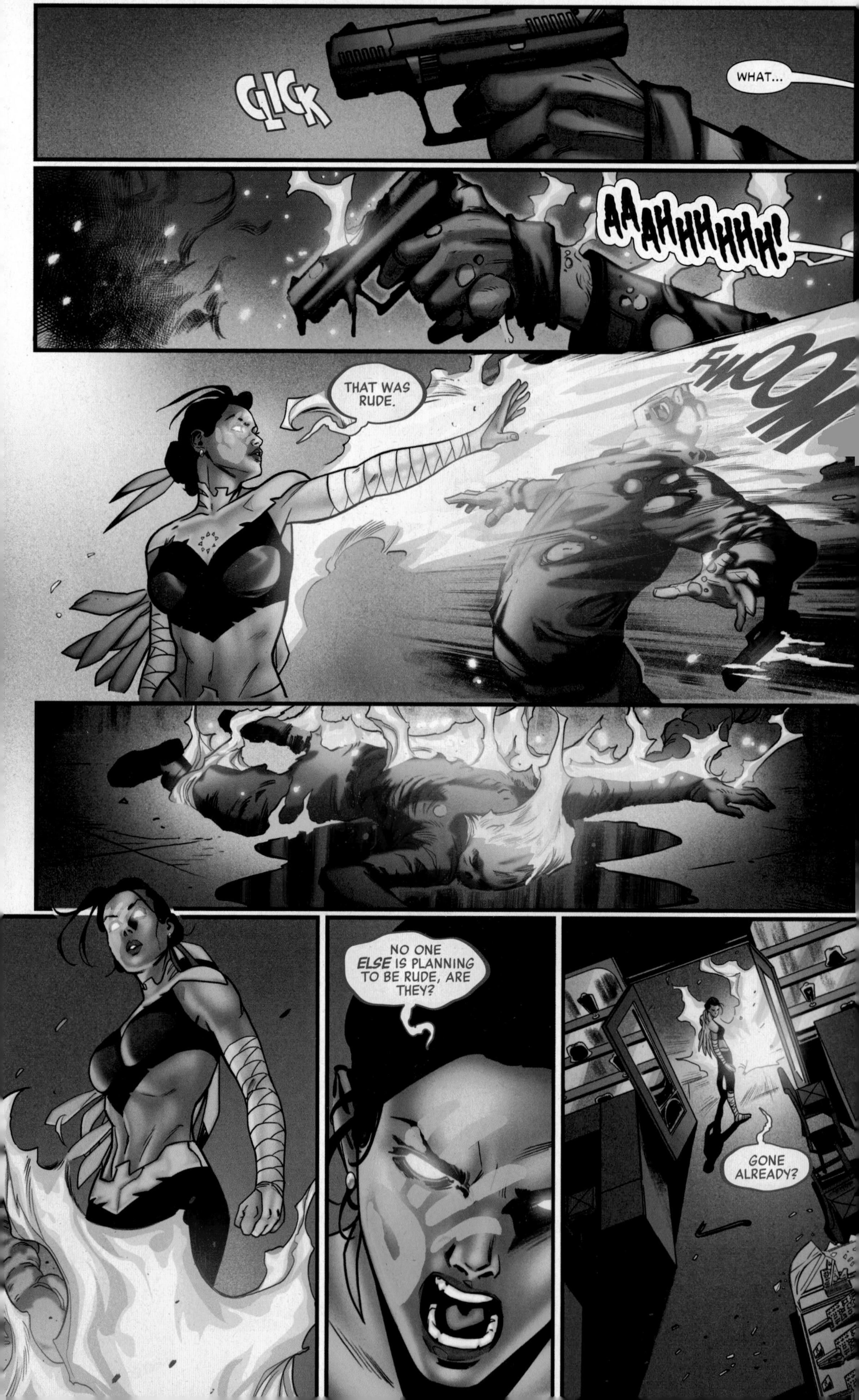
CLICK
WHAT...
AAAHHHHHH!
THAT WAS RUDE.
FWOOM
NO ONE *ELSE* IS PLANNING TO BE RUDE, ARE THEY?
GONE ALREADY?

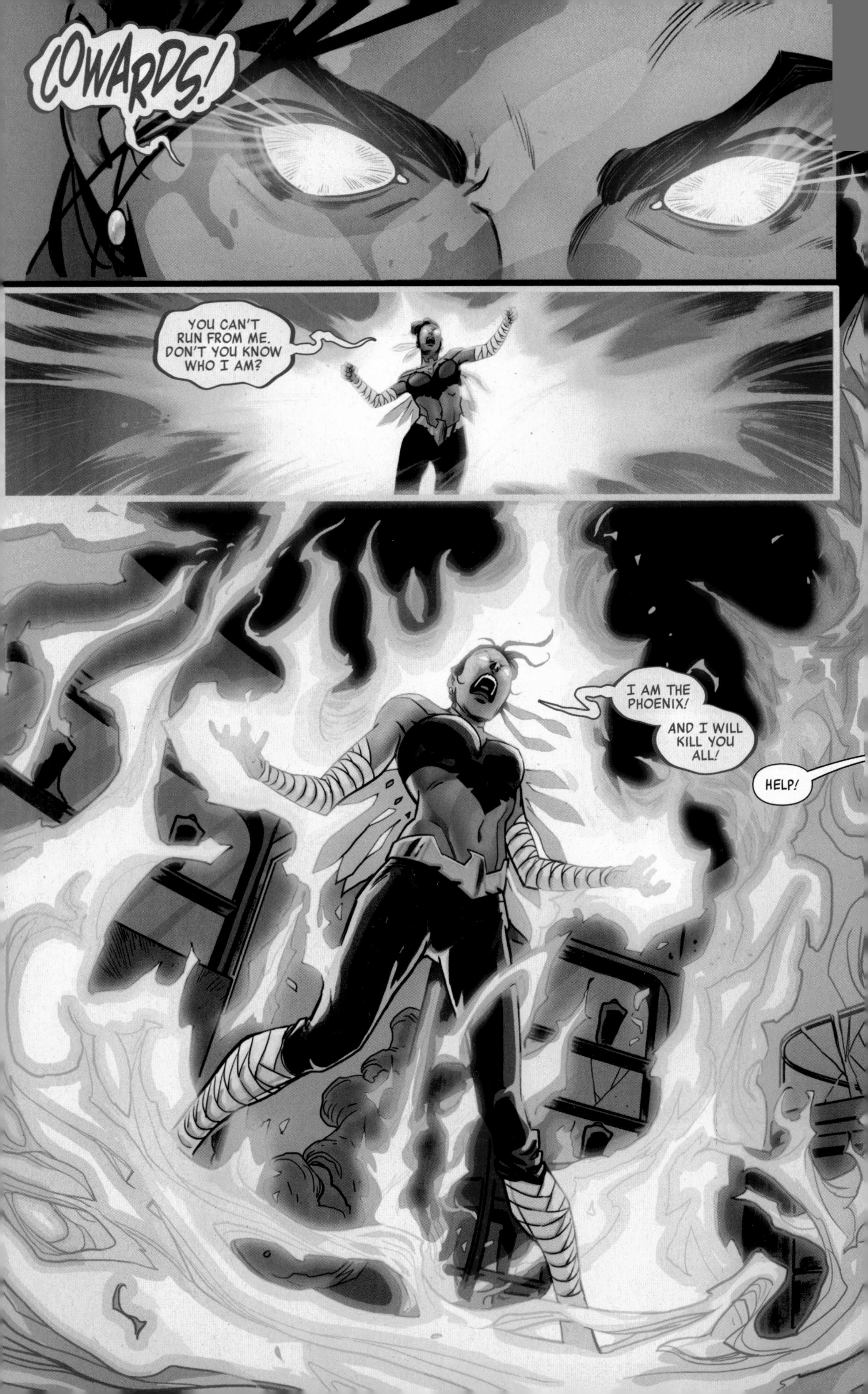
COWARDS!
YOU CAN'T RUN FROM ME. DON'T YOU KNOW WHO I AM?
I AM THE PHOENIX!
AND I WILL KILL YOU ALL!
HELP!

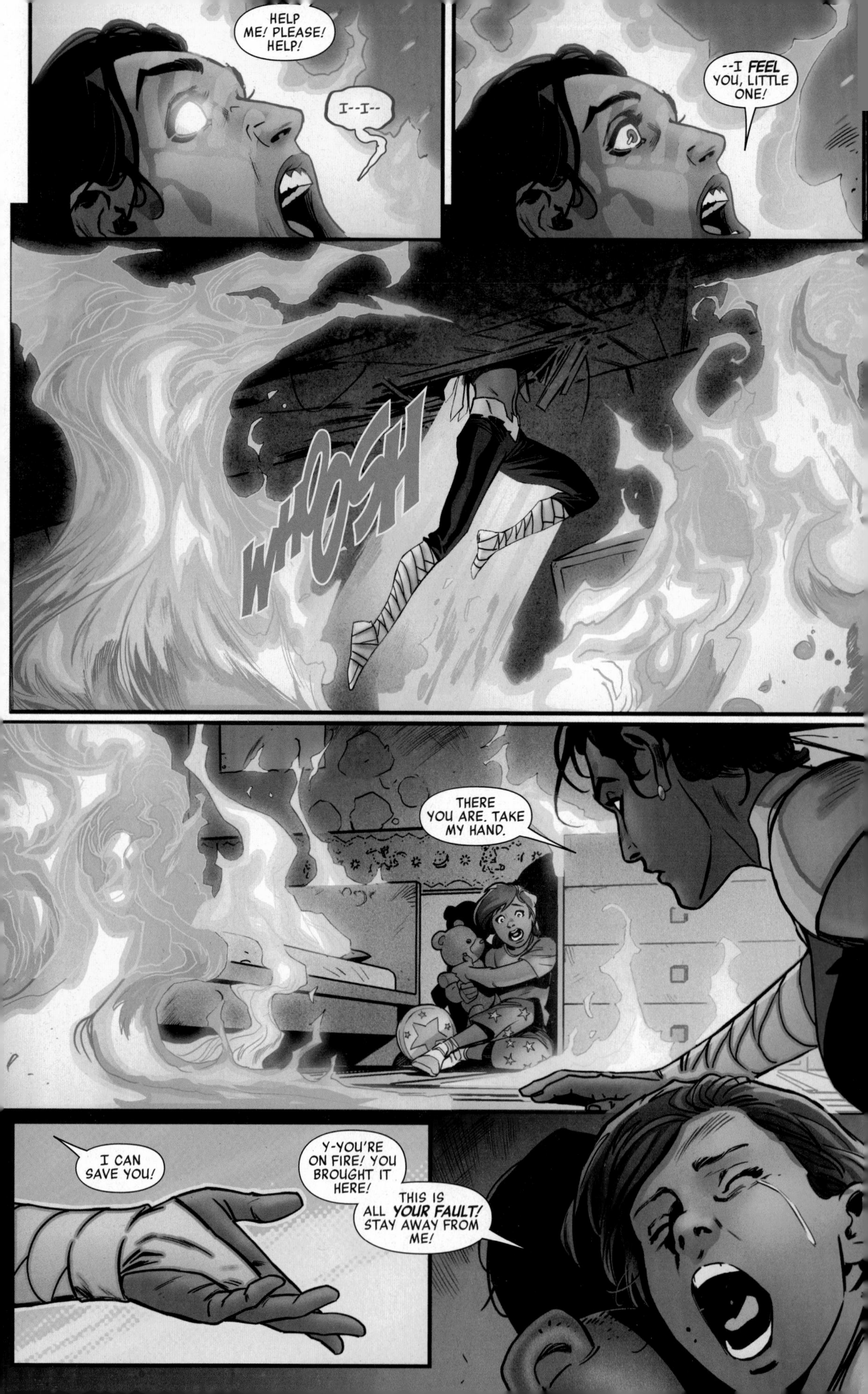
HELP ME! PLEASE! HELP!
I--I--
--I FEEL YOU, LITTLE ONE!
WHOOSH
THERE YOU ARE. TAKE MY HAND.
I CAN SAVE YOU!
Y-YOU'RE ON FIRE! YOU BROUGHT IT HERE!
THIS IS ALL YOUR FAULT! STAY AWAY FROM ME!

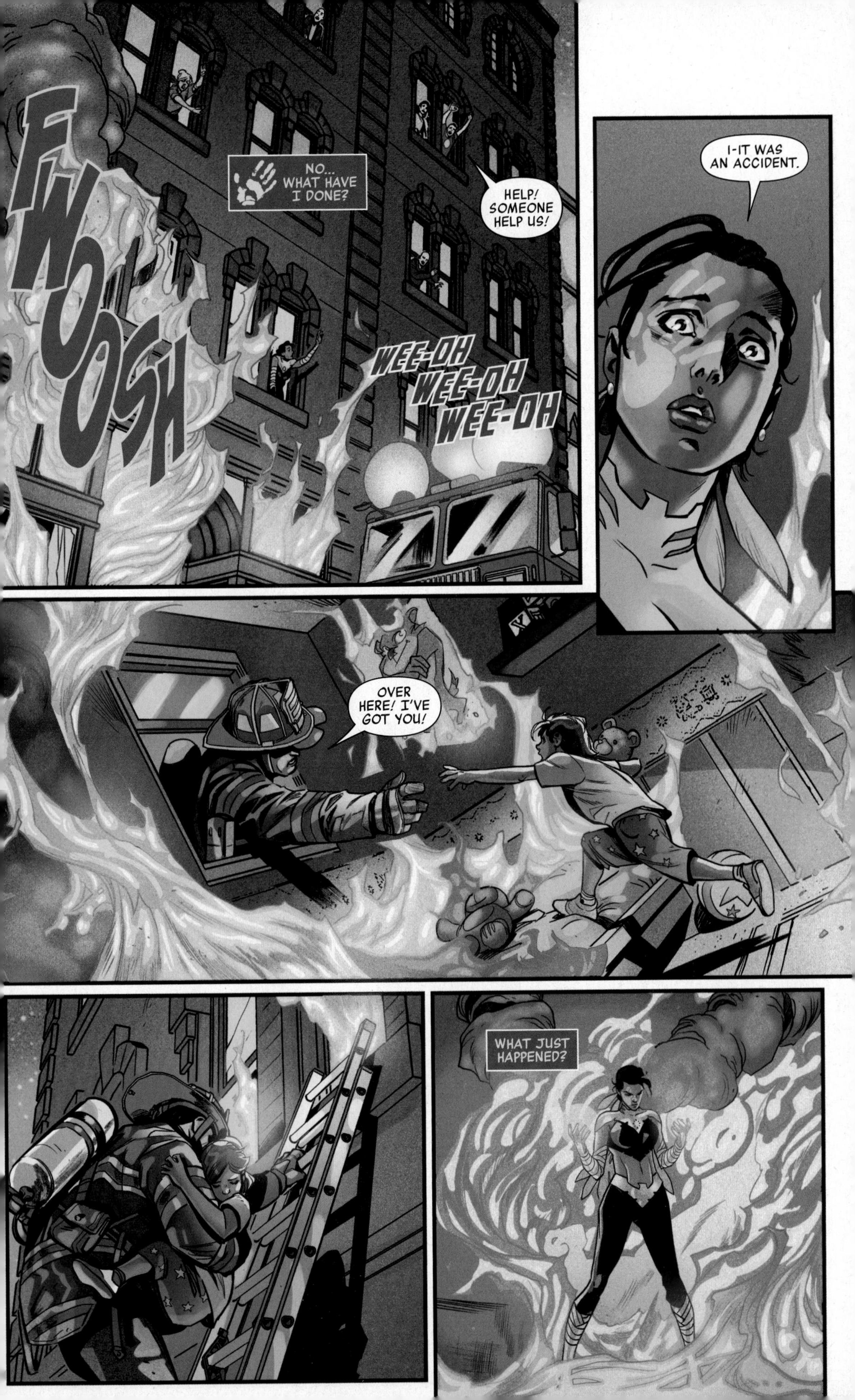
FWOOSH
NO... WHAT HAVE I DONE?
HELP! SOMEONE HELP US!
WEE-OH WEE-OH WEE-OH
I-IT WAS AN ACCIDENT.
OVER HERE! I'VE GOT YOU!
WHAT JUST HAPPENED?

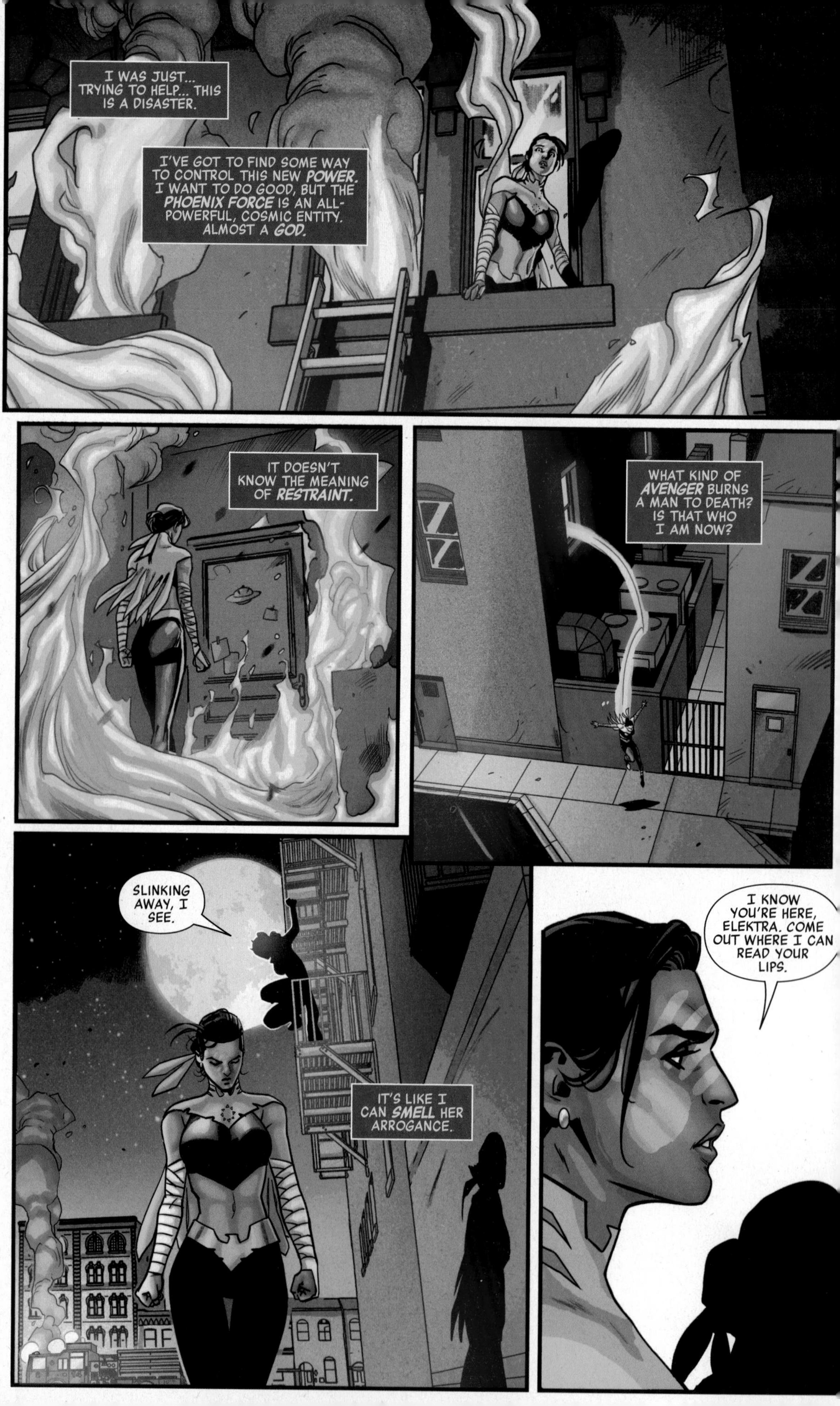
I WAS JUST... TRYING TO HELP... THIS IS A DISASTER.
I'VE GOT TO FIND SOME WAY TO CONTROL THIS NEW POWER. I WANT TO DO GOOD, BUT THE PHOENIX FORCE IS AN ALL-POWERFUL, COSMIC ENTITY. ALMOST A GOD.
IT DOESN'T KNOW THE MEANING OF RESTRAINT.
WHAT KIND OF AVENGER BURNS A MAN TO DEATH? IS THAT WHO I AM NOW?
SLINKING AWAY, I SEE.
IT'S LIKE I CAN SMELL HER ARROGANCE.
I KNOW YOU'RE HERE, ELEKTRA. COME OUT WHERE I CAN READ YOUR LIPS.

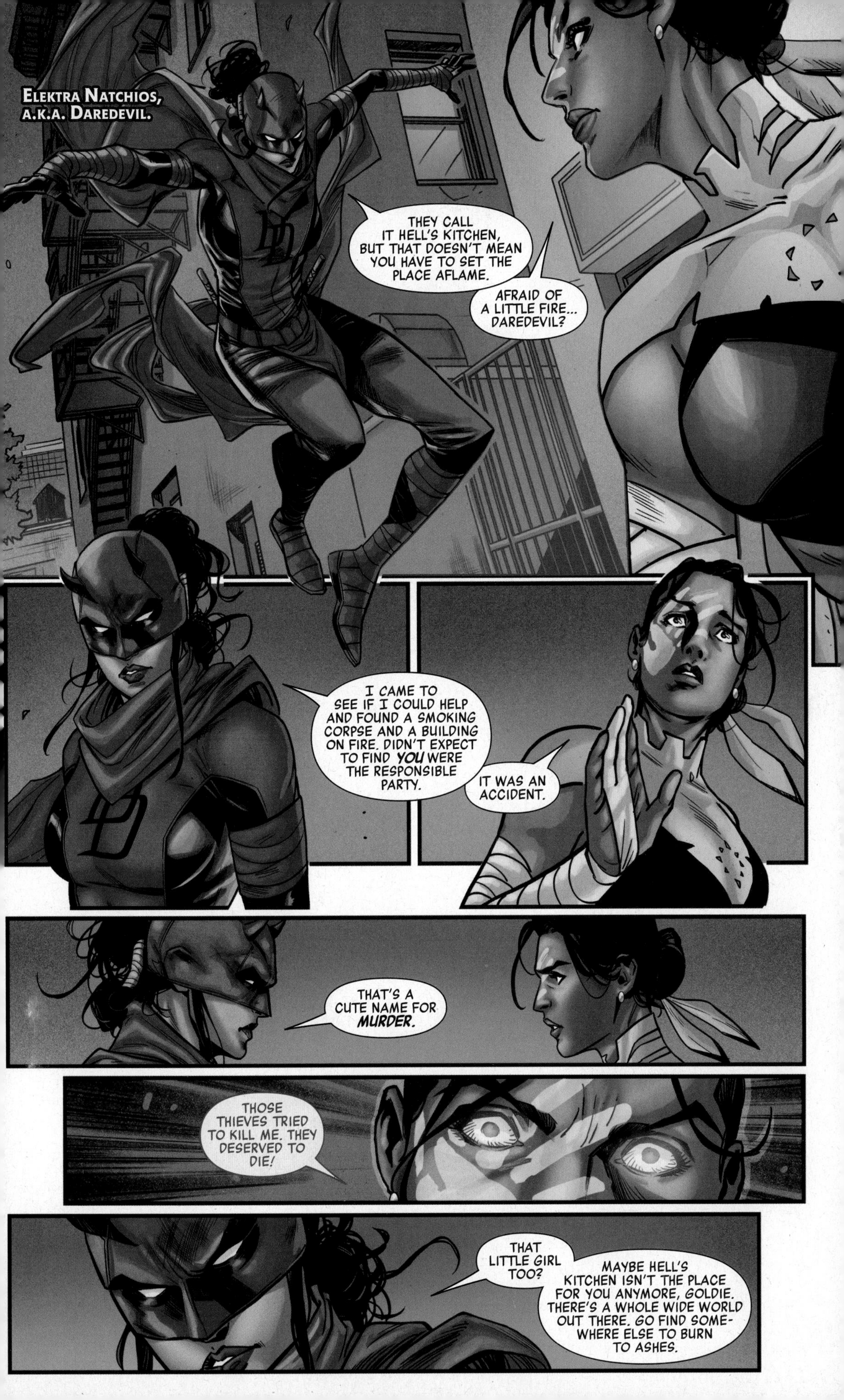
ELEKTRA NATCHIOS, A.K.A. DAREDEVIL.
THEY CALL IT HELL'S KITCHEN, BUT THAT DOESN'T MEAN YOU HAVE TO SET THE PLACE AFLAME.
AFRAID OF A LITTLE FIRE... DAREDEVIL?
I CAME TO SEE IF I COULD HELP AND FOUND A SMOKING CORPSE AND A BUILDING ON FIRE. DIDN'T EXPECT TO FIND *YOU* WERE THE RESPONSIBLE PARTY.
IT WAS AN ACCIDENT.
THAT'S A CUTE NAME FOR *MURDER.*
THOSE THIEVES TRIED TO KILL ME. THEY DESERVED TO DIE!
THAT LITTLE GIRL TOO?
MAYBE HELL'S KITCHEN ISN'T THE PLACE FOR YOU ANYMORE, GOLDIE. THERE'S A WHOLE WIDE WORLD OUT THERE. GO FIND SOME-WHERE ELSE TO BURN TO ASHES.

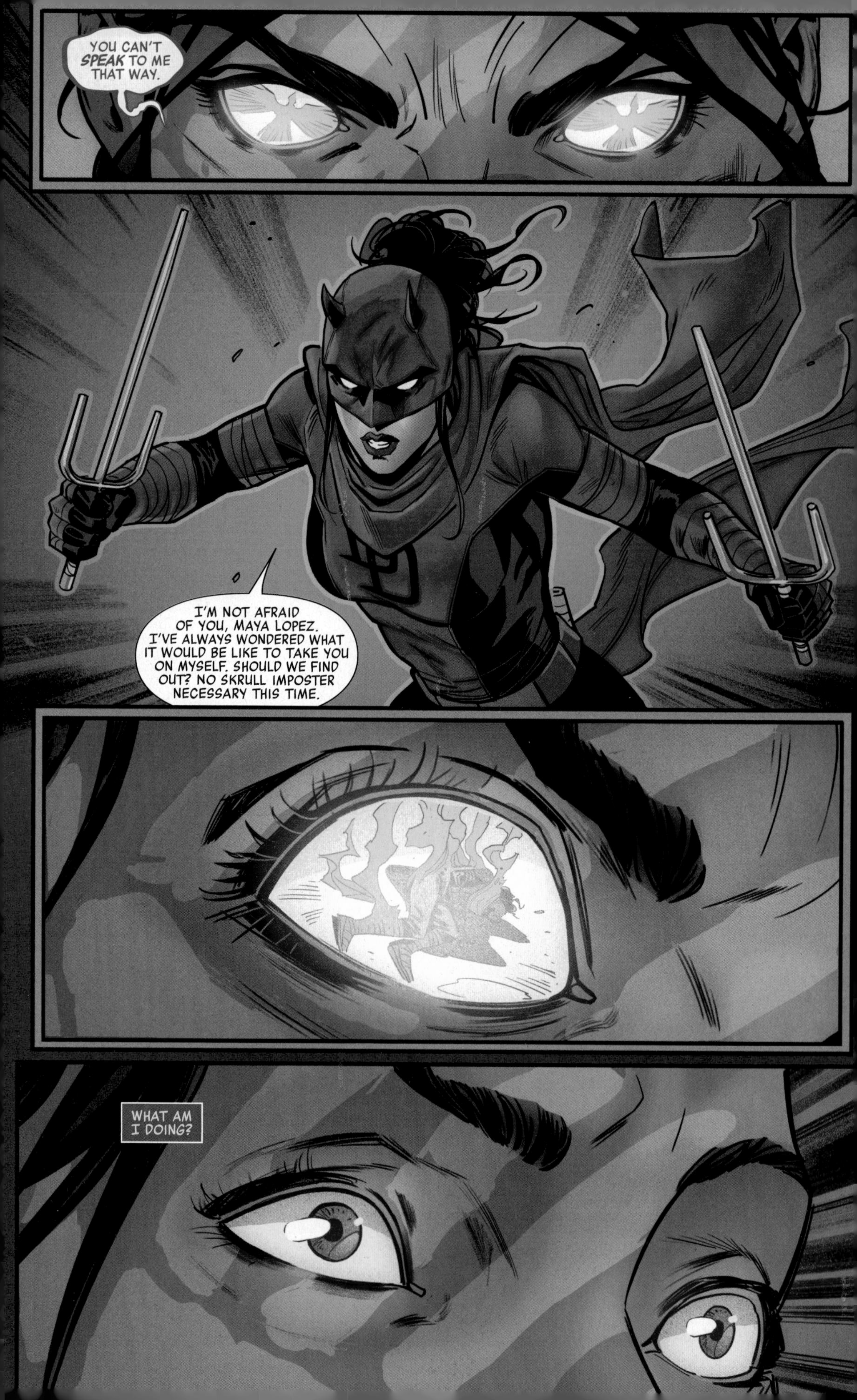
YOU CAN'T SPEAK TO ME THAT WAY.
I'M NOT AFRAID OF YOU, MAYA LOPEZ. I'VE ALWAYS WONDERED WHAT IT WOULD BE LIKE TO TAKE YOU ON MYSELF. SHOULD WE FIND OUT? NO SKRULL IMPOSTER NECESSARY THIS TIME.
WHAT AM I DOING?

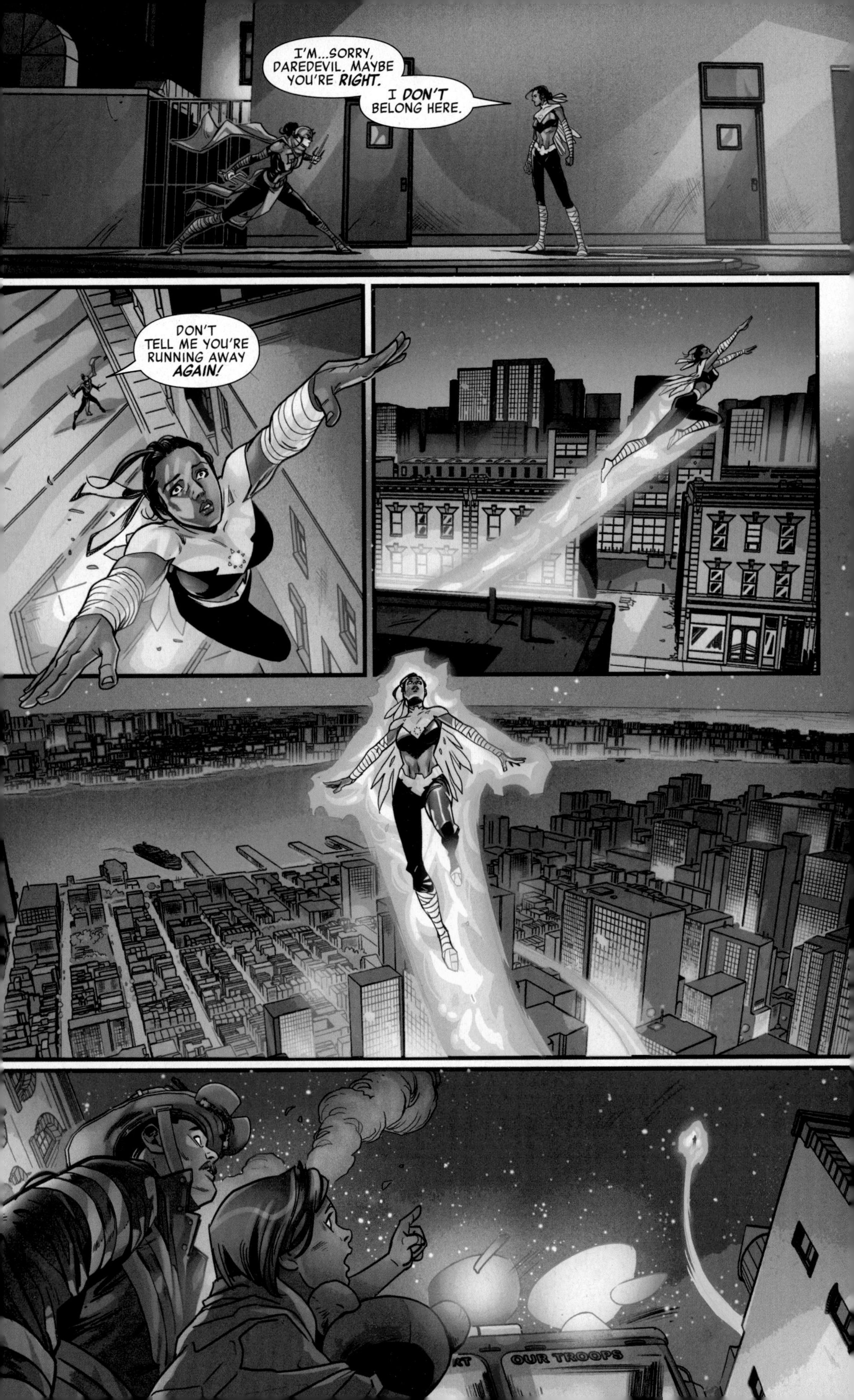
I'M...SORRY, DAREDEVIL. MAYBE YOU'RE RIGHT.
I DON'T BELONG HERE.
DON'T TELL ME YOU'RE RUNNING AWAY AGAIN!
OUR TROOPS

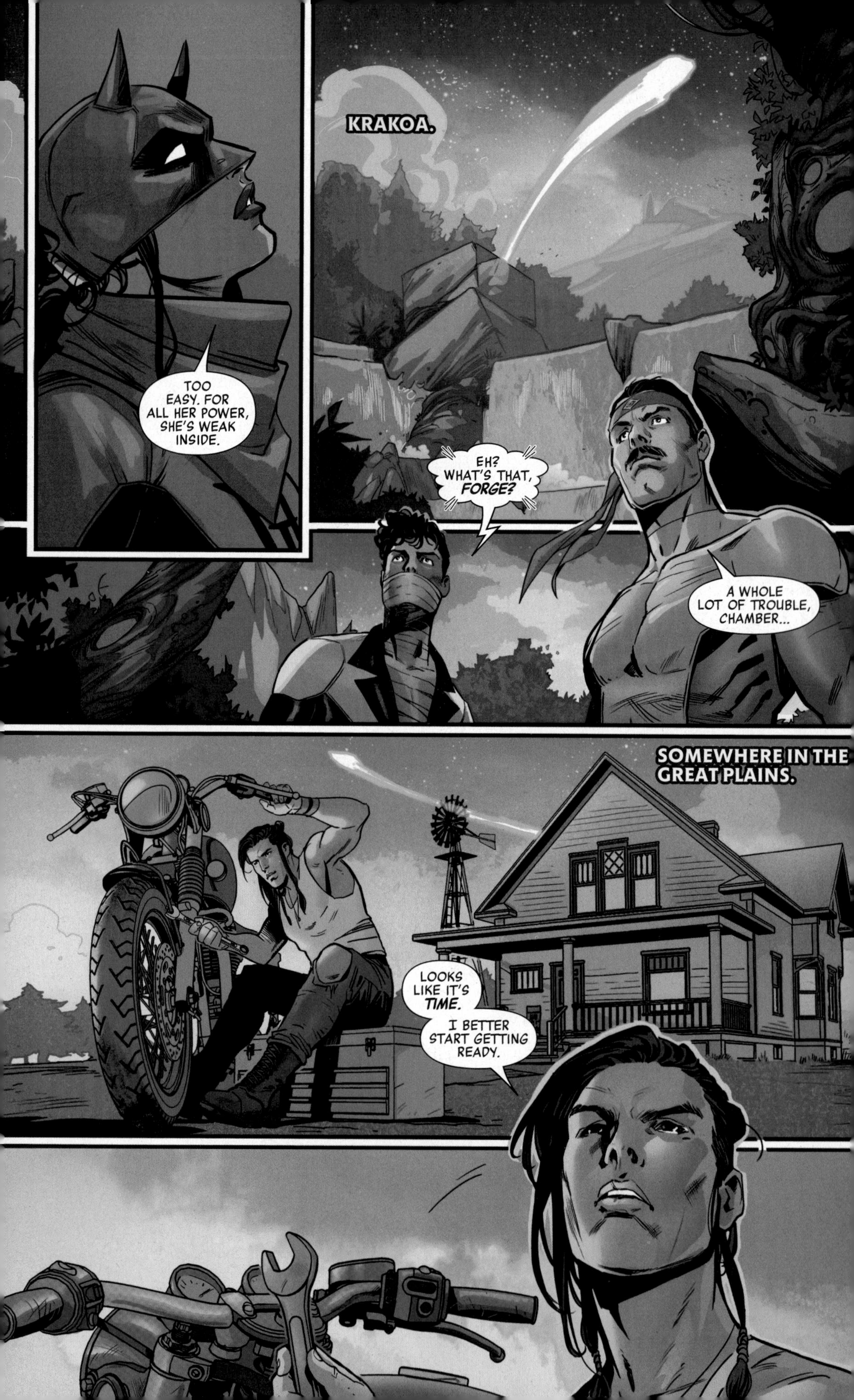
KRAKOA.
TOO EASY. FOR ALL HER POWER, SHE'S WEAK INSIDE.
EH? WHAT'S THAT, FORGE?
A WHOLE LOT OF TROUBLE, CHAMBER...
SOMEWHERE IN THE GREAT PLAINS.
LOOKS LIKE IT'S TIME.
I BETTER START GETTING READY.

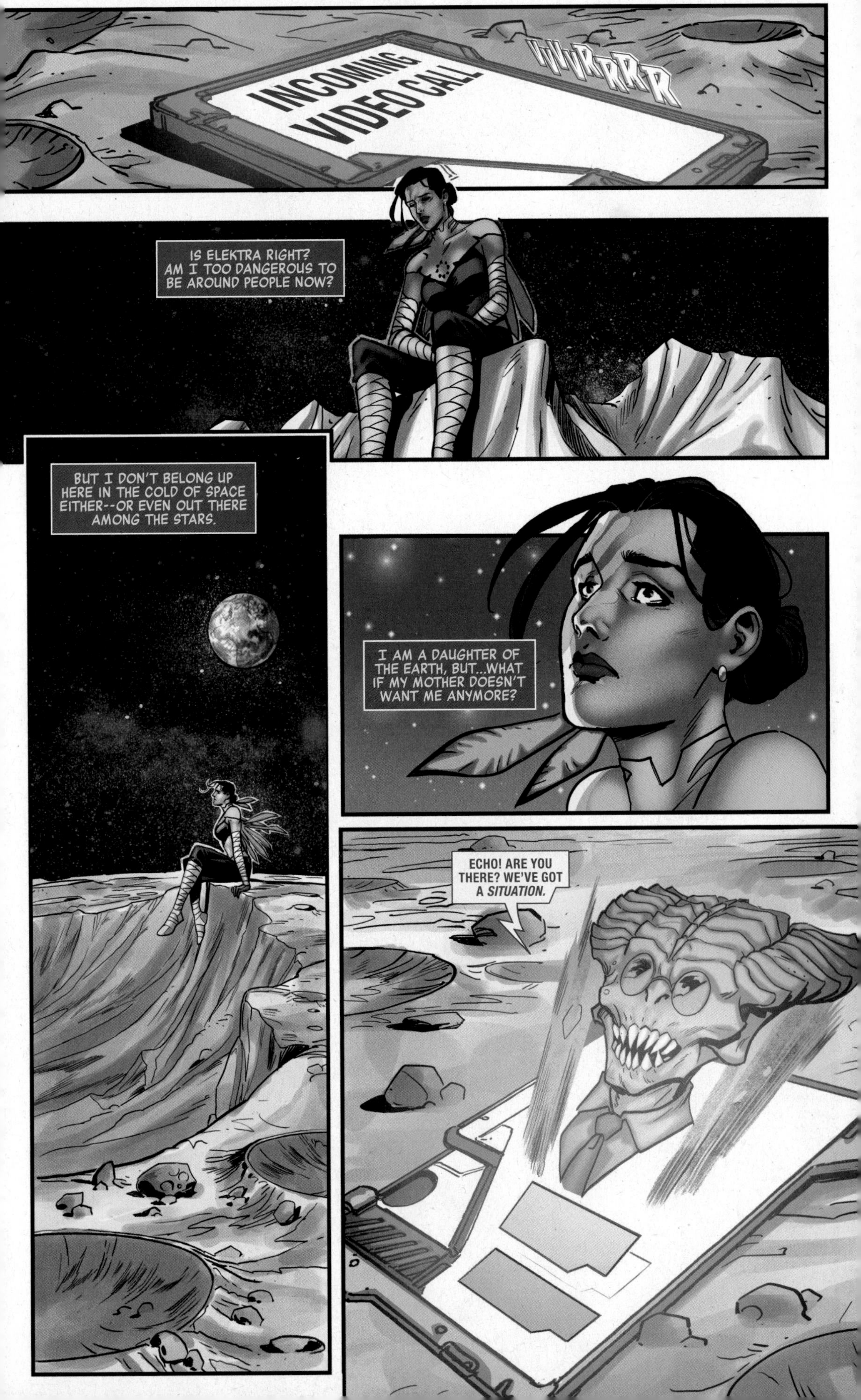
INCOMING VIDEO CALL
VVVRRRR
IS ELEKTRA RIGHT? AM I TOO DANGEROUS TO BE AROUND PEOPLE NOW?
BUT I DON'T BELONG UP HERE IN THE COLD OF SPACE EITHER--OR EVEN OUT THERE AMONG THE STARS.
I AM A DAUGHTER OF THE EARTH, BUT...WHAT IF MY MOTHER DOESN'T WANT ME ANYMORE?
ECHO! ARE YOU THERE? WE'VE GOT A *SITUATION.*

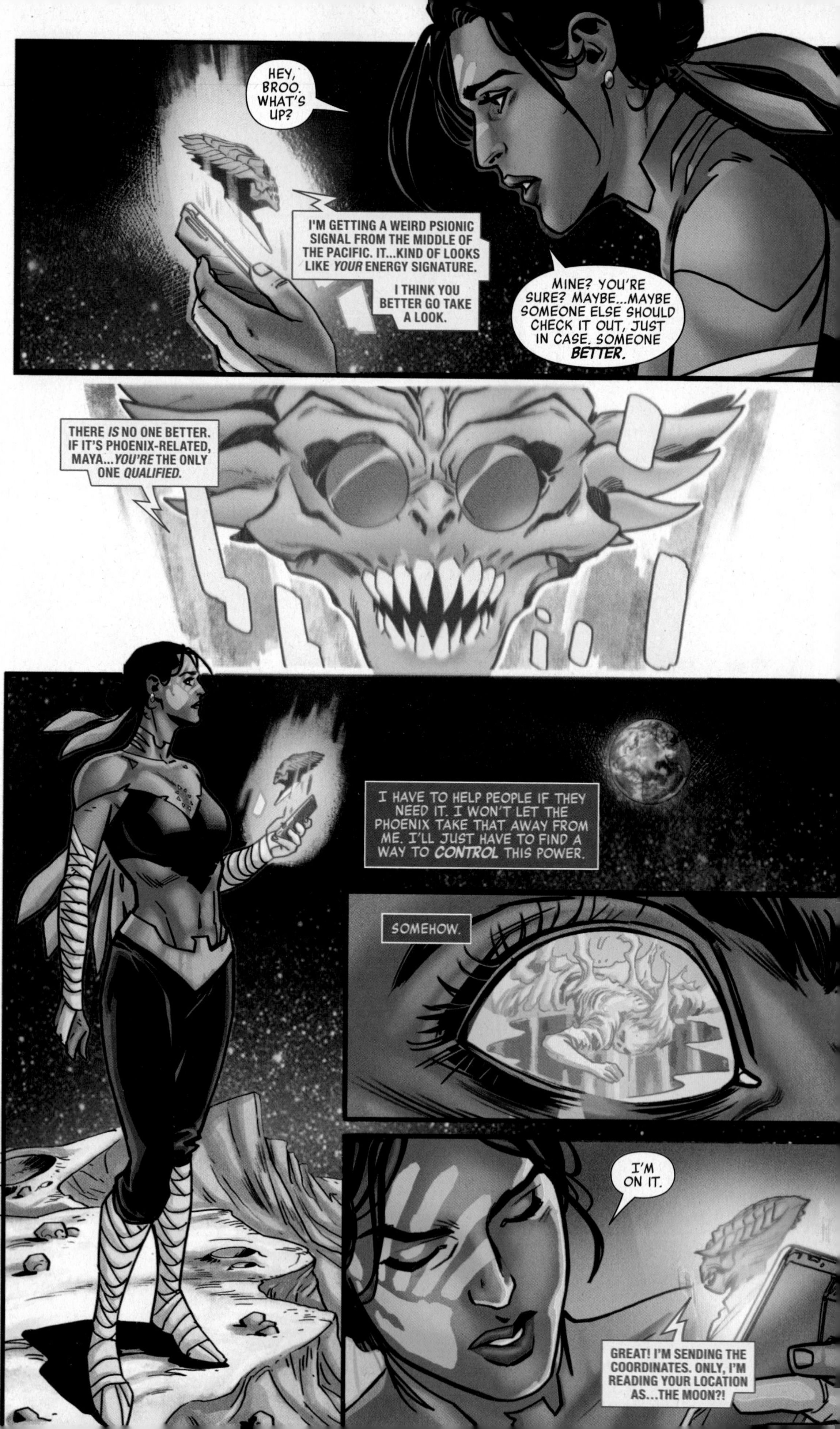

HEY, BROO. WHAT'S UP?
I'M GETTING A WEIRD PSIONIC SIGNAL FROM THE MIDDLE OF THE PACIFIC. IT...KIND OF LOOKS LIKE *YOUR* ENERGY SIGNATURE.
I THINK YOU BETTER GO TAKE A LOOK.
MINE? YOU'RE SURE? MAYBE...MAYBE SOMEONE ELSE SHOULD CHECK IT OUT, JUST IN CASE. SOMEONE *BETTER.*
THERE *IS* NO ONE BETTER. IF IT'S PHOENIX-RELATED, MAYA...*YOU'RE* THE ONLY ONE *QUALIFIED.*
I HAVE TO HELP PEOPLE IF THEY NEED IT. I WON'T LET THE PHOENIX TAKE THAT AWAY FROM ME. I'LL JUST HAVE TO FIND A WAY TO *CONTROL* THIS POWER.
SOMEHOW.
I'M ON IT.
GREAT! I'M SENDING THE COORDINATES. ONLY, I'M READING YOUR LOCATION AS...THE MOON?!

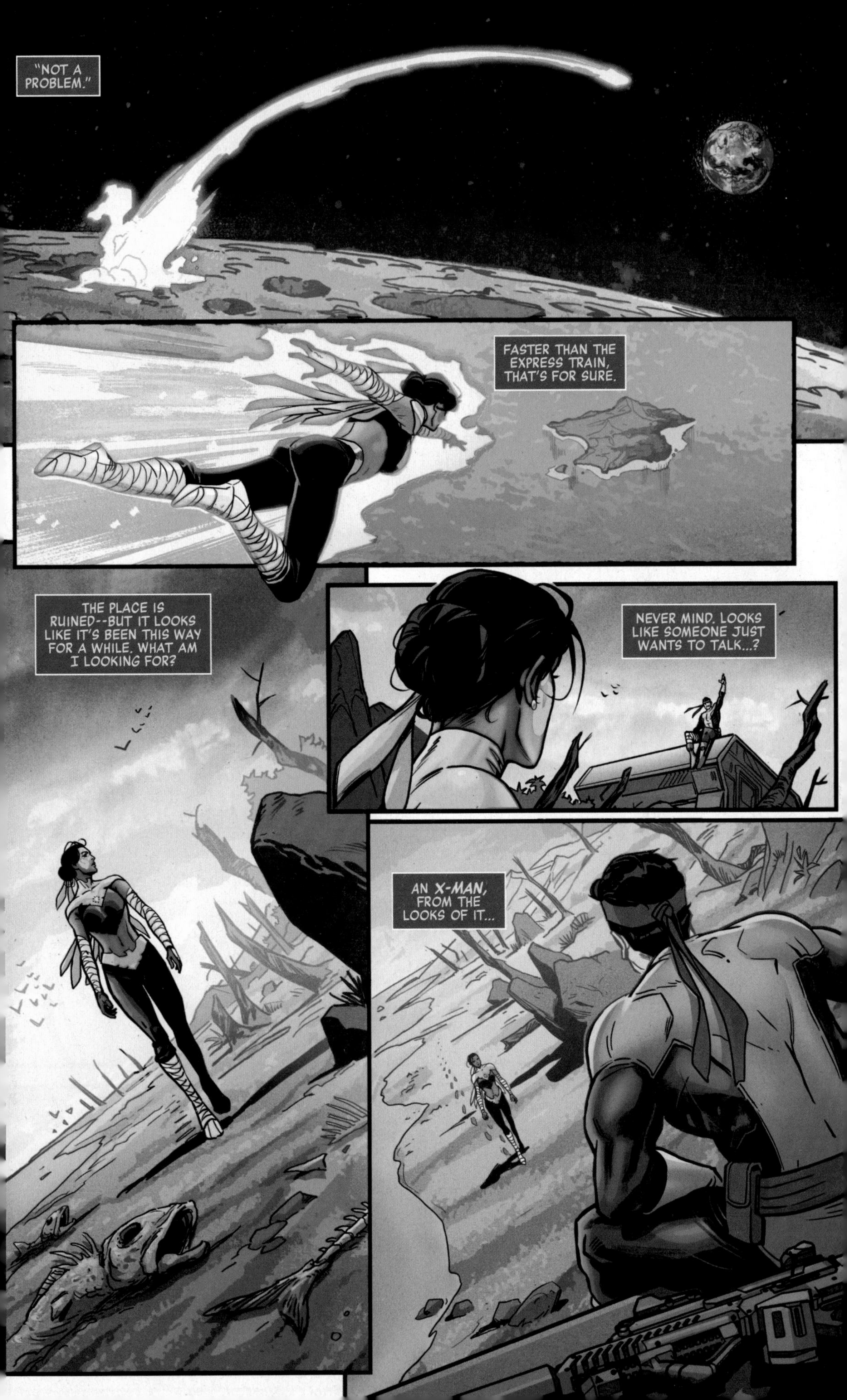
"NOT A PROBLEM."
FASTER THAN THE EXPRESS TRAIN, THAT'S FOR SURE.
THE PLACE IS RUINED--BUT IT LOOKS LIKE IT'S BEEN THIS WAY FOR A WHILE. WHAT AM I LOOKING FOR?
NEVER MIND. LOOKS LIKE SOMEONE JUST WANTS TO TALK...?
AN X-MAN, FROM THE LOOKS OF IT...

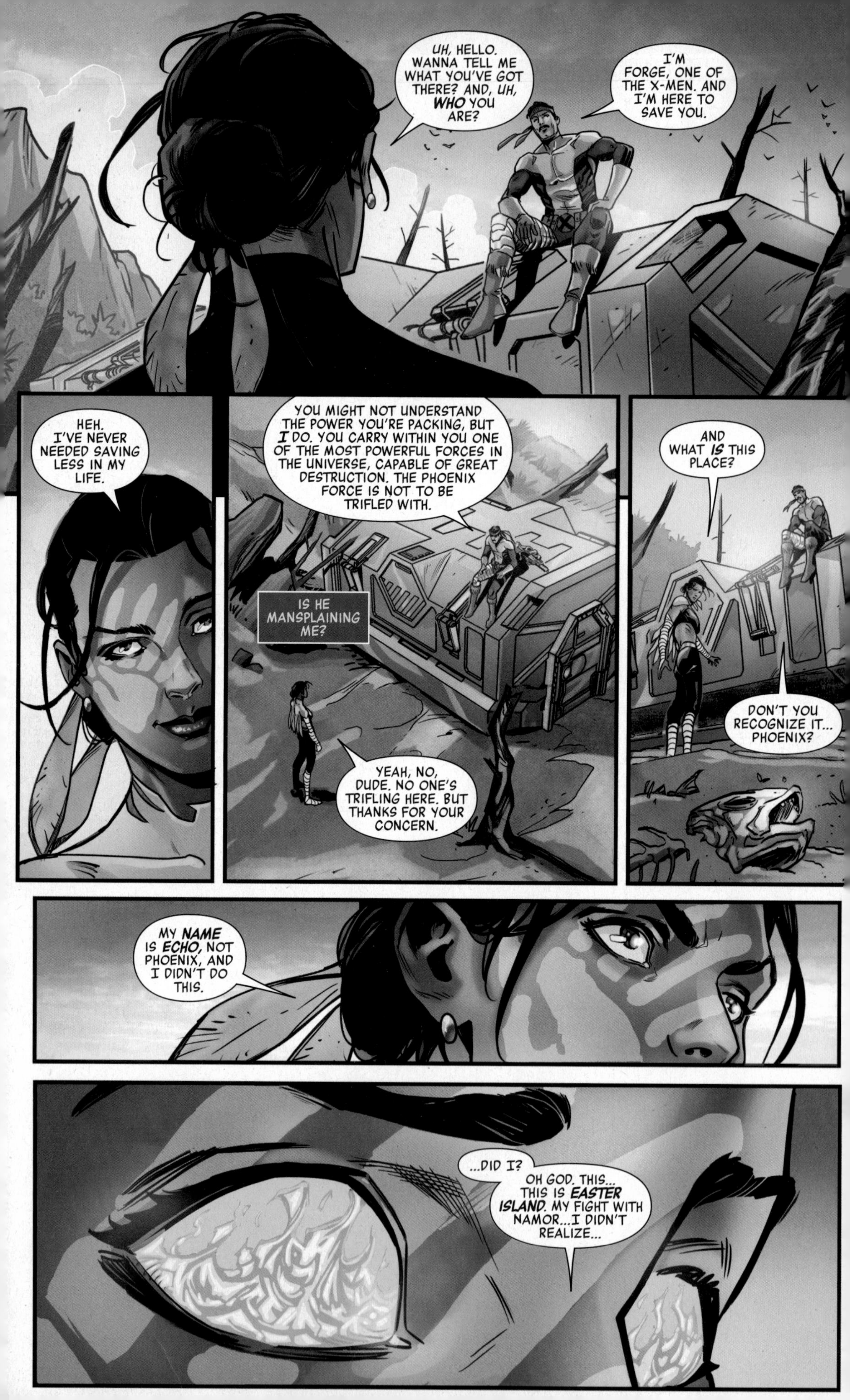
UH, HELLO. WANNA TELL ME WHAT YOU'VE GOT THERE? AND, UH, WHO YOU ARE?
I'M FORGE, ONE OF THE X-MEN. AND I'M HERE TO SAVE YOU.
HEH. I'VE NEVER NEEDED SAVING LESS IN MY LIFE.
YOU MIGHT NOT UNDERSTAND THE POWER YOU'RE PACKING, BUT I DO. YOU CARRY WITHIN YOU ONE OF THE MOST POWERFUL FORCES IN THE UNIVERSE, CAPABLE OF GREAT DESTRUCTION. THE PHOENIX FORCE IS NOT TO BE TRIFLED WITH.
IS HE MANSPLAINING ME?
YEAH, NO, DUDE. NO ONE'S TRIFLING HERE. BUT THANKS FOR YOUR CONCERN.
AND WHAT IS THIS PLACE?
DON'T YOU RECOGNIZE IT... PHOENIX?
MY NAME IS ECHO, NOT PHOENIX, AND I DIDN'T DO THIS.
...DID I?
OH GOD. THIS... THIS IS EASTER ISLAND. MY FIGHT WITH NAMOR...I DIDN'T REALIZE...

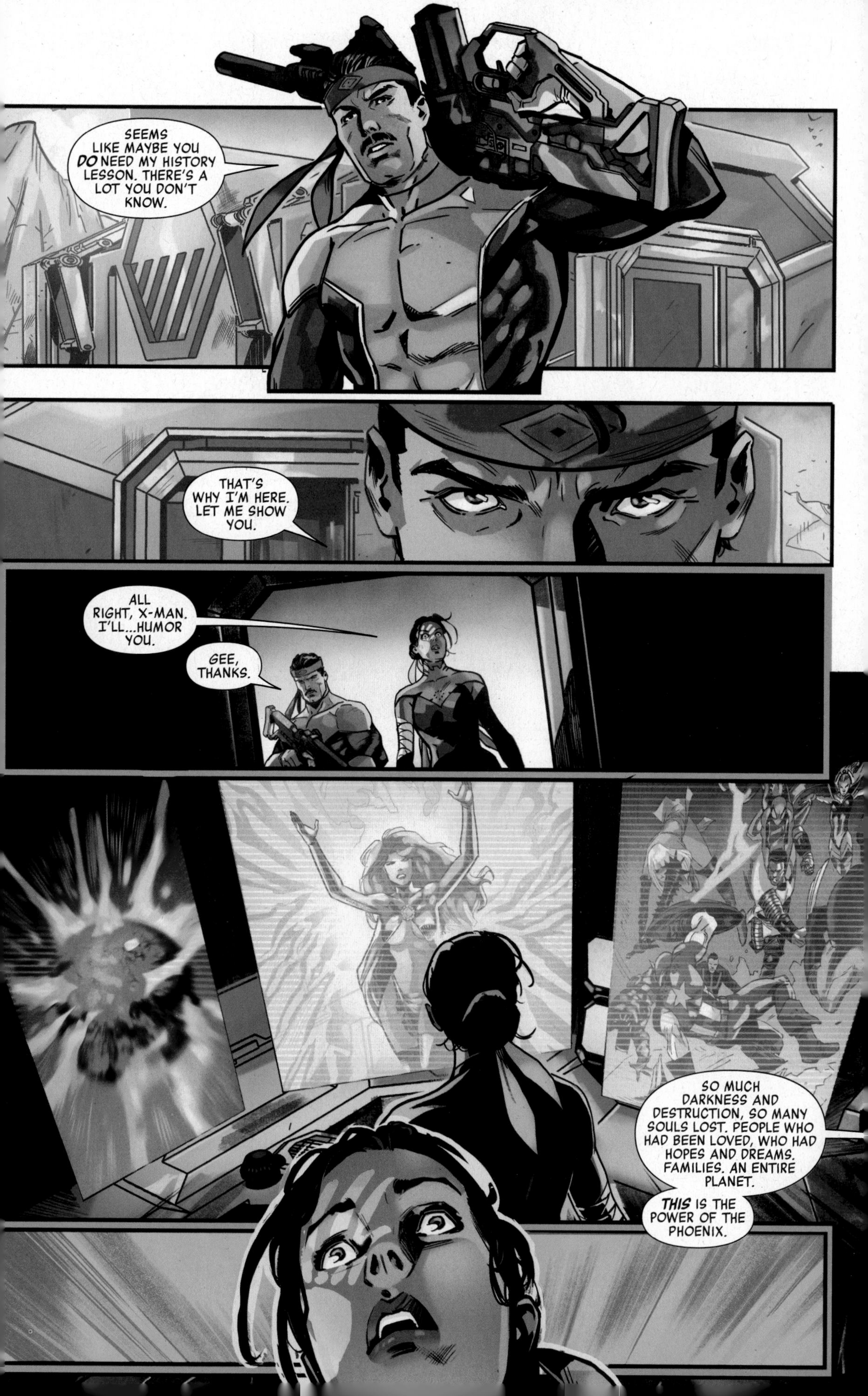
SEEMS LIKE MAYBE YOU DO NEED MY HISTORY LESSON. THERE'S A LOT YOU DON'T KNOW.
THAT'S WHY I'M HERE. LET ME SHOW YOU.
ALL RIGHT, X-MAN. I'LL...HUMOR YOU.
GEE, THANKS.
SO MUCH DARKNESS AND DESTRUCTION, SO MANY SOULS LOST. PEOPLE WHO HAD BEEN LOVED, WHO HAD HOPES AND DREAMS. FAMILIES. AN ENTIRE PLANET.
THIS IS THE POWER OF THE PHOENIX.

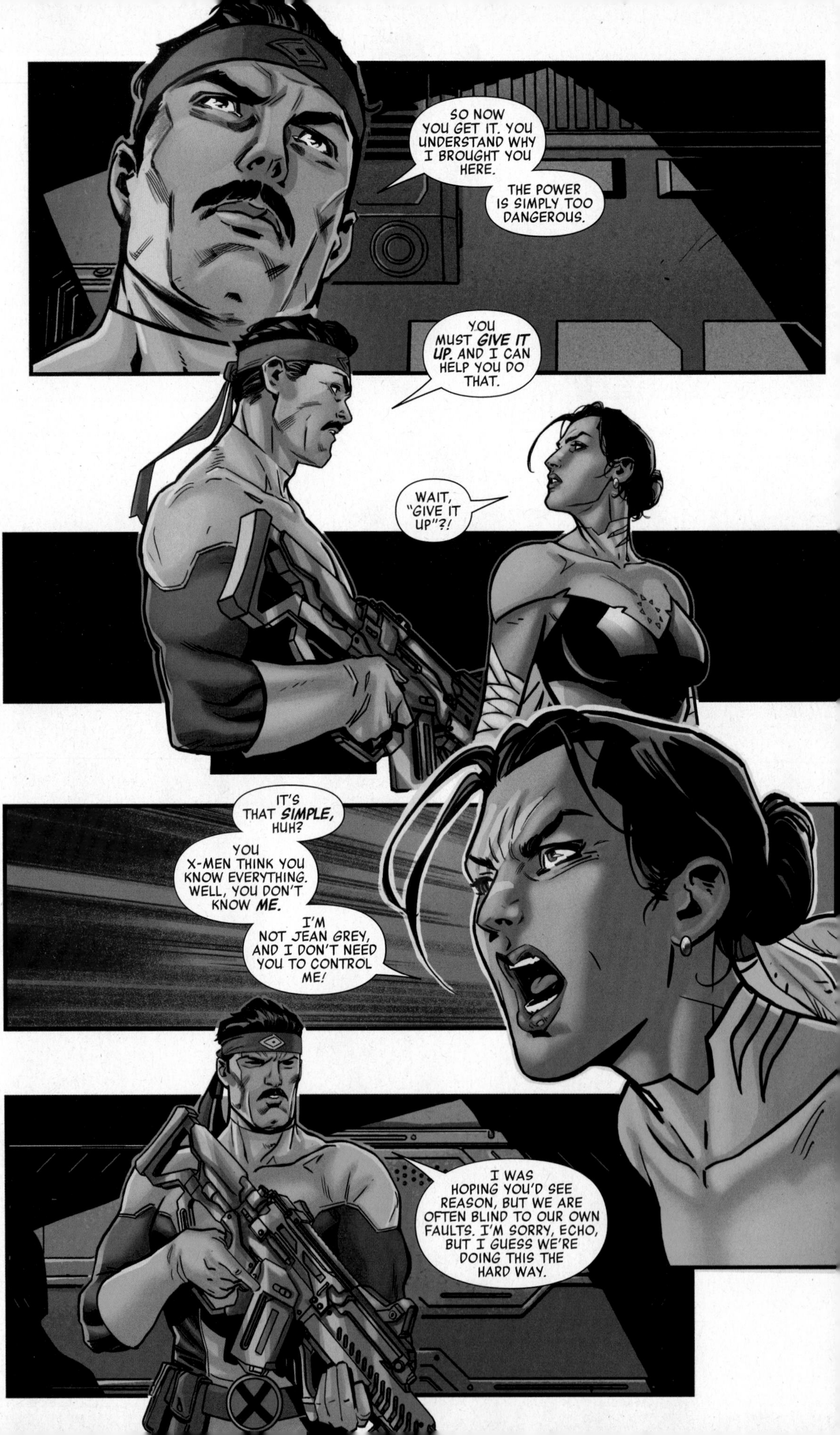
SO NOW YOU GET IT. YOU UNDERSTAND WHY I BROUGHT YOU HERE.
THE POWER IS SIMPLY TOO DANGEROUS.
YOU MUST GIVE IT UP. AND I CAN HELP YOU DO THAT.
WAIT, "GIVE IT UP"?!
IT'S THAT SIMPLE, HUH?
YOU X-MEN THINK YOU KNOW EVERYTHING. WELL, YOU DON'T KNOW ME.
I'M NOT JEAN GREY, AND I DON'T NEED YOU TO CONTROL ME!
I WAS HOPING YOU'D SEE REASON, BUT WE ARE OFTEN BLIND TO OUR OWN FAULTS. I'M SORRY, ECHO, BUT I GUESS WE'RE DOING THIS THE HARD WAY.

AGH!

BZCHRT

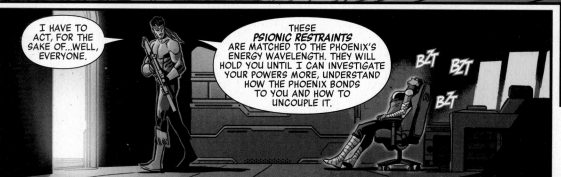

I HAVE TO ACT, FOR THE SAKE OF...WELL, EVERYONE.

THESE **PSIONIC RESTRAINTS** ARE MATCHED TO THE PHOENIX'S ENERGY WAVELENGTH. THEY WILL HOLD YOU UNTIL I CAN INVESTIGATE YOUR POWERS MORE, UNDERSTAND HOW THE PHOENIX BONDS TO YOU AND HOW TO UNCOUPLE IT.

BZT BZT BZT

THIS ISN'T FOREVER, ECHO. WITH TIME, I'LL FIND A WAY TO RELEASE YOU, FROM ALL OF IT. I PROMISE.

RUMBLE

XAVIER WON'T LIKE THIS, BUT SOMEONE HAD TO DO SOMETHING WHILE WE STILL COULD. HAVEN'T WE MUTANTS SEEN THIS HAPPEN OVER AND OVER AGAIN? STILL, I DO...

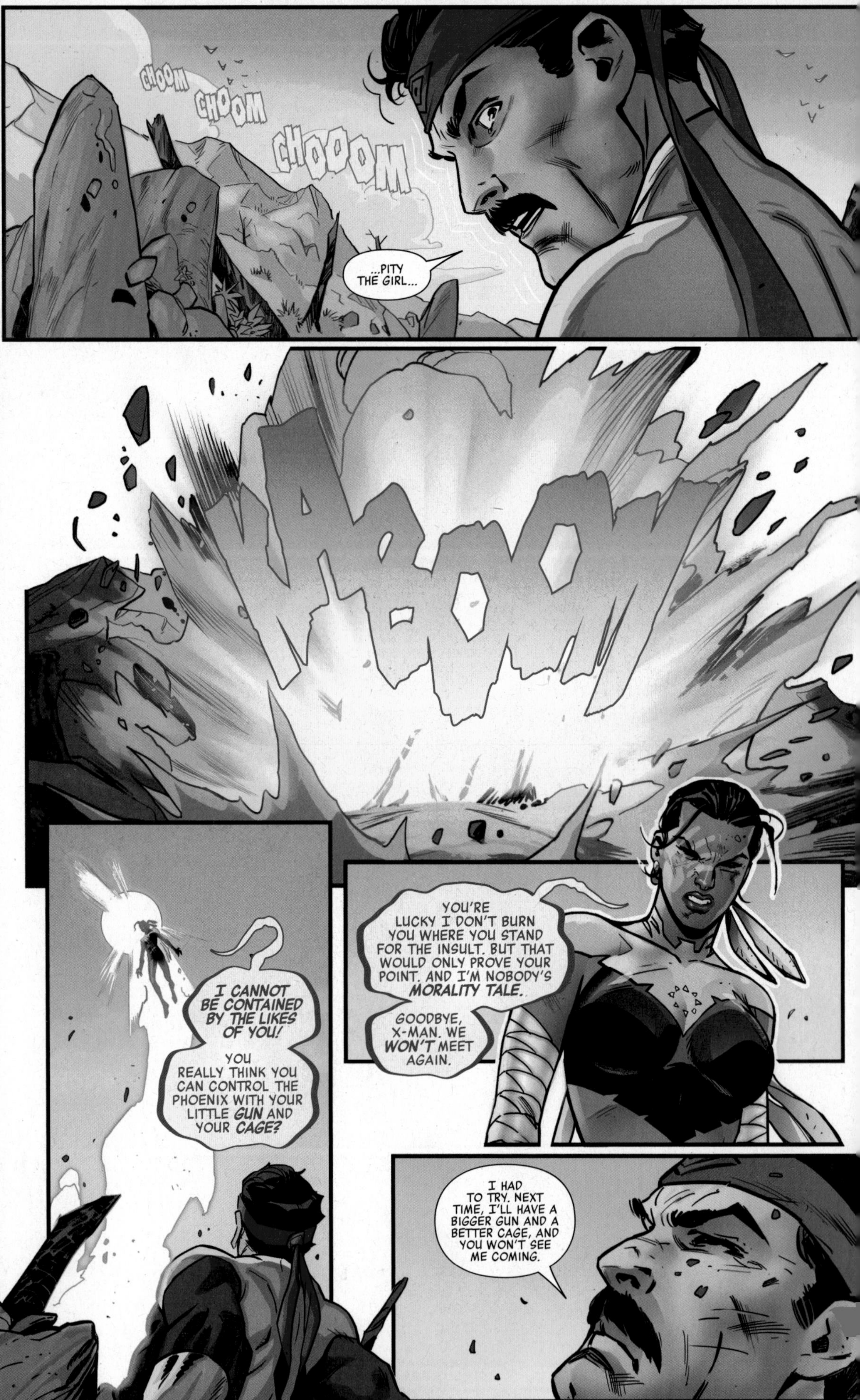
CHOOM
CHOOM
CHOOOM
...PITY THE GIRL...
KABOOM
I CANNOT BE CONTAINED BY THE LIKES OF YOU!
YOU REALLY THINK YOU CAN CONTROL THE PHOENIX WITH YOUR LITTLE GUN AND YOUR CAGE?
YOU'RE LUCKY I DON'T BURN YOU WHERE YOU STAND FOR THE INSULT. BUT THAT WOULD ONLY PROVE YOUR POINT. AND I'M NOBODY'S MORALITY TALE.
GOODBYE, X-MAN. WE WON'T MEET AGAIN.
I HAD TO TRY. NEXT TIME, I'LL HAVE A BIGGER GUN AND A BETTER CAGE, AND YOU WON'T SEE ME COMING.

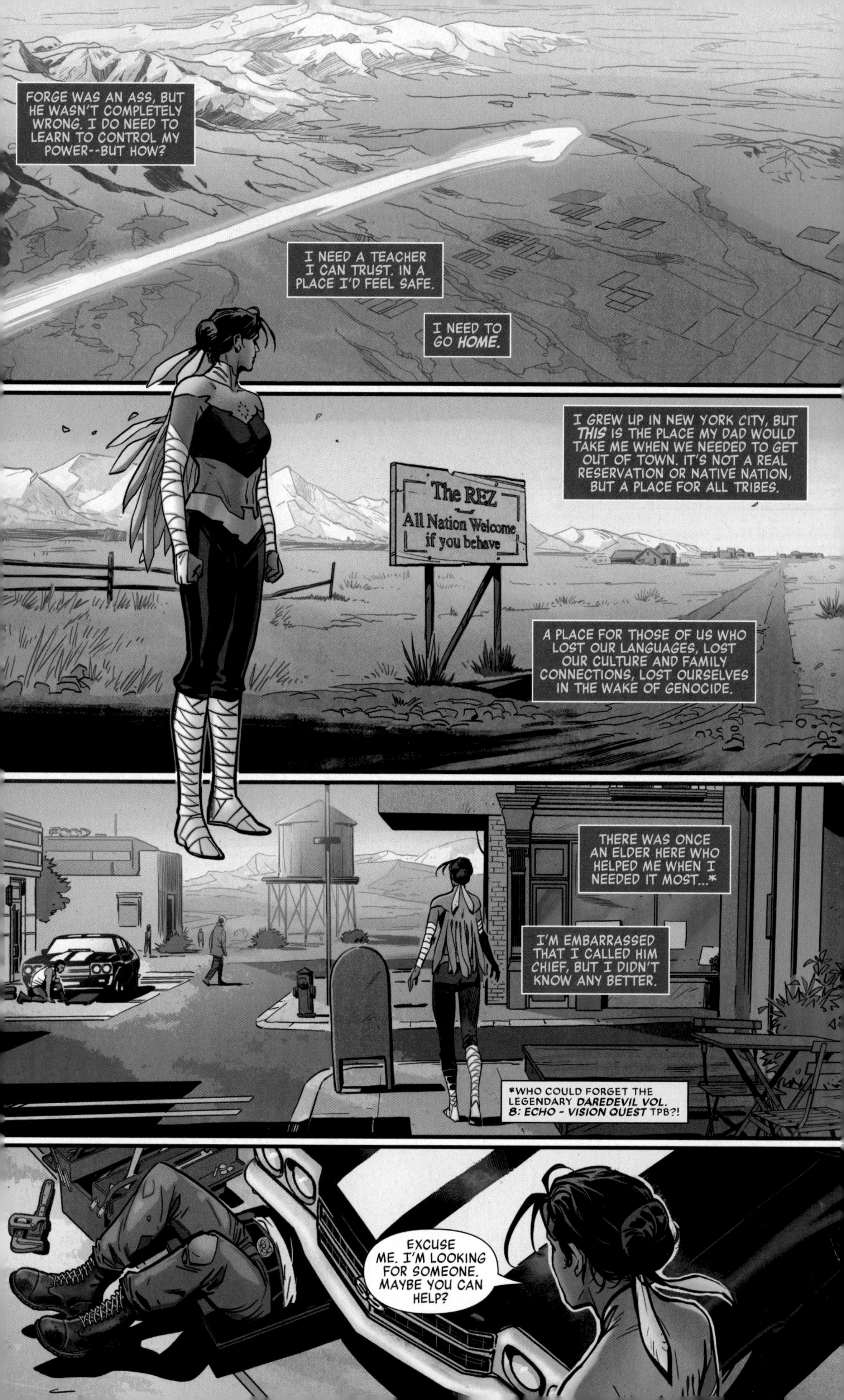
FORGE WAS AN ASS, BUT HE WASN'T COMPLETELY WRONG. I DO NEED TO LEARN TO CONTROL MY POWER--BUT HOW?
I NEED A TEACHER I CAN TRUST. IN A PLACE I'D FEEL SAFE.
I NEED TO GO HOME.
I GREW UP IN NEW YORK CITY, BUT THIS IS THE PLACE MY DAD WOULD TAKE ME WHEN WE NEEDED TO GET OUT OF TOWN. IT'S NOT A REAL RESERVATION OR NATIVE NATION, BUT A PLACE FOR ALL TRIBES.
The REZ
All Nation Welcome
if you behave
A PLACE FOR THOSE OF US WHO LOST OUR LANGUAGES, LOST OUR CULTURE AND FAMILY CONNECTIONS, LOST OURSELVES IN THE WAKE OF GENOCIDE.
FOOD
THERE WAS ONCE AN ELDER HERE WHO HELPED ME WHEN I NEEDED IT MOST...*
I'M EMBARRASSED THAT I CALLED HIM CHIEF, BUT I DIDN'T KNOW ANY BETTER.
*WHO COULD FORGET THE LEGENDARY DAREDEVIL VOL. 8: ECHO - VISION QUEST TPB?!
EXCUSE ME. I'M LOOKING FOR SOMEONE. MAYBE YOU CAN HELP?

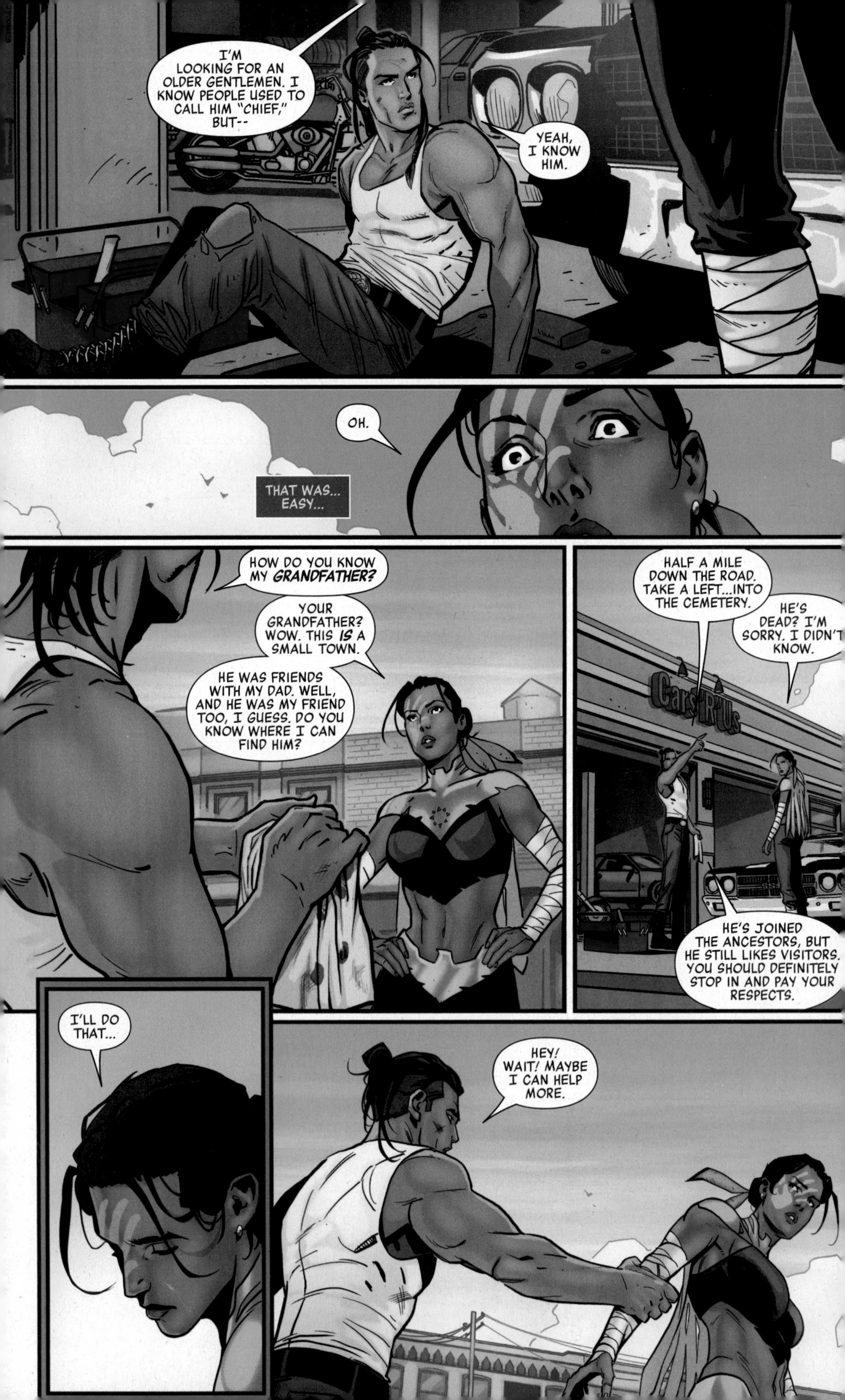
I'M LOOKING FOR AN OLDER GENTLEMEN. I KNOW PEOPLE USED TO CALL HIM "CHIEF," BUT--
YEAH, I KNOW HIM.
OH.
THAT WAS... EASY...
HOW DO YOU KNOW MY GRANDFATHER?
YOUR GRANDFATHER? WOW. THIS IS A SMALL TOWN.
HE WAS FRIENDS WITH MY DAD. WELL, AND HE WAS MY FRIEND TOO, I GUESS. DO YOU KNOW WHERE I CAN FIND HIM?
HALF A MILE DOWN THE ROAD. TAKE A LEFT...INTO THE CEMETERY.
HE'S DEAD? I'M SORRY. I DIDN'T KNOW.
Cars 'R' Us
HE'S JOINED THE ANCESTORS, BUT HE STILL LIKES VISITORS. YOU SHOULD DEFINITELY STOP IN AND PAY YOUR RESPECTS.
I'LL DO THAT...
HEY! WAIT! MAYBE I CAN HELP MORE.

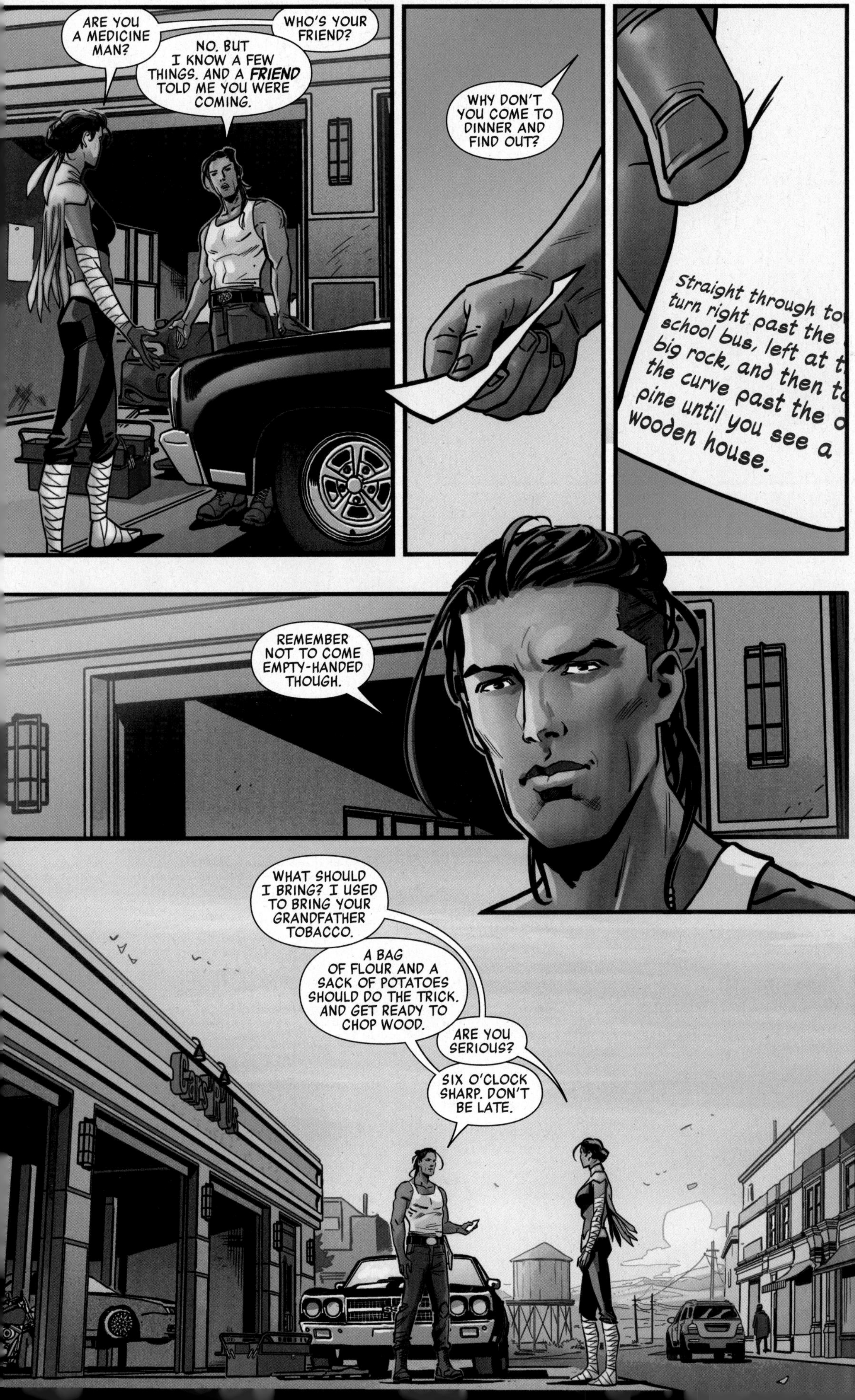
ARE YOU A MEDICINE MAN?
WHO'S YOUR FRIEND?
NO. BUT I KNOW A FEW THINGS. AND A FRIEND TOLD ME YOU WERE COMING.
WHY DON'T YOU COME TO DINNER AND FIND OUT?
Straight through to
turn right past the
school bus, left at
big rock, and then t
the curve past the
pine until you see a
wooden house.
REMEMBER NOT TO COME EMPTY-HANDED THOUGH.
WHAT SHOULD I BRING? I USED TO BRING YOUR GRANDFATHER TOBACCO.
A BAG OF FLOUR AND A SACK OF POTATOES SHOULD DO THE TRICK. AND GET READY TO CHOP WOOD.
ARE YOU SERIOUS?
SIX O'CLOCK SHARP. DON'T BE LATE.

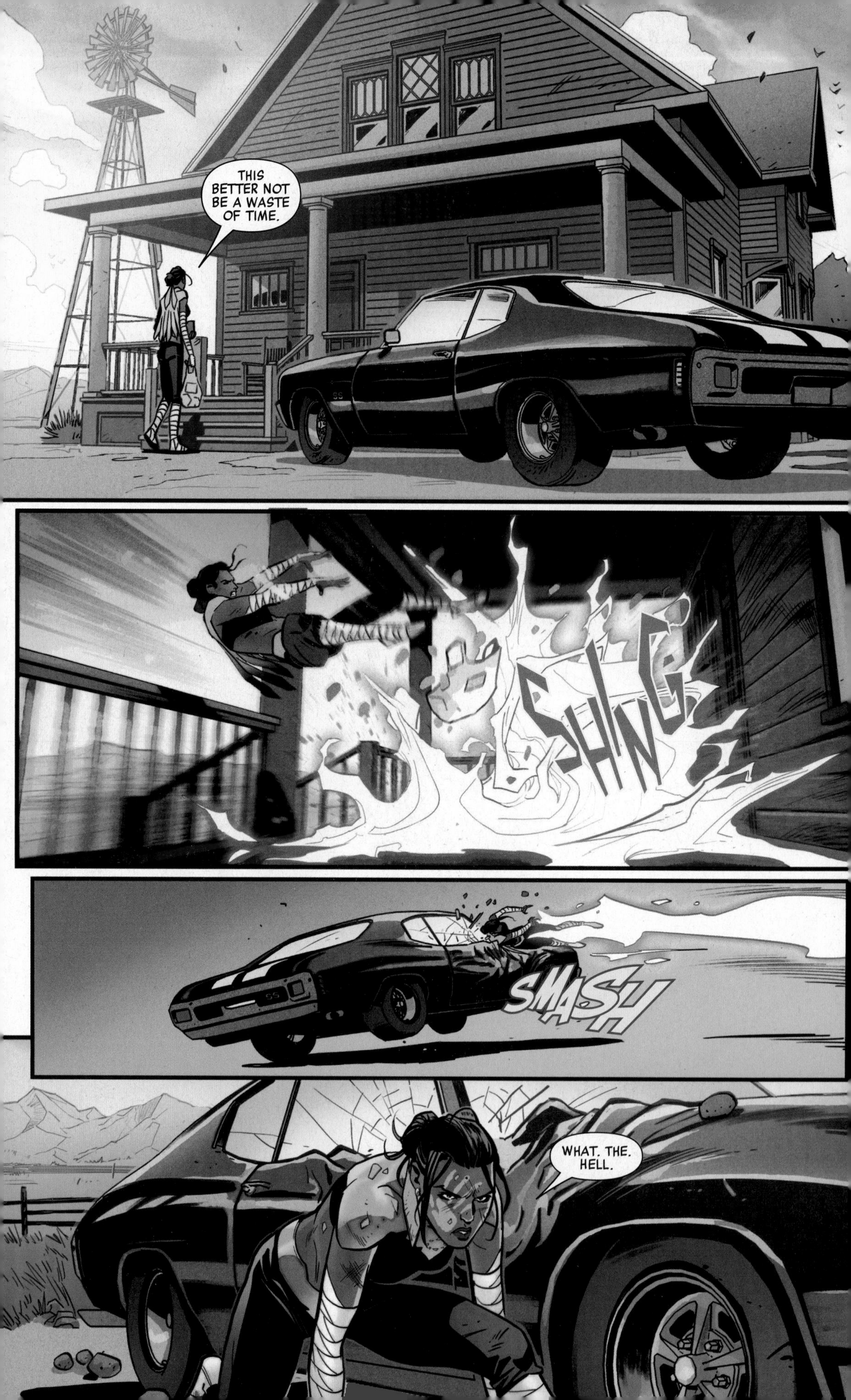
THIS BETTER NOT BE A WASTE OF TIME.
SHING
SMASH
WHAT. THE. HELL.

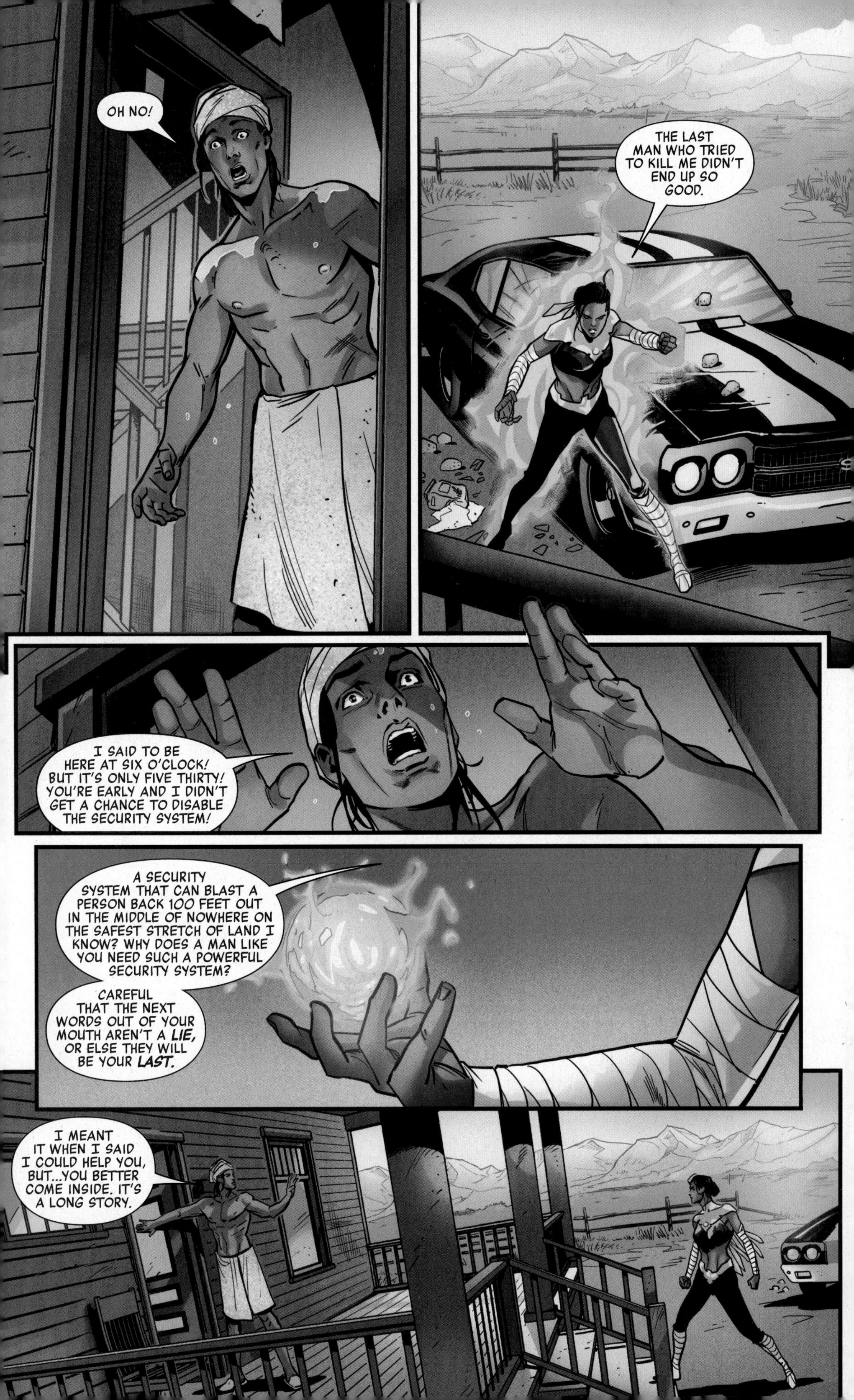
OH NO!
THE LAST MAN WHO TRIED TO KILL ME DIDN'T END UP SO GOOD.
I SAID TO BE HERE AT SIX O'CLOCK! BUT IT'S ONLY FIVE THIRTY! YOU'RE EARLY AND I DIDN'T GET A CHANCE TO DISABLE THE SECURITY SYSTEM!
A SECURITY SYSTEM THAT CAN BLAST A PERSON BACK 100 FEET OUT IN THE MIDDLE OF NOWHERE ON THE SAFEST STRETCH OF LAND I KNOW? WHY DOES A MAN LIKE YOU NEED SUCH A POWERFUL SECURITY SYSTEM?
CAREFUL THAT THE NEXT WORDS OUT OF YOUR MOUTH AREN'T A LIE, OR ELSE THEY WILL BE YOUR LAST.
I MEANT IT WHEN I SAID I COULD HELP YOU, BUT...YOU BETTER COME INSIDE. IT'S A LONG STORY.

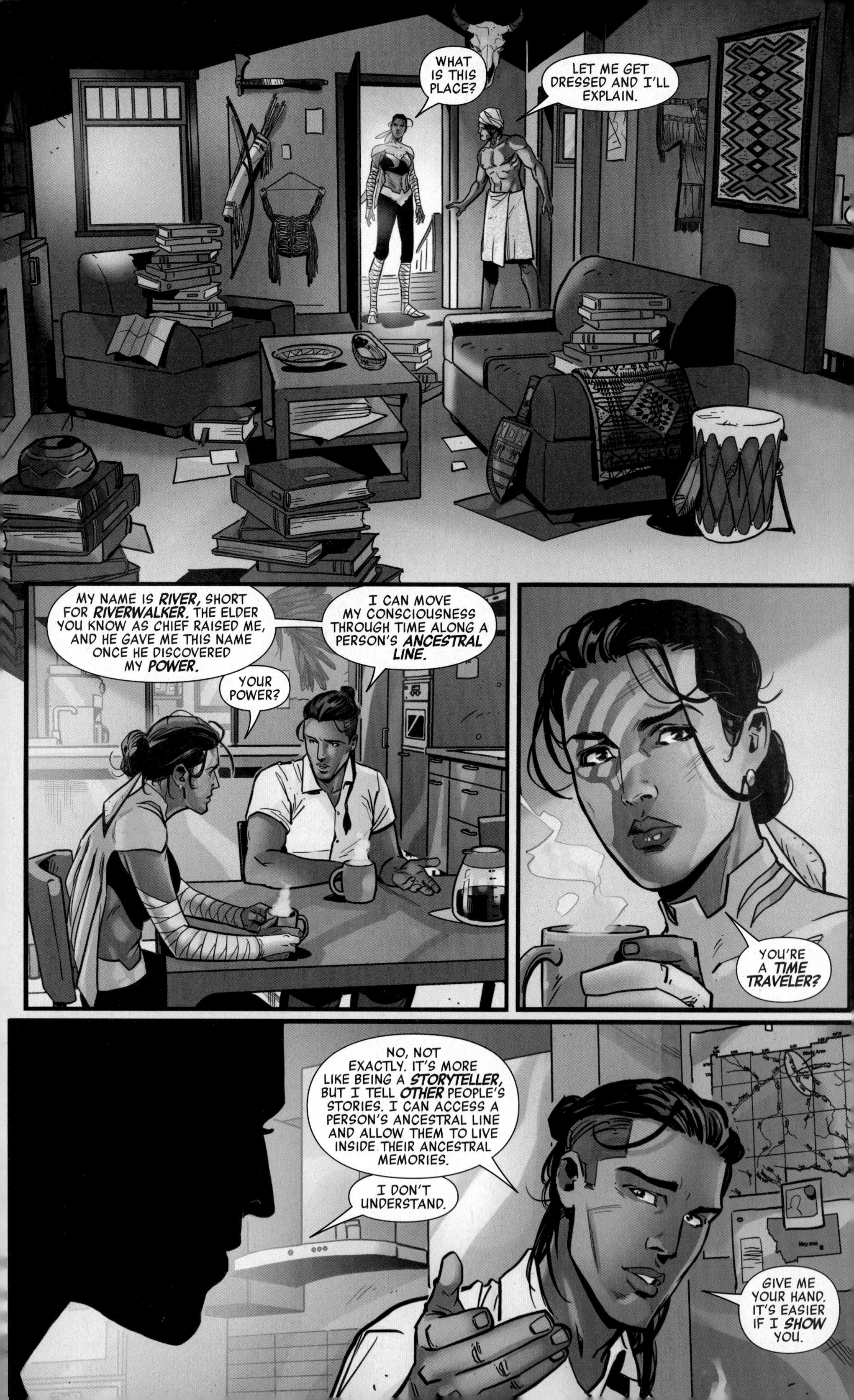
WHAT IS THIS PLACE?
LET ME GET DRESSED AND I'LL EXPLAIN.
MY NAME IS RIVER, SHORT FOR RIVERWALKER. THE ELDER YOU KNOW AS CHIEF RAISED ME, AND HE GAVE ME THIS NAME ONCE HE DISCOVERED MY POWER.
YOUR POWER?
I CAN MOVE MY CONSCIOUSNESS THROUGH TIME ALONG A PERSON'S ANCESTRAL LINE.
YOU'RE A TIME TRAVELER?
NO, NOT EXACTLY. IT'S MORE LIKE BEING A STORYTELLER, BUT I TELL OTHER PEOPLE'S STORIES. I CAN ACCESS A PERSON'S ANCESTRAL LINE AND ALLOW THEM TO LIVE INSIDE THEIR ANCESTRAL MEMORIES.
I DON'T UNDERSTAND.
GIVE ME YOUR HAND. IT'S EASIER IF I SHOW YOU.

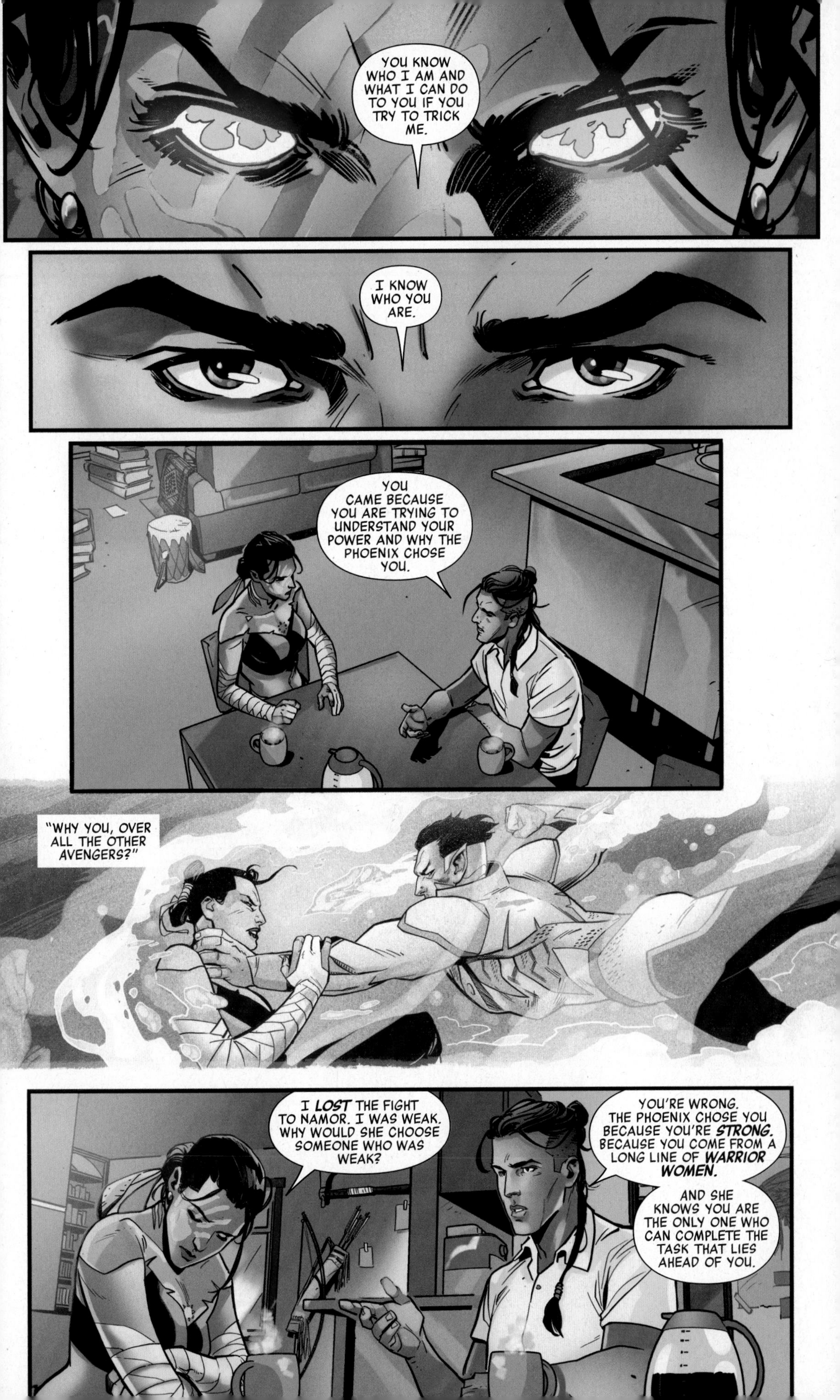
YOU KNOW WHO I AM AND WHAT I CAN DO TO YOU IF YOU TRY TO TRICK ME.
I KNOW WHO YOU ARE.
YOU CAME BECAUSE YOU ARE TRYING TO UNDERSTAND YOUR POWER AND WHY THE PHOENIX CHOSE YOU.
"WHY YOU, OVER ALL THE OTHER AVENGERS?"
I **LOST** THE FIGHT TO NAMOR. I WAS WEAK. WHY WOULD SHE CHOOSE SOMEONE WHO WAS WEAK?
YOU'RE WRONG. THE PHOENIX CHOSE YOU BECAUSE YOU'RE **STRONG.** BECAUSE YOU COME FROM A LONG LINE OF **WARRIOR WOMEN.**
AND SHE KNOWS YOU ARE THE ONLY ONE WHO CAN COMPLETE THE TASK THAT LIES AHEAD OF YOU.

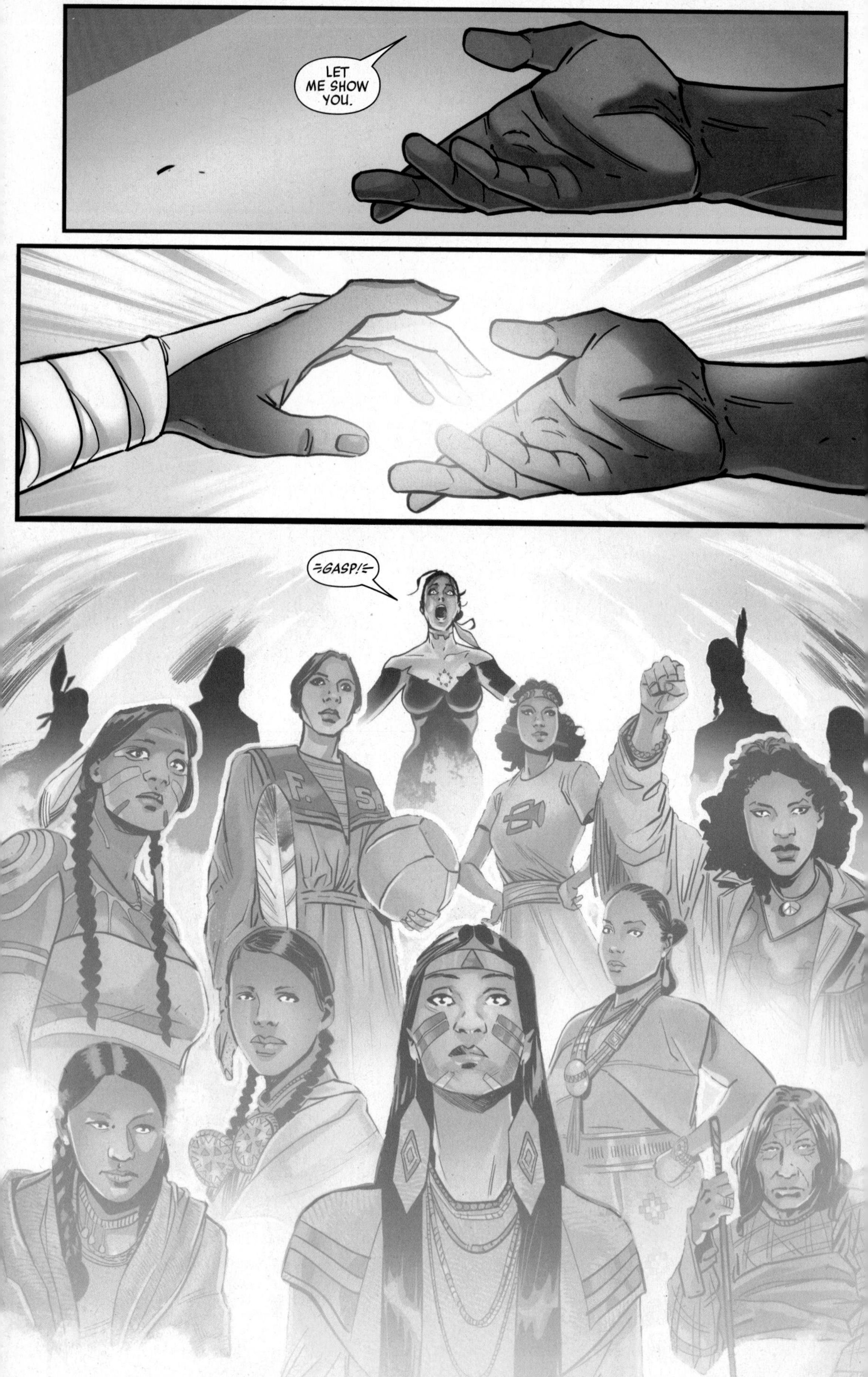
LET ME SHOW YOU.
=GASP!=

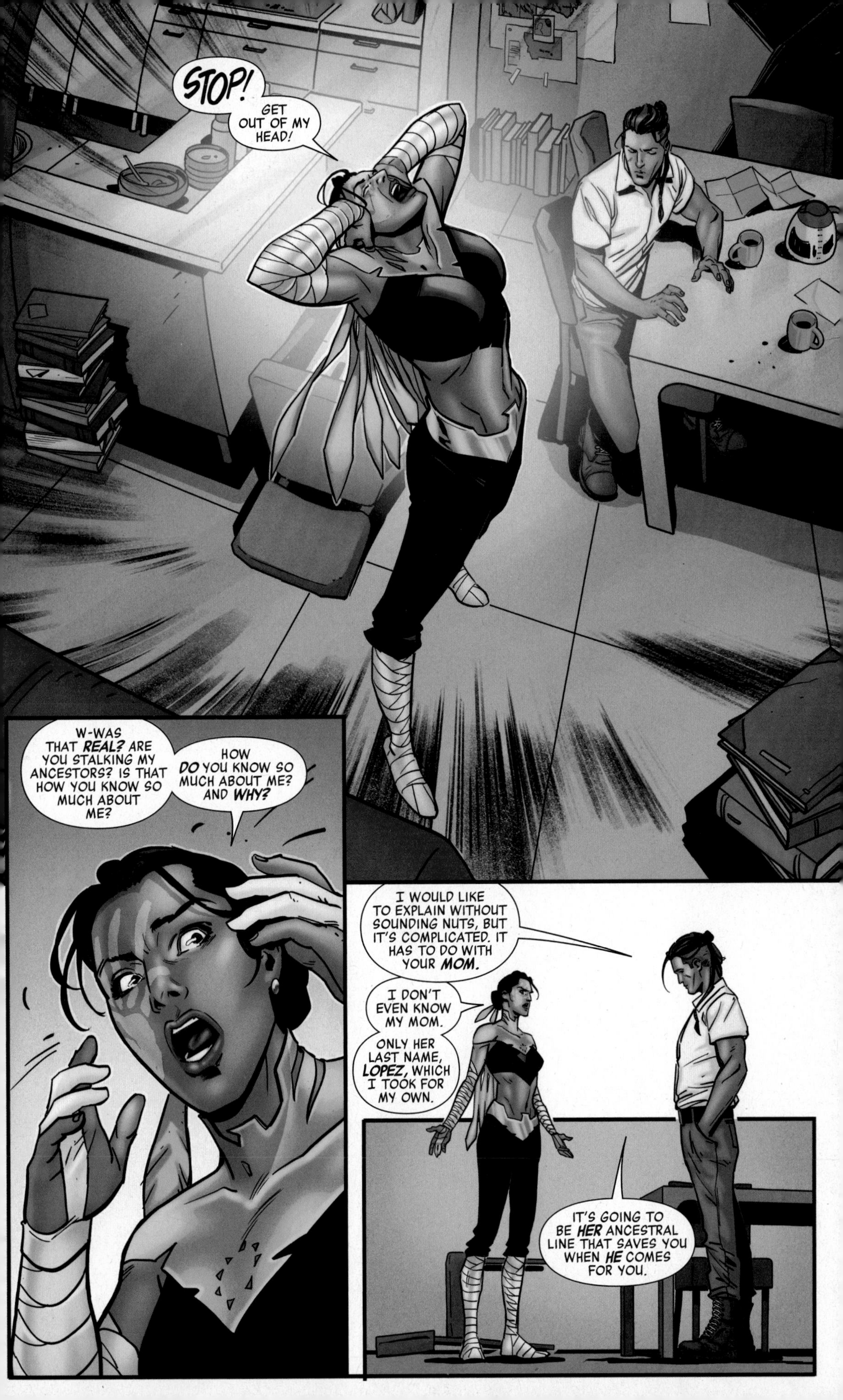
STOP!
GET OUT OF MY HEAD!
W-WAS THAT REAL? ARE YOU STALKING MY ANCESTORS? IS THAT HOW YOU KNOW SO MUCH ABOUT ME?
HOW DO YOU KNOW SO MUCH ABOUT ME? AND WHY?
I WOULD LIKE TO EXPLAIN WITHOUT SOUNDING NUTS, BUT IT'S COMPLICATED. IT HAS TO DO WITH YOUR MOM.
I DON'T EVEN KNOW MY MOM.
ONLY HER LAST NAME, LOPEZ, WHICH I TOOK FOR MY OWN.
IT'S GOING TO BE HER ANCESTRAL LINE THAT SAVES YOU WHEN HE COMES FOR YOU.

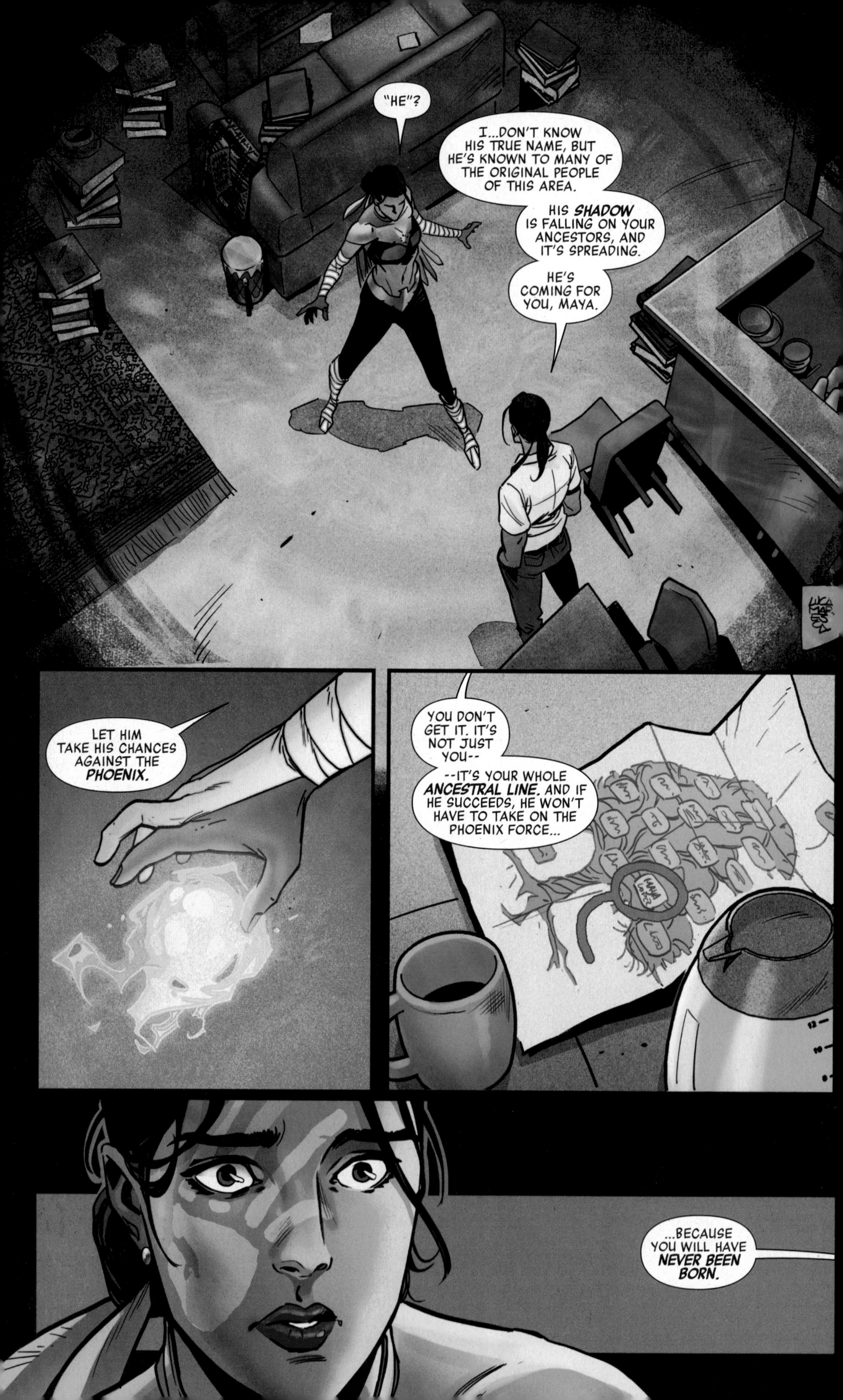
"HE"?
I...DON'T KNOW HIS TRUE NAME, BUT HE'S KNOWN TO MANY OF THE ORIGINAL PEOPLE OF THIS AREA.
HIS SHADOW IS FALLING ON YOUR ANCESTORS, AND IT'S SPREADING.
HE'S COMING FOR YOU, MAYA.
LET HIM TAKE HIS CHANCES AGAINST THE PHOENIX.
YOU DON'T GET IT. IT'S NOT JUST YOU--
--IT'S YOUR WHOLE ANCESTRAL LINE. AND IF HE SUCCEEDS, HE WON'T HAVE TO TAKE ON THE PHOENIX FORCE...
...BECAUSE YOU WILL HAVE NEVER BEEN BORN.

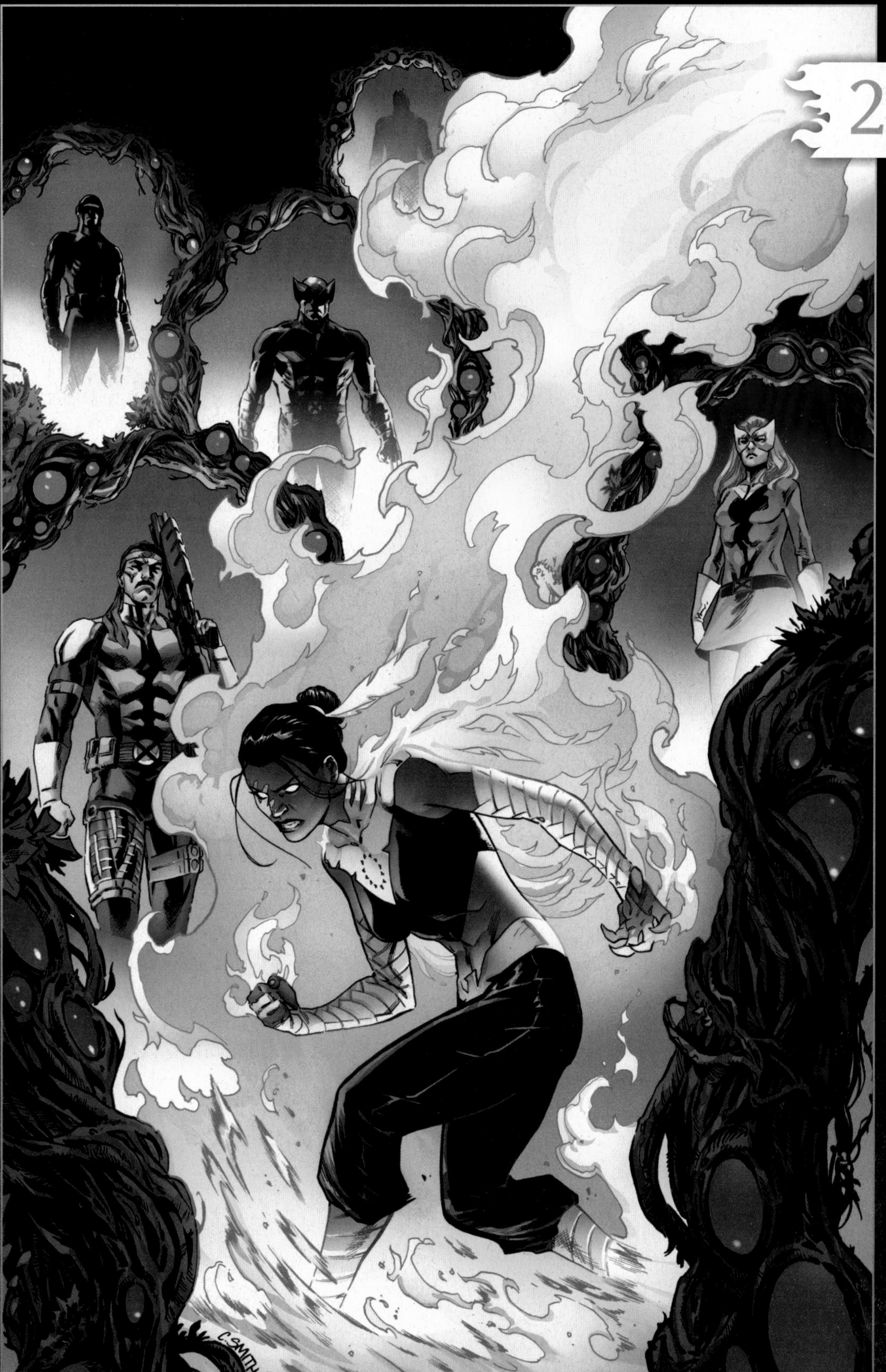

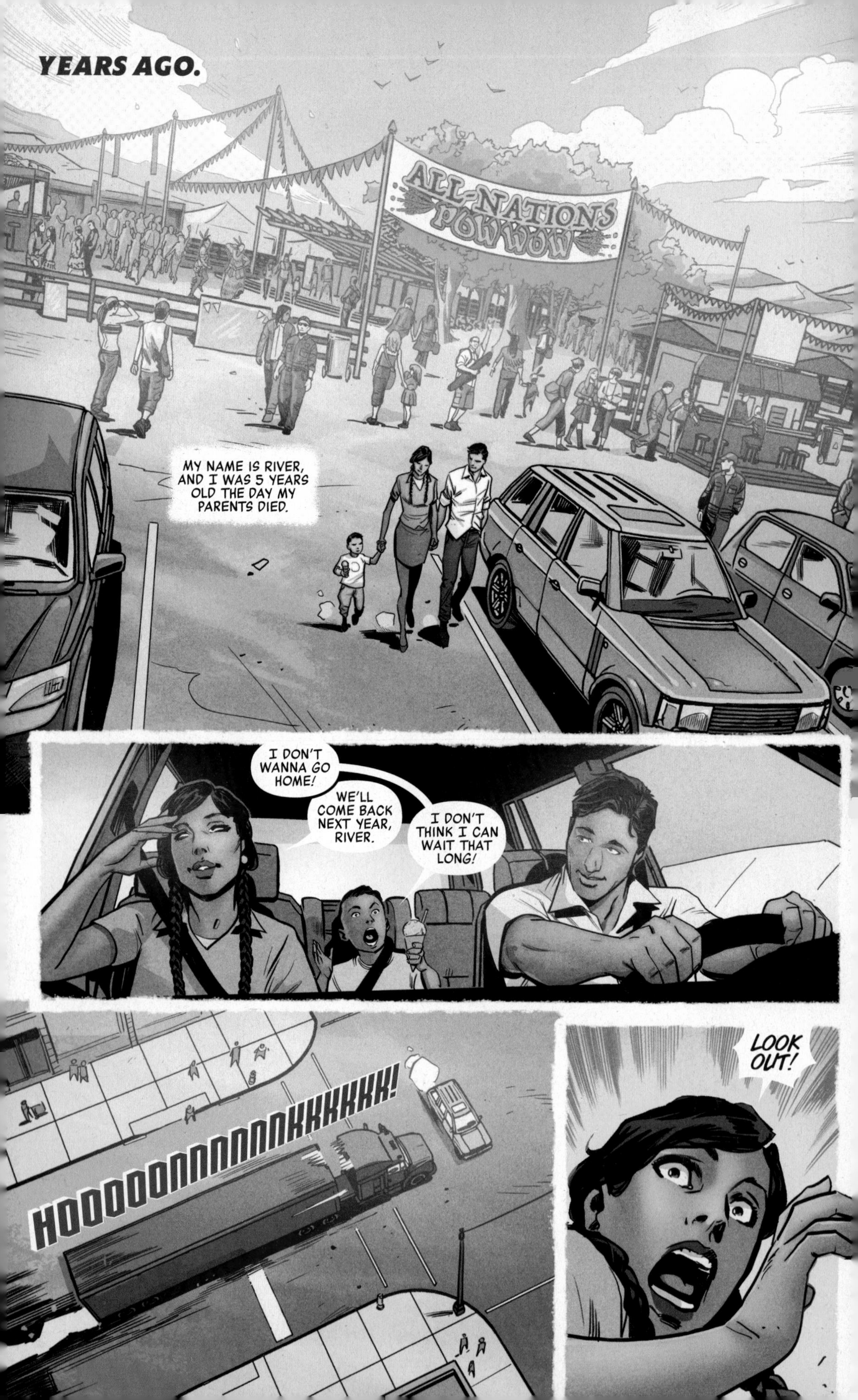
YEARS AGO.
ALL-NATIONS POW WOW
MY NAME IS RIVER, AND I WAS 5 YEARS OLD THE DAY MY PARENTS DIED.
I DON'T WANNA GO HOME!
WE'LL COME BACK NEXT YEAR, RIVER.
I DON'T THINK I CAN WAIT THAT LONG!
HOOOOONNNNNNKKKKKK!
LOOK OUT!

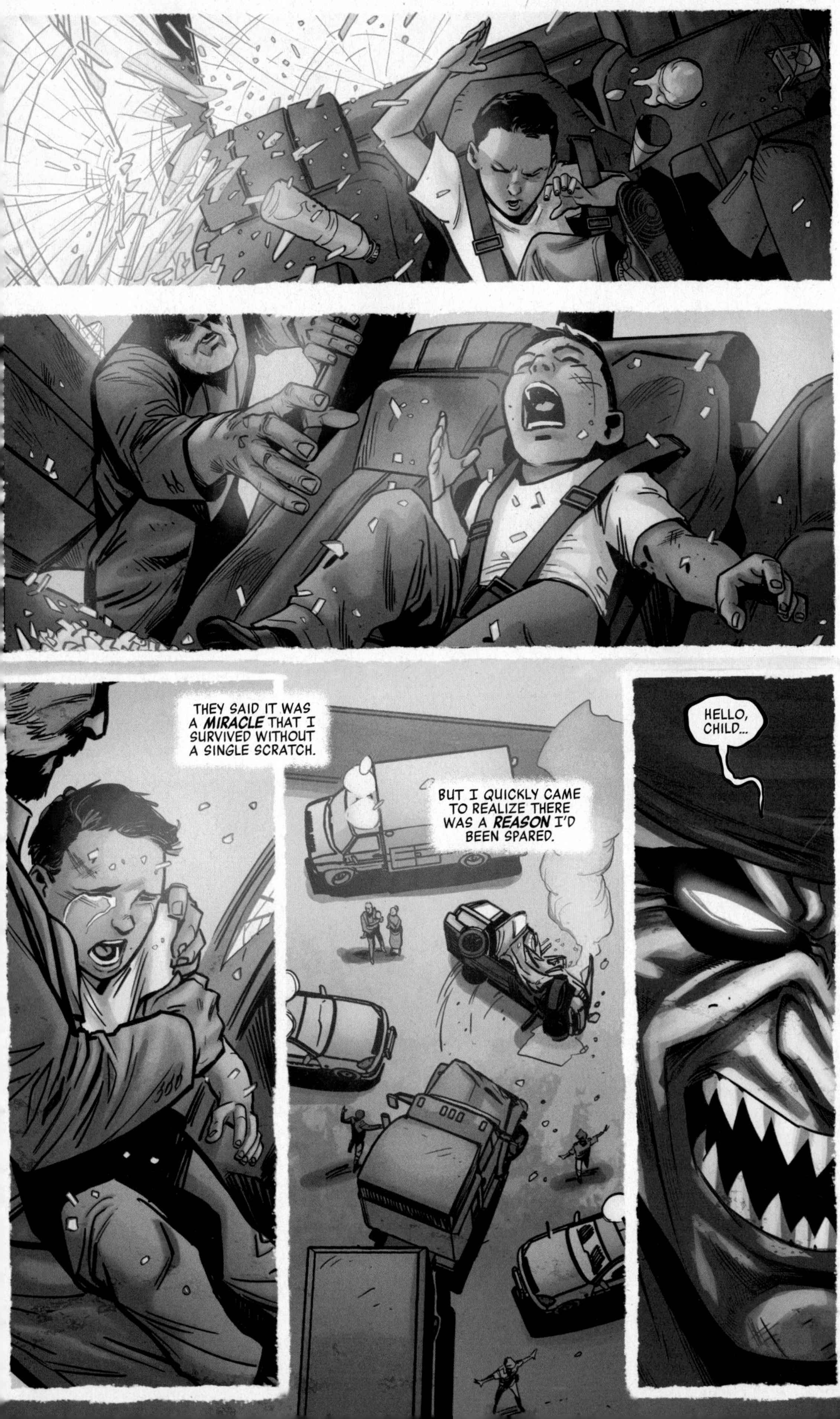
THEY SAID IT WAS A MIRACLE THAT I SURVIVED WITHOUT A SINGLE SCRATCH.
BUT I QUICKLY CAME TO REALIZE THERE WAS A REASON I'D BEEN SPARED.
HELLO, CHILD...

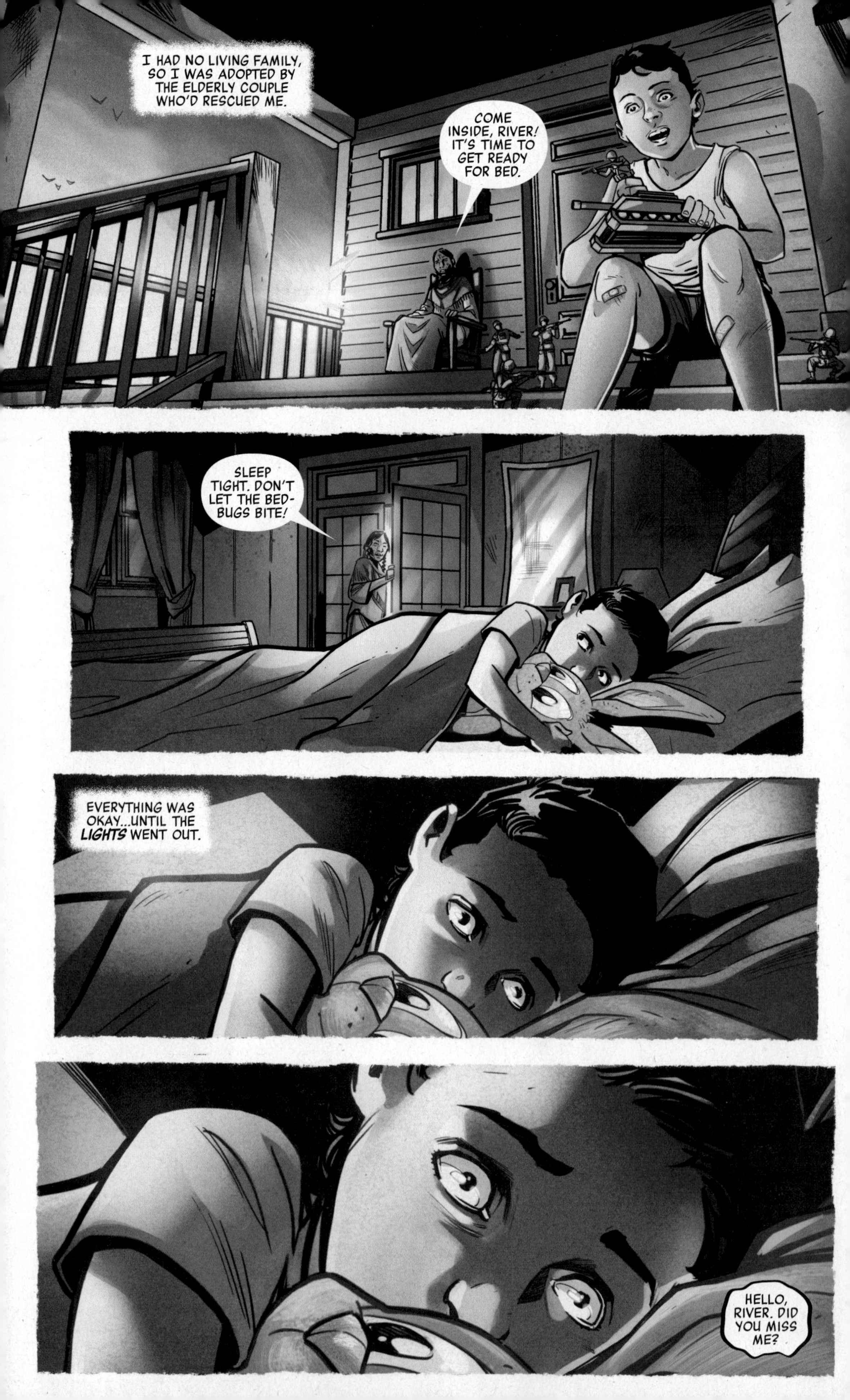
I HAD NO LIVING FAMILY, SO I WAS ADOPTED BY THE ELDERLY COUPLE WHO'D RESCUED ME.
COME INSIDE, RIVER! IT'S TIME TO GET READY FOR BED.
SLEEP TIGHT. DON'T LET THE BED-BUGS BITE!
EVERYTHING WAS OKAY...UNTIL THE *LIGHTS* WENT OUT.
HELLO, RIVER. DID YOU MISS ME?

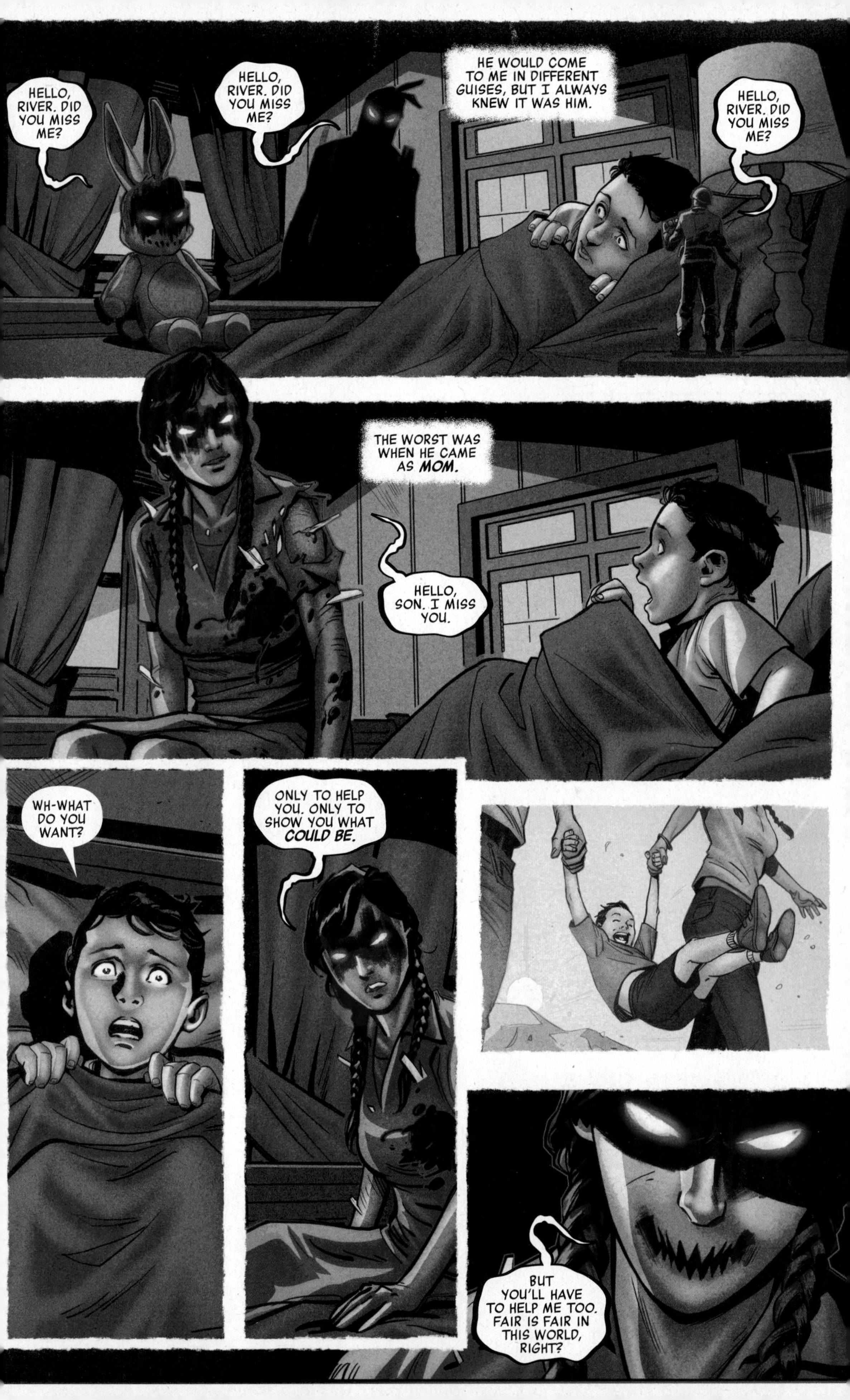
HELLO, RIVER. DID YOU MISS ME?
HELLO, RIVER. DID YOU MISS ME?
HE WOULD COME TO ME IN DIFFERENT GUISES, BUT I ALWAYS KNEW IT WAS HIM.
HELLO, RIVER. DID YOU MISS ME?
THE WORST WAS WHEN HE CAME AS MOM.
HELLO, SON. I MISS YOU.
WH-WHAT DO YOU WANT?
ONLY TO HELP YOU. ONLY TO SHOW YOU WHAT COULD BE.
BUT YOU'LL HAVE TO HELP ME TOO. FAIR IS FAIR IN THIS WORLD, RIGHT?

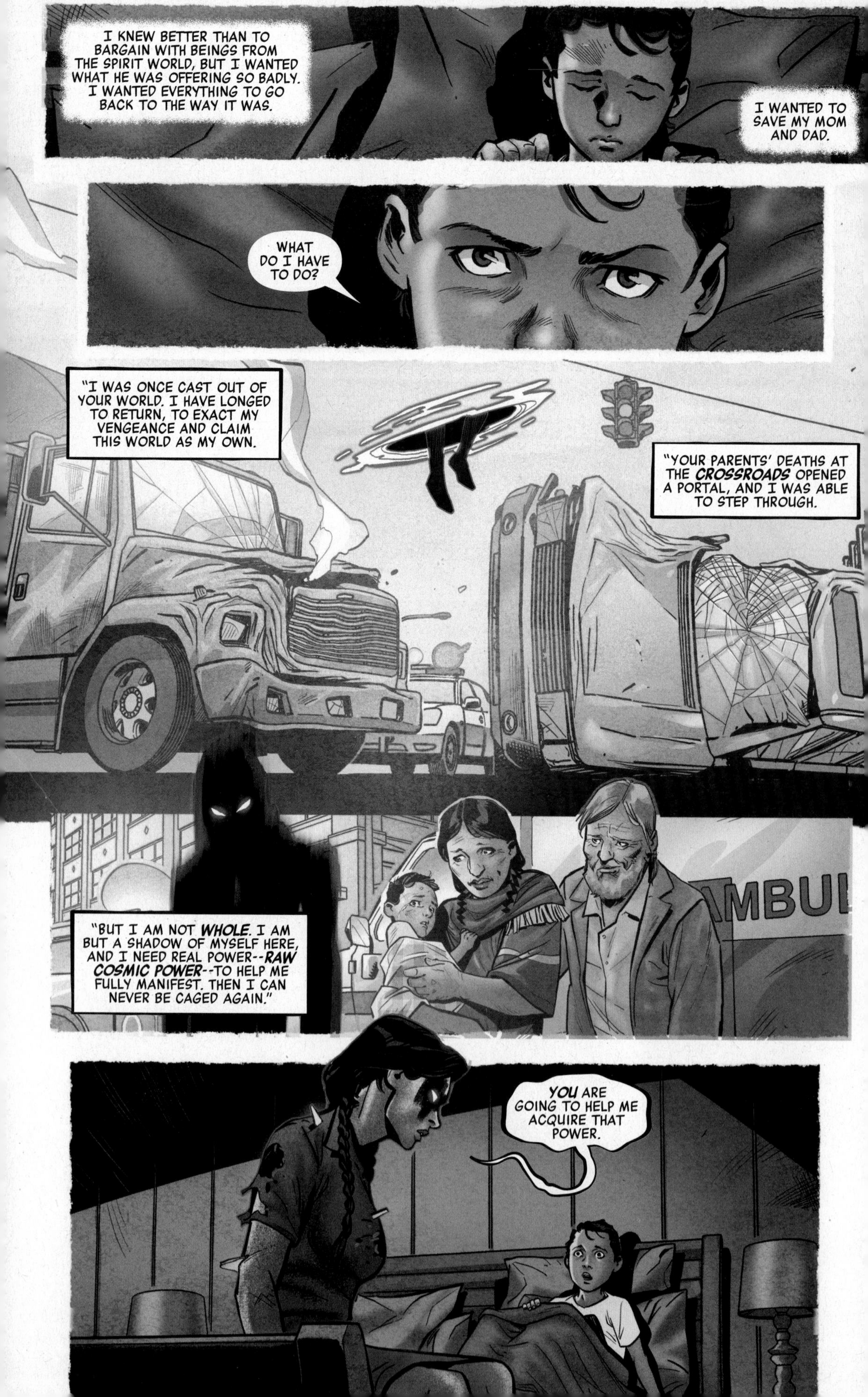
I KNEW BETTER THAN TO BARGAIN WITH BEINGS FROM THE SPIRIT WORLD, BUT I WANTED WHAT HE WAS OFFERING SO BADLY. I WANTED EVERYTHING TO GO BACK TO THE WAY IT WAS.
I WANTED TO SAVE MY MOM AND DAD.
WHAT DO I HAVE TO DO?
"I WAS ONCE CAST OUT OF YOUR WORLD. I HAVE LONGED TO RETURN, TO EXACT MY VENGEANCE AND CLAIM THIS WORLD AS MY OWN.
"YOUR PARENTS' DEATHS AT THE CROSSROADS OPENED A PORTAL, AND I WAS ABLE TO STEP THROUGH.
AMBUL
"BUT I AM NOT WHOLE. I AM BUT A SHADOW OF MYSELF HERE, AND I NEED REAL POWER--RAW COSMIC POWER--TO HELP ME FULLY MANIFEST. THEN I CAN NEVER BE CAGED AGAIN."
YOU ARE GOING TO HELP ME ACQUIRE THAT POWER.

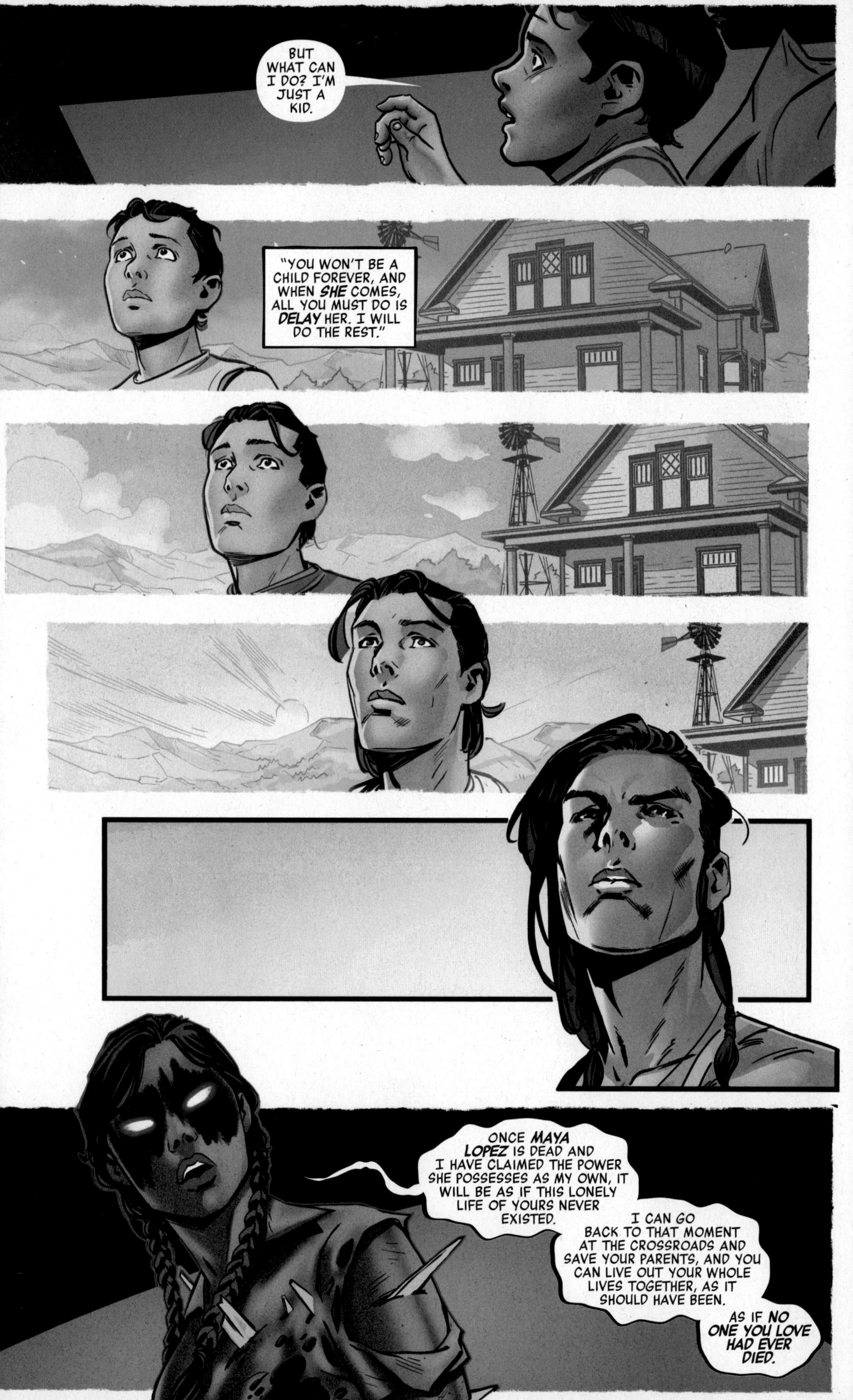
BUT WHAT CAN I DO? I'M JUST A KID.
"YOU WON'T BE A CHILD FOREVER, AND WHEN SHE COMES, ALL YOU MUST DO IS DELAY HER. I WILL DO THE REST."
ONCE MAYA LOPEZ IS DEAD AND I HAVE CLAIMED THE POWER SHE POSSESSES AS MY OWN, IT WILL BE AS IF THIS LONELY LIFE OF YOURS NEVER EXISTED.
I CAN GO BACK TO THAT MOMENT AT THE CROSSROADS AND SAVE YOUR PARENTS, AND YOU CAN LIVE OUT YOUR WHOLE LIVES TOGETHER, AS IT SHOULD HAVE BEEN.
AS IF NO ONE YOU LOVE HAD EVER DIED.

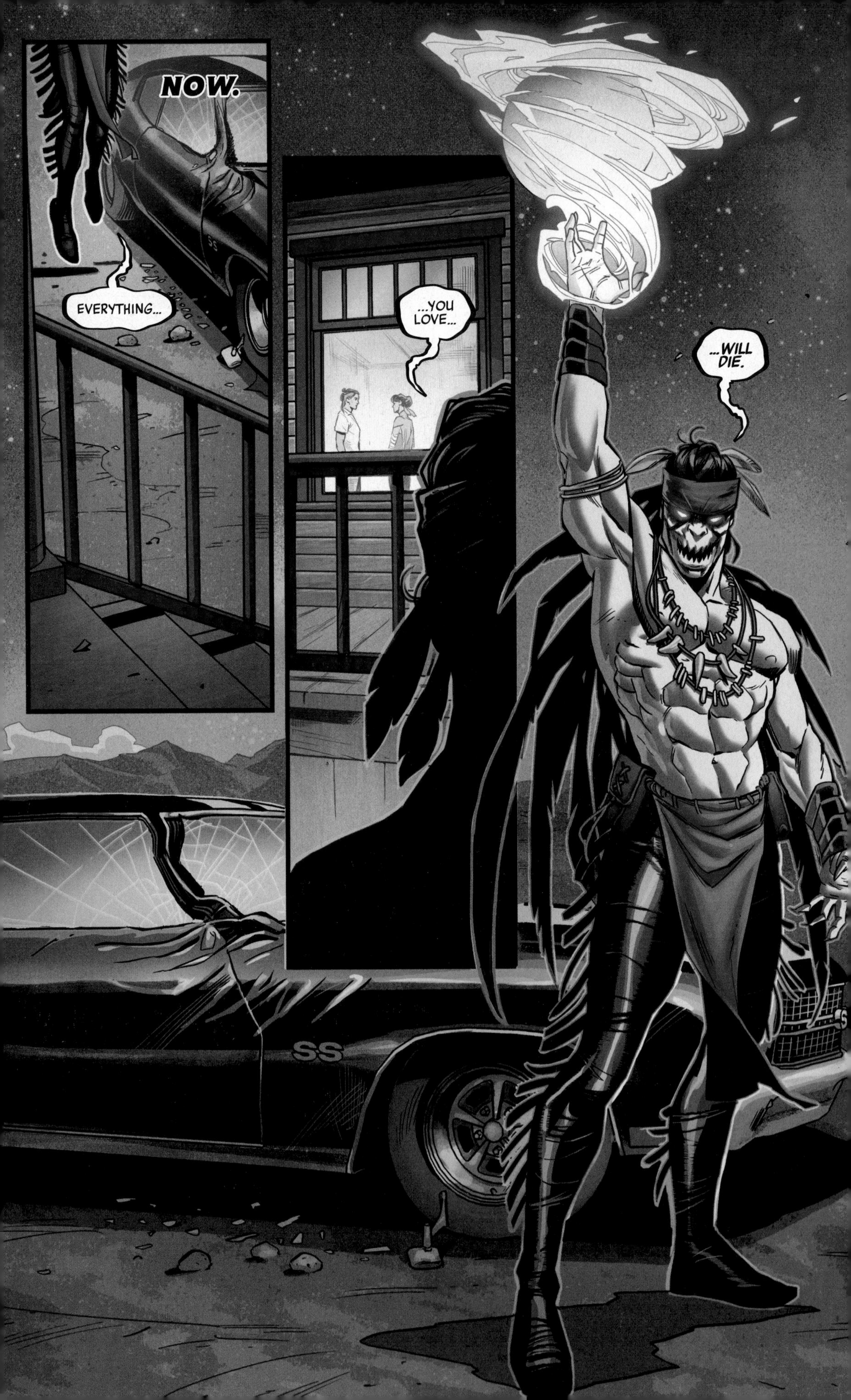
NOW.
EVERYTHING...
...YOU LOVE...
...WILL DIE.
SS

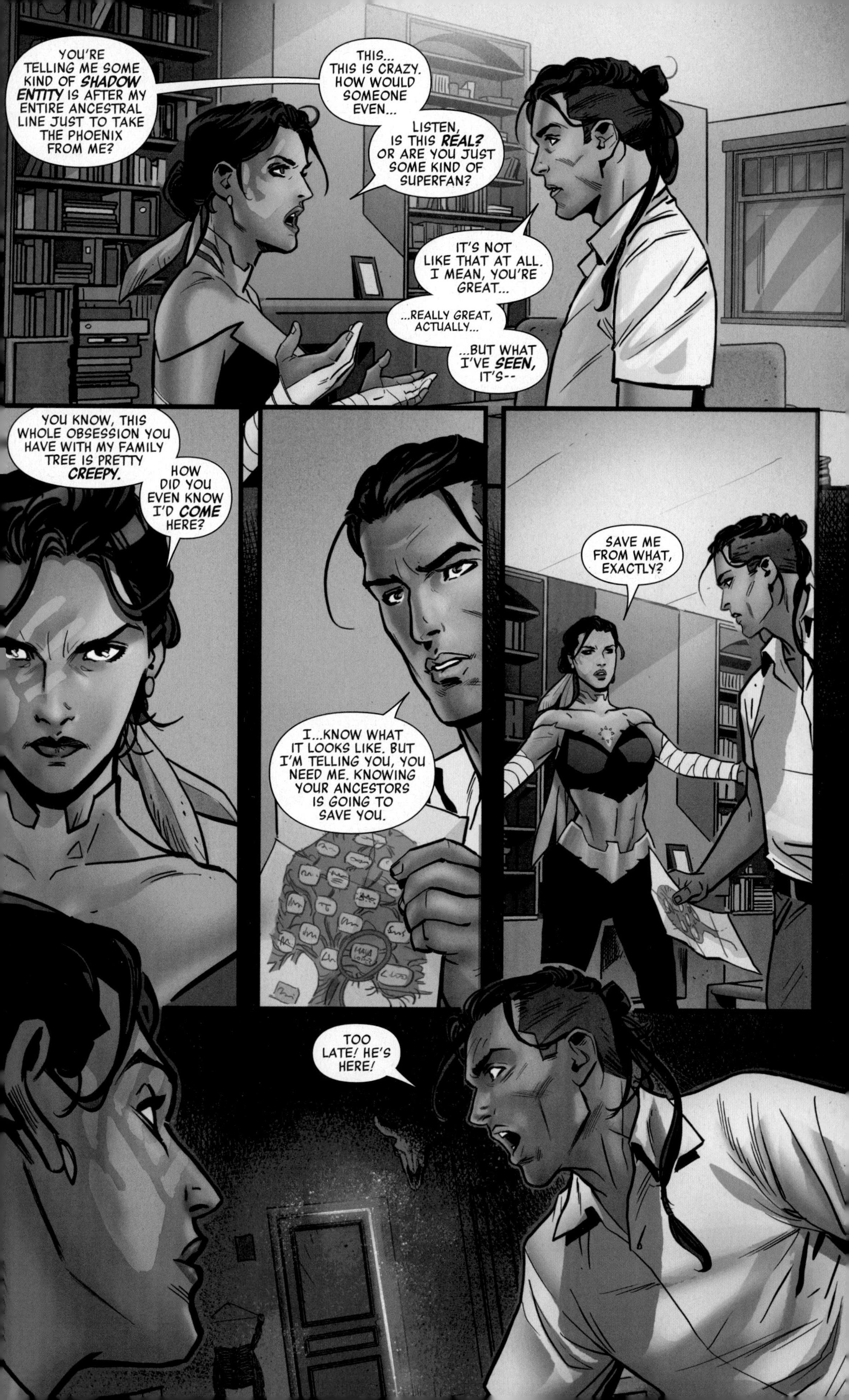
YOU'RE TELLING ME SOME KIND OF SHADOW ENTITY IS AFTER MY ENTIRE ANCESTRAL LINE JUST TO TAKE THE PHOENIX FROM ME?
THIS... THIS IS CRAZY. HOW WOULD SOMEONE EVEN...
LISTEN, IS THIS REAL? OR ARE YOU JUST SOME KIND OF SUPERFAN?
IT'S NOT LIKE THAT AT ALL. I MEAN, YOU'RE GREAT...
...REALLY GREAT, ACTUALLY...
...BUT WHAT I'VE SEEN, IT'S--
YOU KNOW, THIS WHOLE OBSESSION YOU HAVE WITH MY FAMILY TREE IS PRETTY CREEPY.
HOW DID YOU EVEN KNOW I'D COME HERE?
I...KNOW WHAT IT LOOKS LIKE. BUT I'M TELLING YOU, YOU NEED ME. KNOWING YOUR ANCESTORS IS GOING TO SAVE YOU.
SAVE ME FROM WHAT, EXACTLY?
TOO LATE! HE'S HERE!

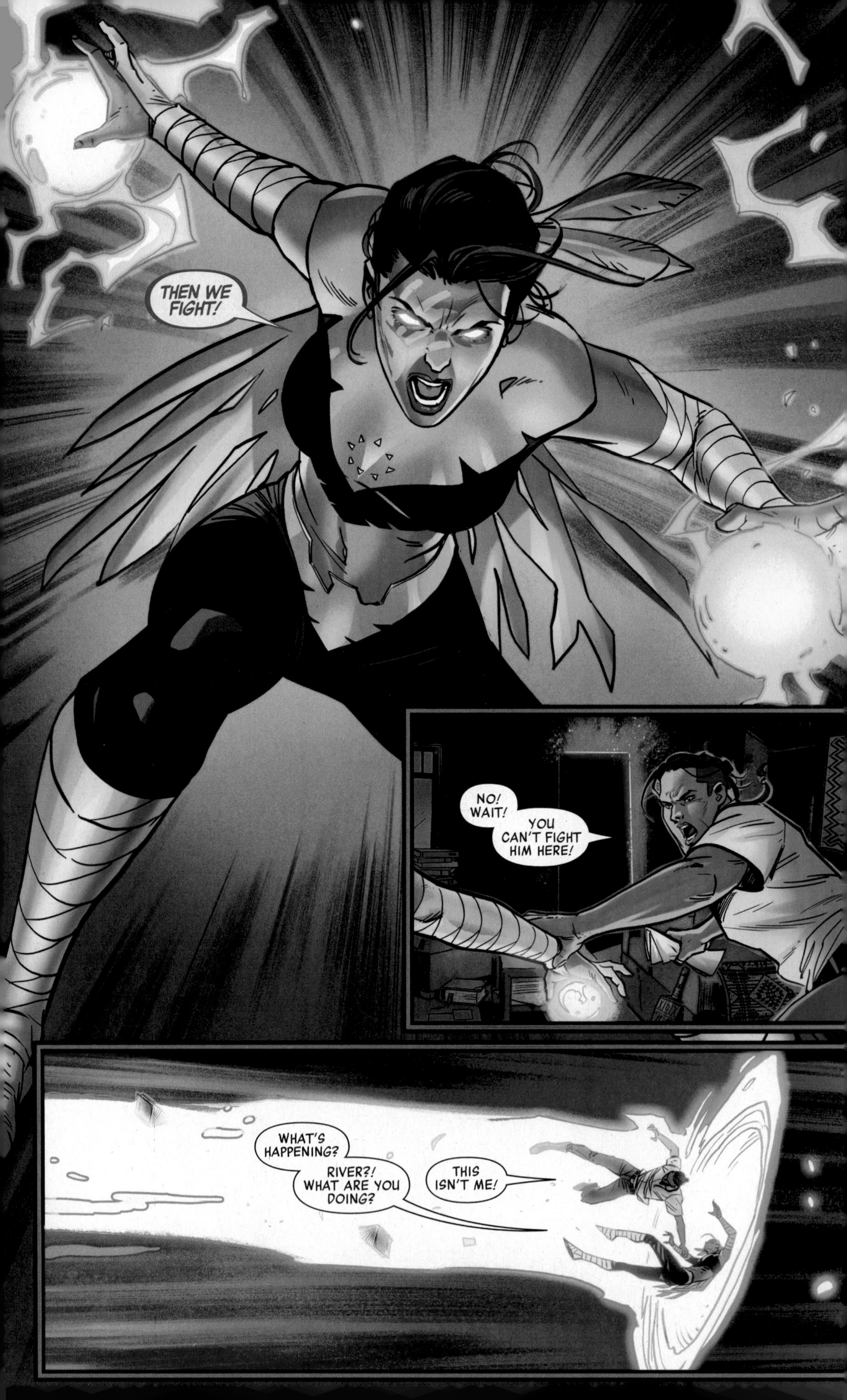
THEN WE FIGHT!
NO! WAIT!
YOU CAN'T FIGHT HIM HERE!
WHAT'S HAPPENING?
RIVER?! WHAT ARE YOU DOING?
THIS ISN'T ME!

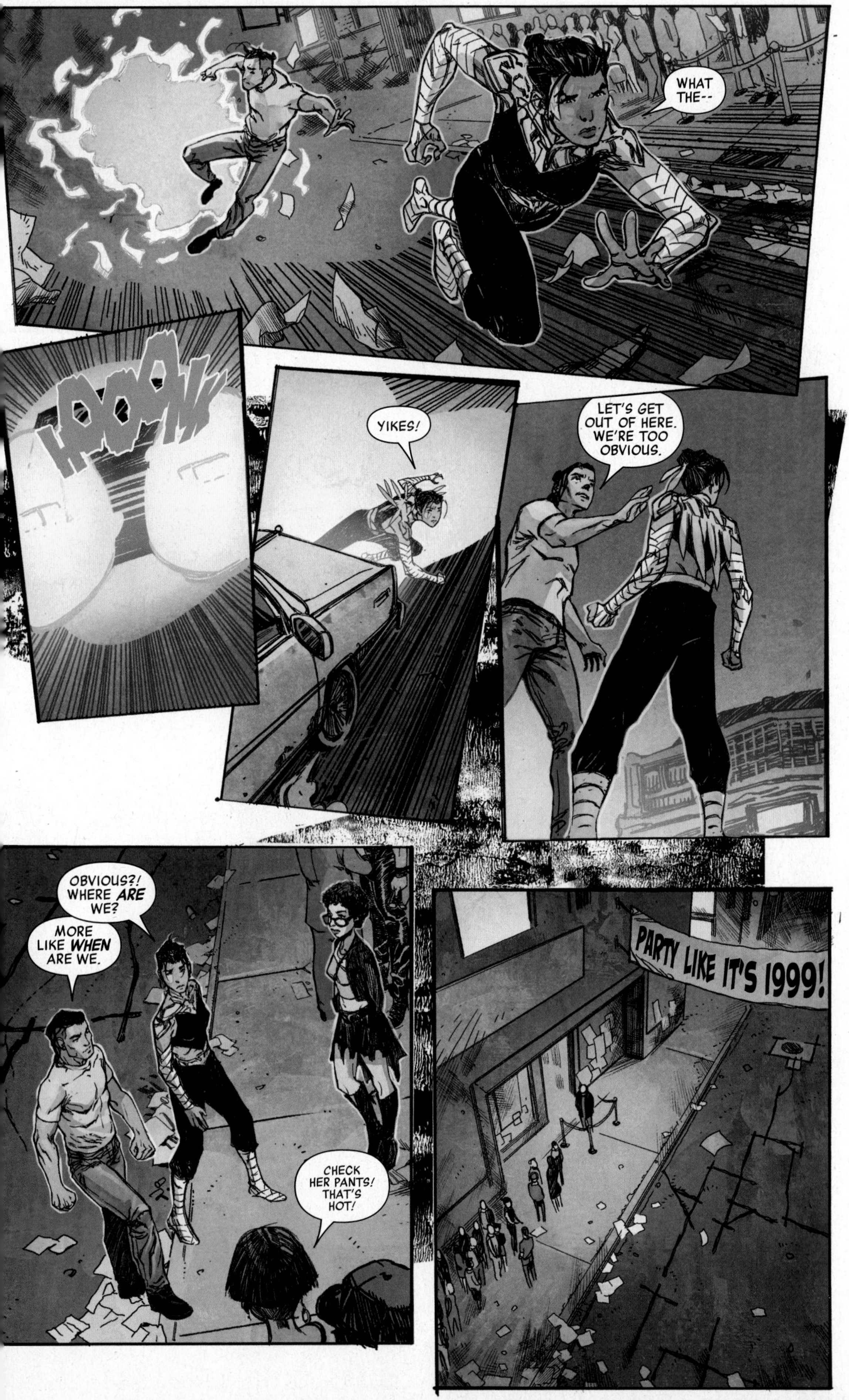
WHAT THE--
YIKES!
LET'S GET OUT OF HERE. WE'RE TOO OBVIOUS.
OBVIOUS?! WHERE *ARE* WE?
MORE LIKE *WHEN* ARE WE.
CHECK HER PANTS! THAT'S HOT!
PARTY LIKE IT'S 1999!

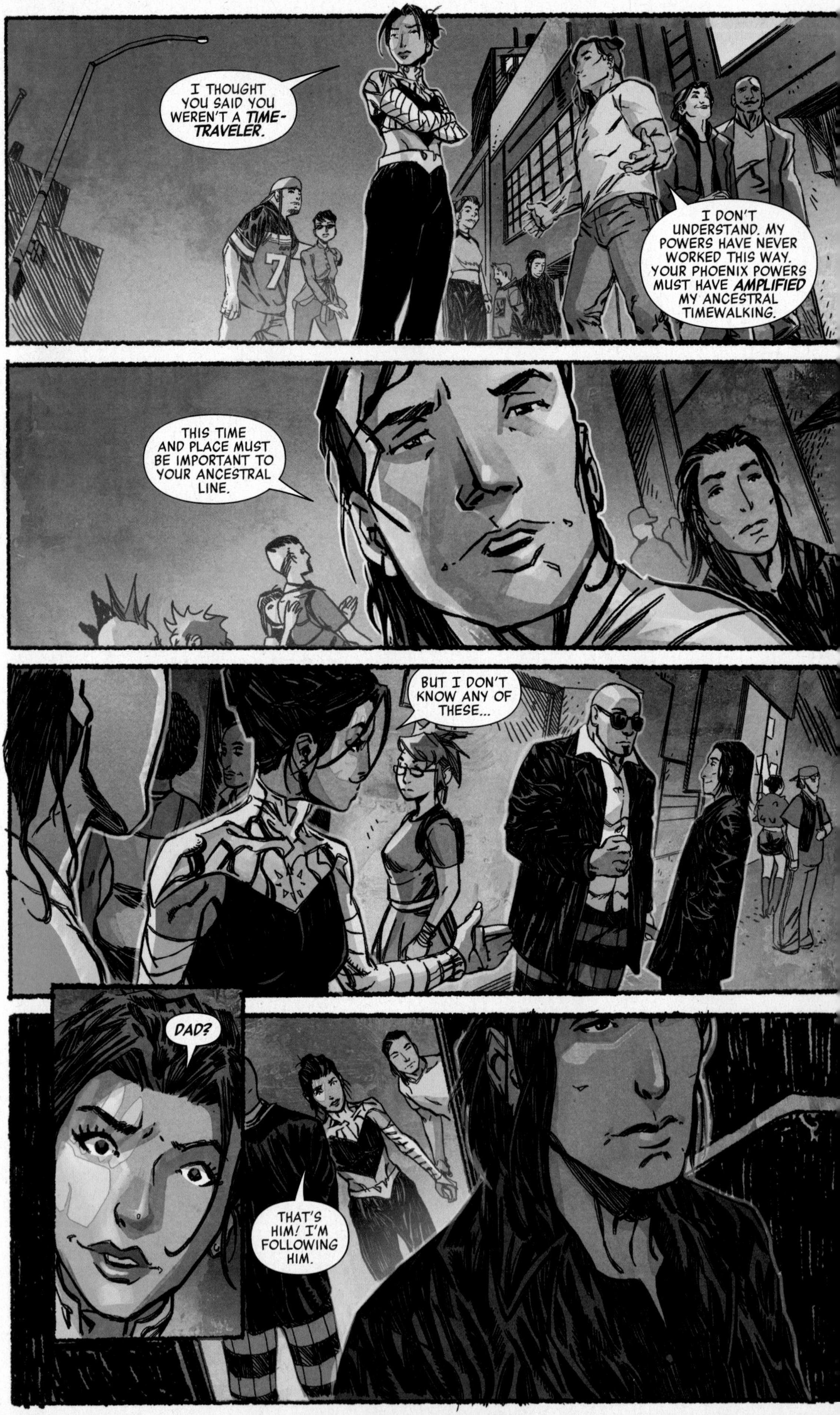
I THOUGHT YOU SAID YOU WEREN'T A *TIME-TRAVELER*.
I DON'T UNDERSTAND. MY POWERS HAVE NEVER WORKED THIS WAY. YOUR PHOENIX POWERS MUST HAVE *AMPLIFIED* MY ANCESTRAL TIMEWALKING.
THIS TIME AND PLACE MUST BE IMPORTANT TO YOUR ANCESTRAL LINE.
BUT I DON'T KNOW ANY OF THESE...
DAD?
THAT'S HIM! I'M FOLLOWING HIM.

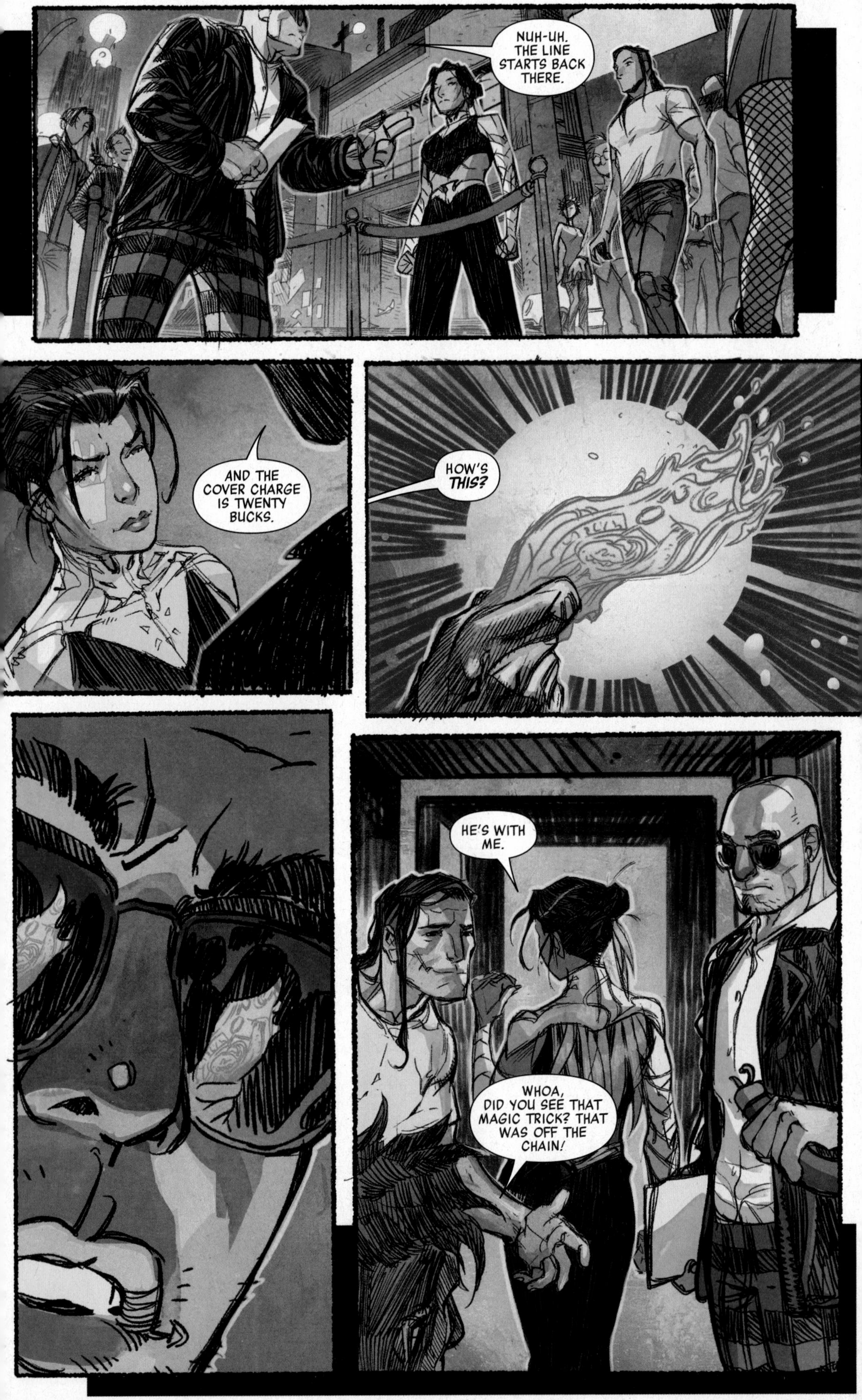
NUH-UH. THE LINE STARTS BACK THERE.
AND THE COVER CHARGE IS TWENTY BUCKS.
HOW'S *THIS?*
HE'S WITH ME.
WHOA, DID YOU SEE THAT MAGIC TRICK? THAT WAS OFF THE CHAIN!

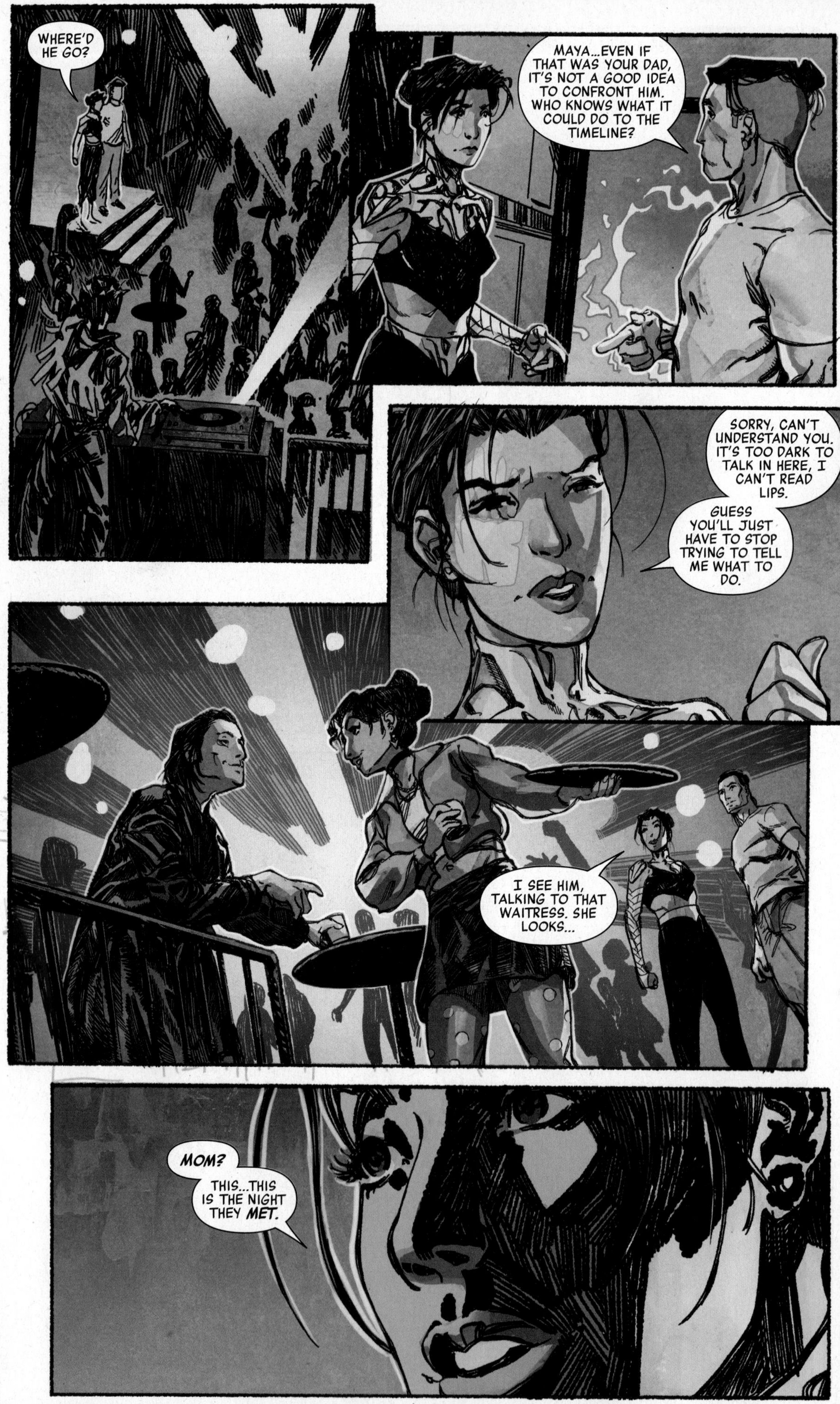
WHERE'D HE GO?
MAYA...EVEN IF THAT WAS YOUR DAD, IT'S NOT A GOOD IDEA TO CONFRONT HIM. WHO KNOWS WHAT IT COULD DO TO THE TIMELINE?
SORRY, CAN'T UNDERSTAND YOU. IT'S TOO DARK TO TALK IN HERE, I CAN'T READ LIPS.
GUESS YOU'LL JUST HAVE TO STOP TRYING TO TELL ME WHAT TO DO.
I SEE HIM, TALKING TO THAT WAITRESS. SHE LOOKS...
MOM?
THIS...THIS IS THE NIGHT THEY MET.

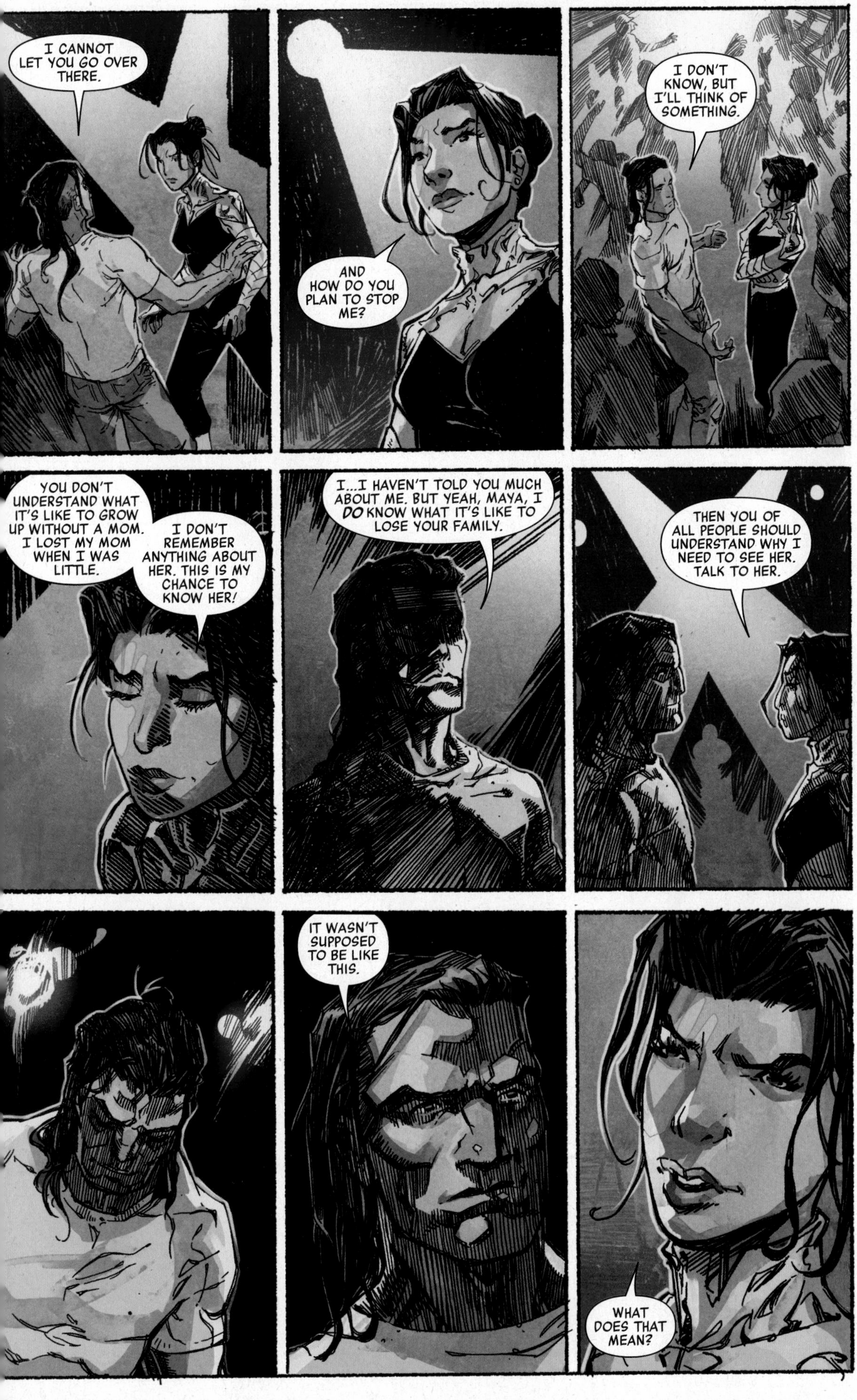
I CANNOT LET YOU GO OVER THERE.
AND HOW DO YOU PLAN TO STOP ME?
I DON'T KNOW, BUT I'LL THINK OF SOMETHING.
YOU DON'T UNDERSTAND WHAT IT'S LIKE TO GROW UP WITHOUT A MOM. I LOST MY MOM WHEN I WAS LITTLE.
I DON'T REMEMBER ANYTHING ABOUT HER. THIS IS MY CHANCE TO KNOW HER!
I...I HAVEN'T TOLD YOU MUCH ABOUT ME. BUT YEAH, MAYA, I *DO* KNOW WHAT IT'S LIKE TO LOSE YOUR FAMILY.
THEN YOU OF ALL PEOPLE SHOULD UNDERSTAND WHY I NEED TO SEE HER. TALK TO HER.
IT WASN'T SUPPOSED TO BE LIKE THIS.
WHAT DOES THAT MEAN?

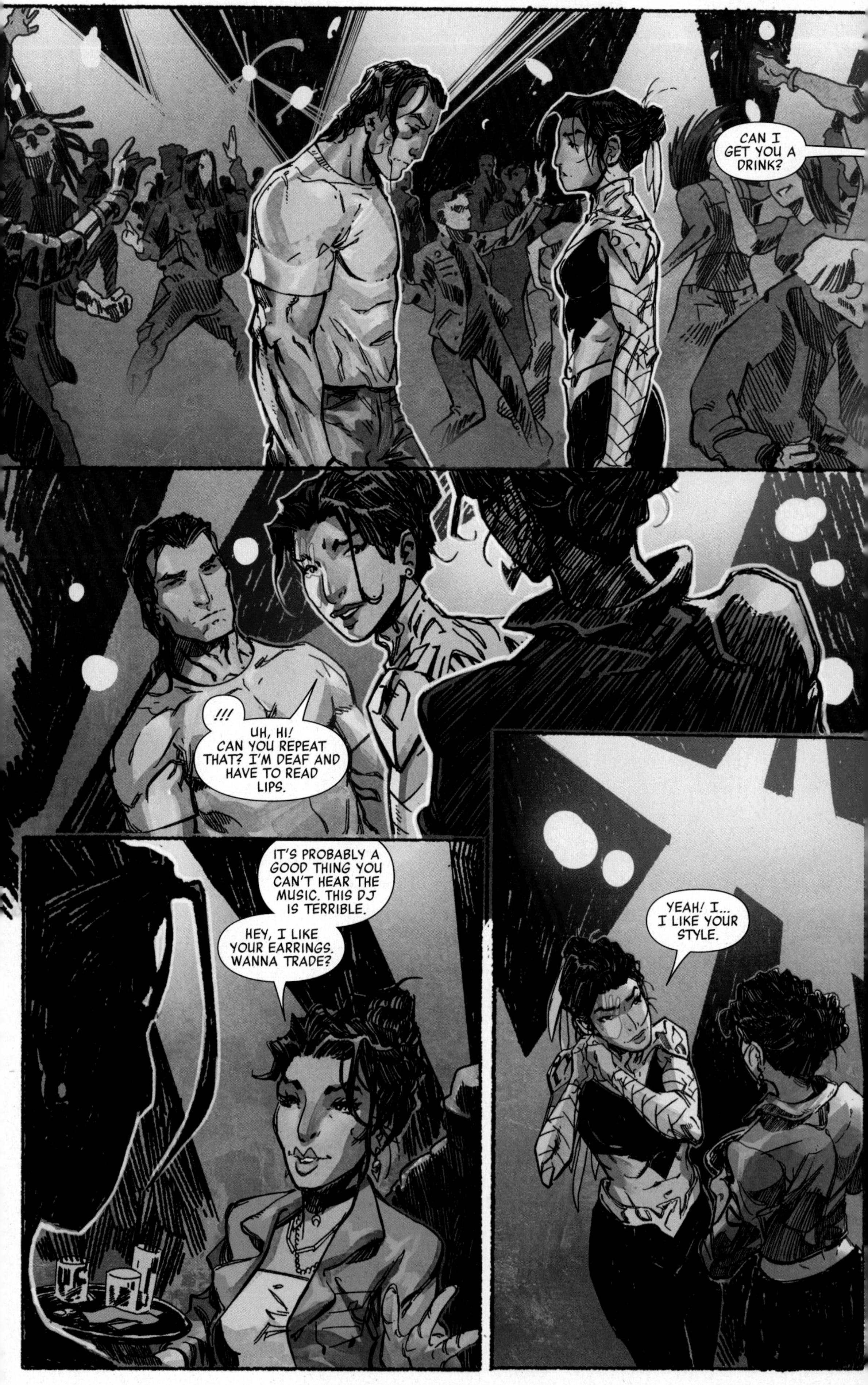
CAN I GET YOU A DRINK?
!!!
UH, HI! CAN YOU REPEAT THAT? I'M DEAF AND HAVE TO READ LIPS.
IT'S PROBABLY A GOOD THING YOU CAN'T HEAR THE MUSIC. THIS DJ IS TERRIBLE.
HEY, I LIKE YOUR EARRINGS. WANNA TRADE?
YEAH! I... I LIKE YOUR STYLE.

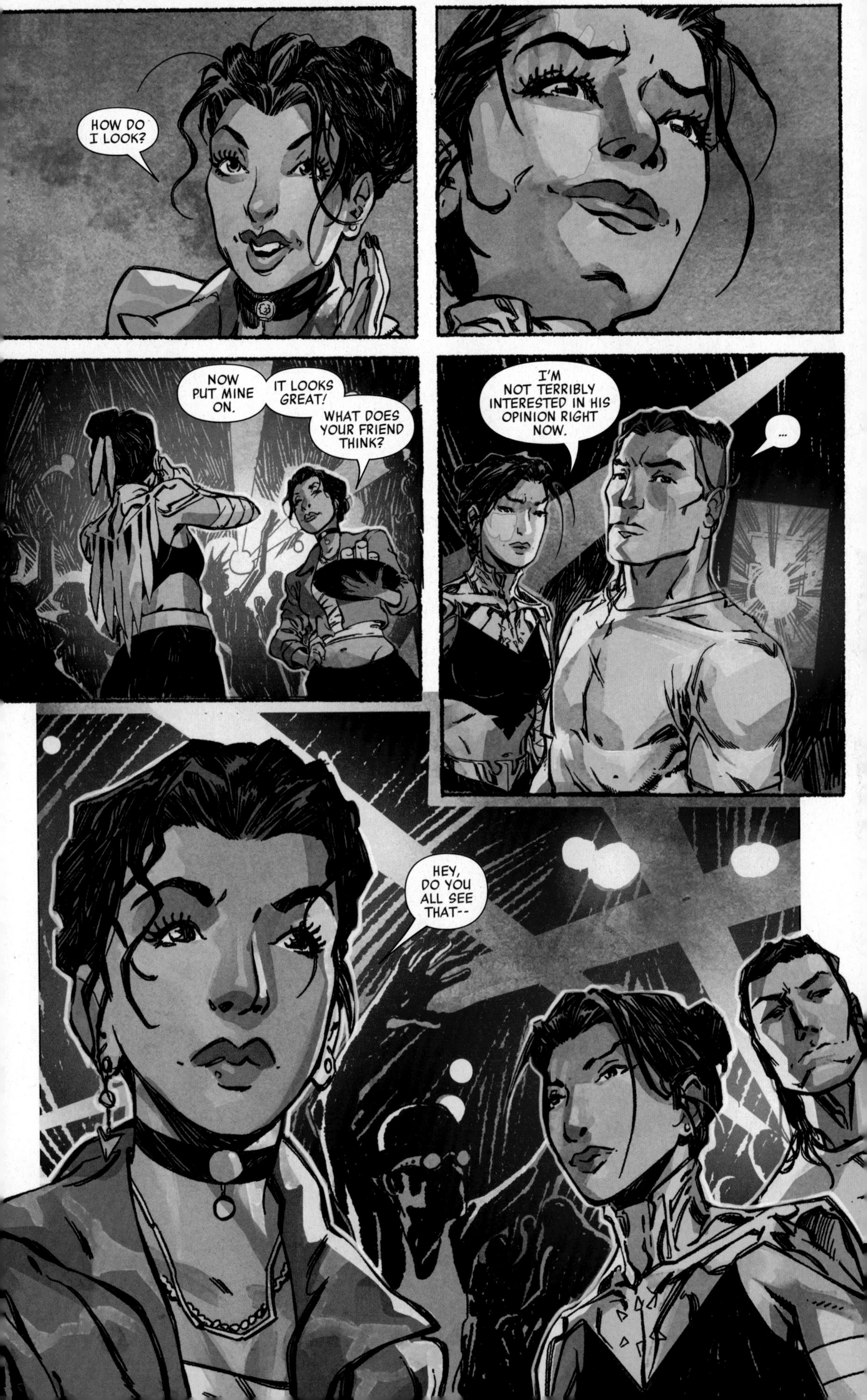
HOW DO I LOOK?
NOW PUT MINE ON.
IT LOOKS GREAT!
WHAT DOES YOUR FRIEND THINK?
I'M NOT TERRIBLY INTERESTED IN HIS OPINION RIGHT NOW.
...
HEY, DO YOU ALL SEE THAT--

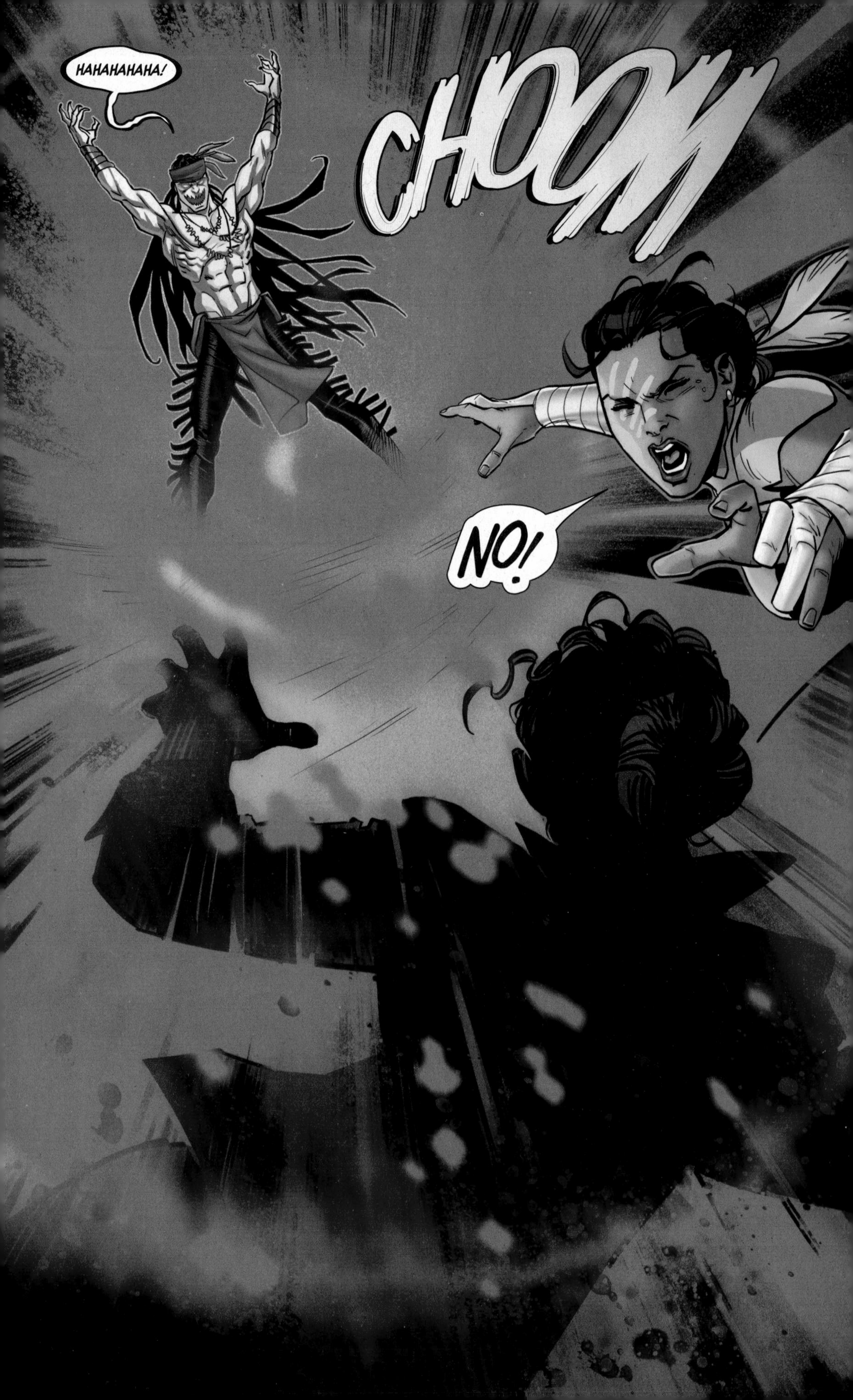
HAHAHAHAHA!
CHOOM
NO!

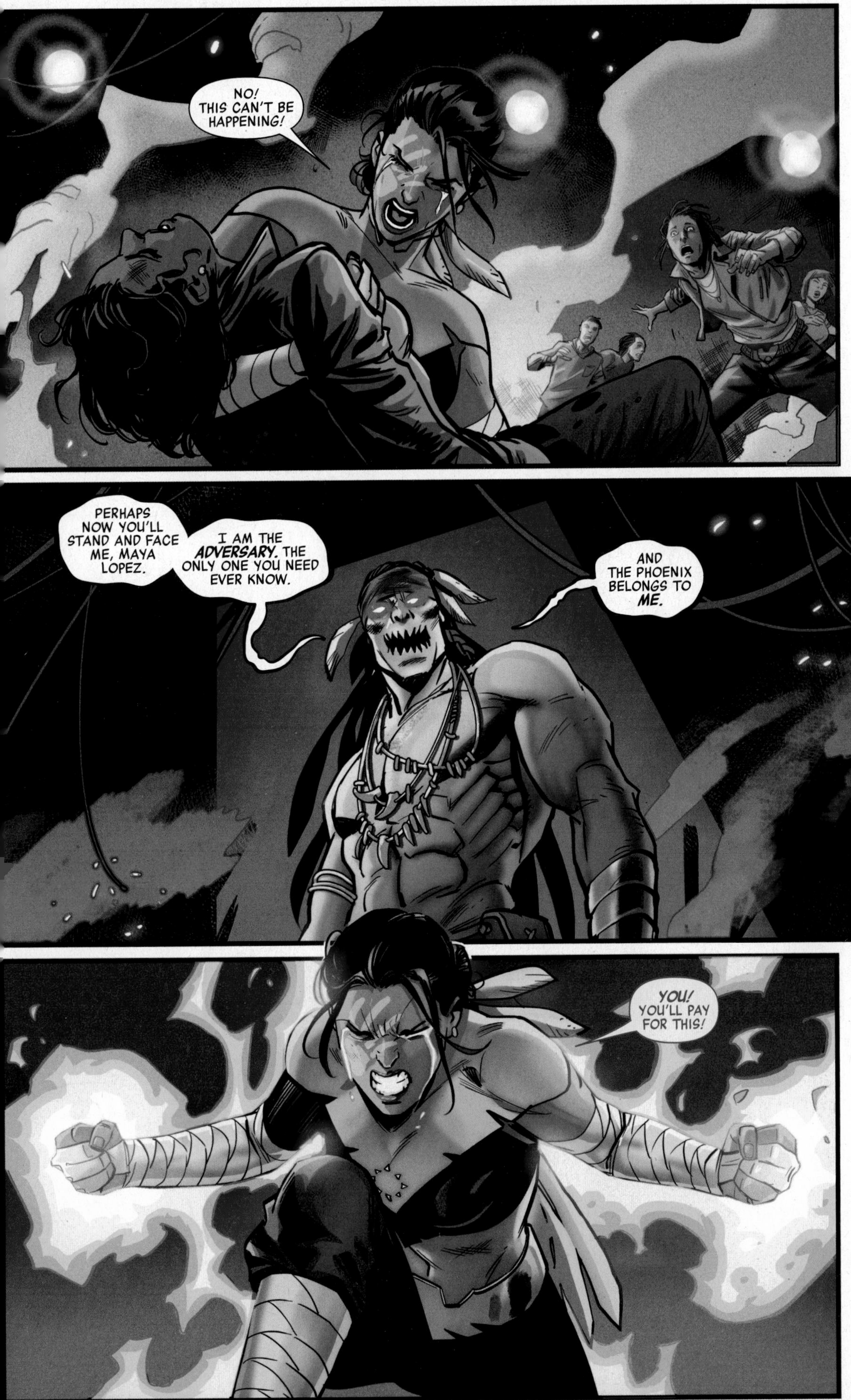
NO! THIS CAN'T BE HAPPENING!
PERHAPS NOW YOU'LL STAND AND FACE ME, MAYA LOPEZ.
I AM THE ADVERSARY. THE ONLY ONE YOU NEED EVER KNOW.
AND THE PHOENIX BELONGS TO ME.
YOU! YOU'LL PAY FOR THIS!

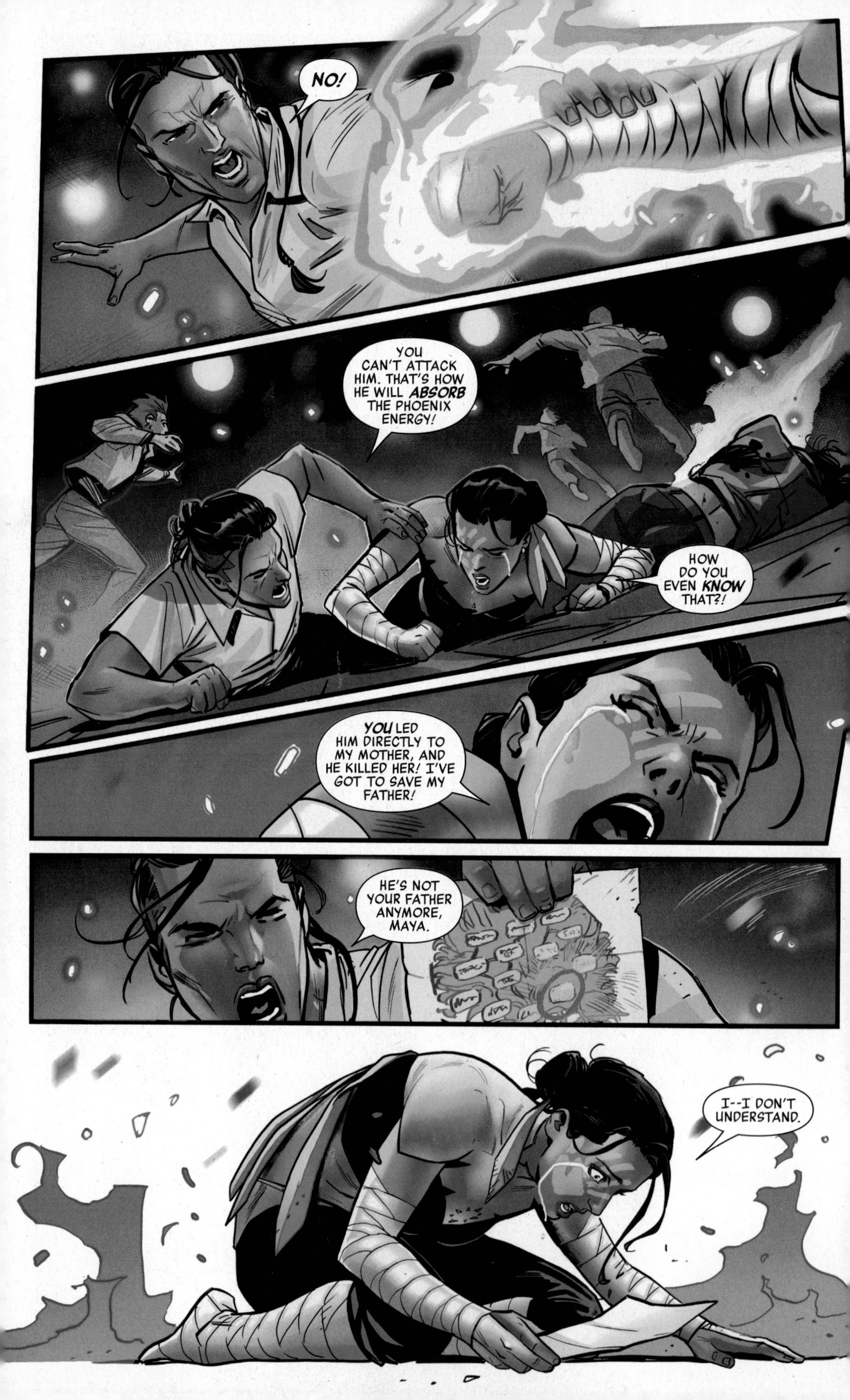
NO!
YOU CAN'T ATTACK HIM. THAT'S HOW HE WILL ABSORB THE PHOENIX ENERGY!
HOW DO YOU EVEN KNOW THAT?!
YOU LED HIM DIRECTLY TO MY MOTHER, AND HE KILLED HER! I'VE GOT TO SAVE MY FATHER!
HE'S NOT YOUR FATHER ANYMORE, MAYA.
I--I DON'T UNDERSTAND.

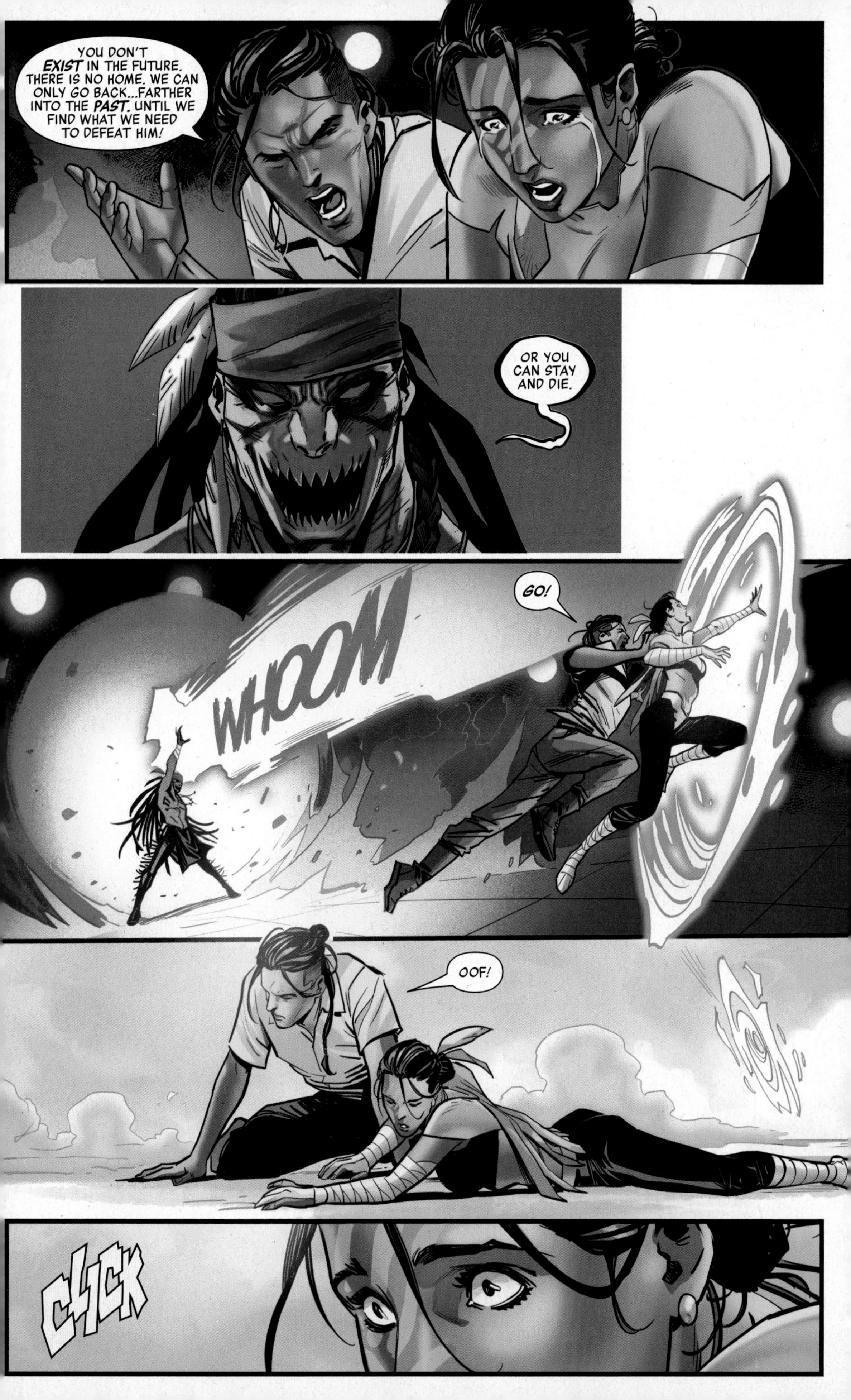
YOU DON'T EXIST IN THE FUTURE. THERE IS NO HOME. WE CAN ONLY GO BACK...FARTHER INTO THE PAST. UNTIL WE FIND WHAT WE NEED TO DEFEAT HIM!
OR YOU CAN STAY AND DIE.
WHOOM
GO!
OOF!
CLICK

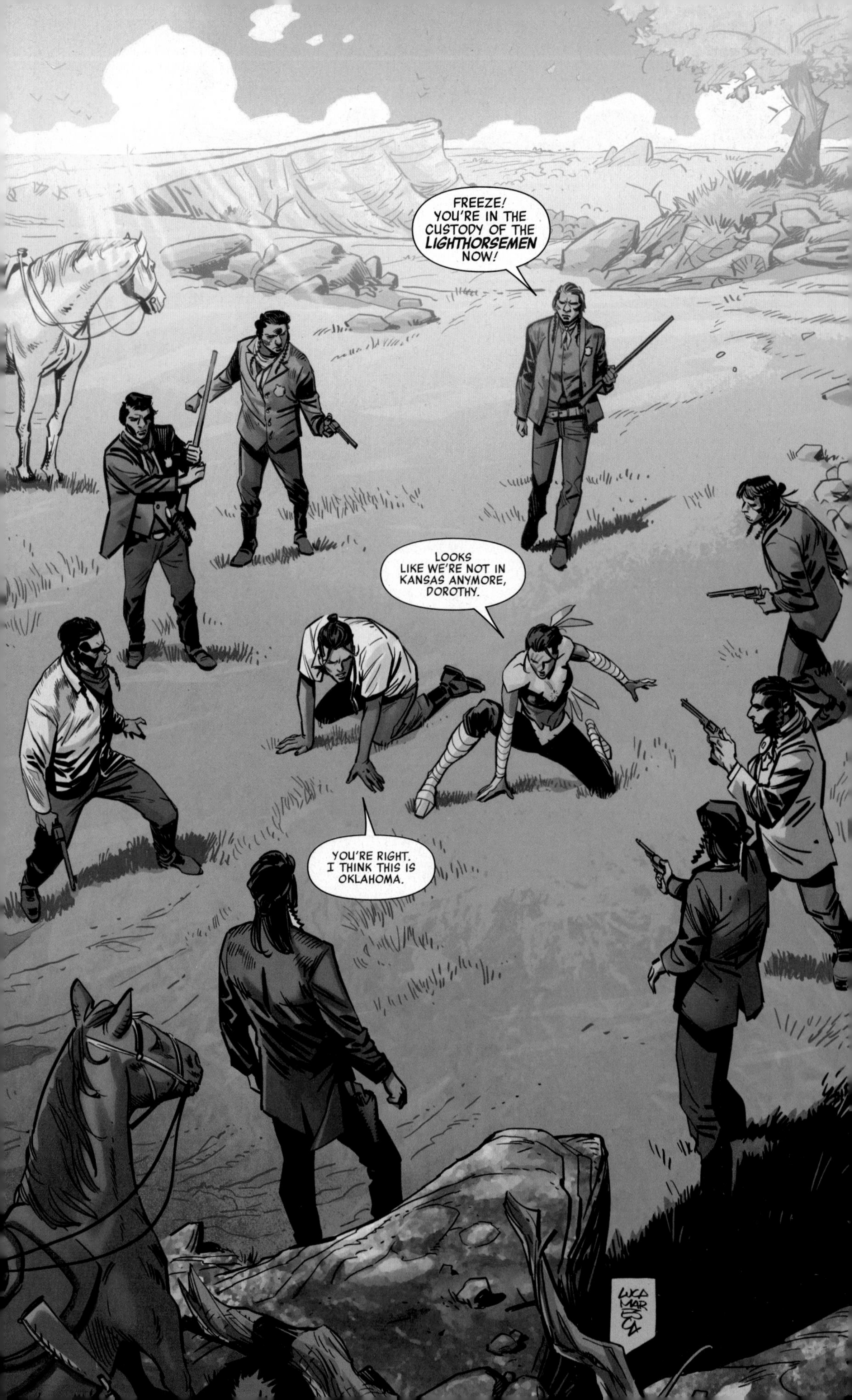
FREEZE! YOU'RE IN THE CUSTODY OF THE LIGHTHORSEMEN NOW!
LOOKS LIKE WE'RE NOT IN KANSAS ANYMORE, DOROTHY.
YOU'RE RIGHT. I THINK THIS IS OKLAHOMA.

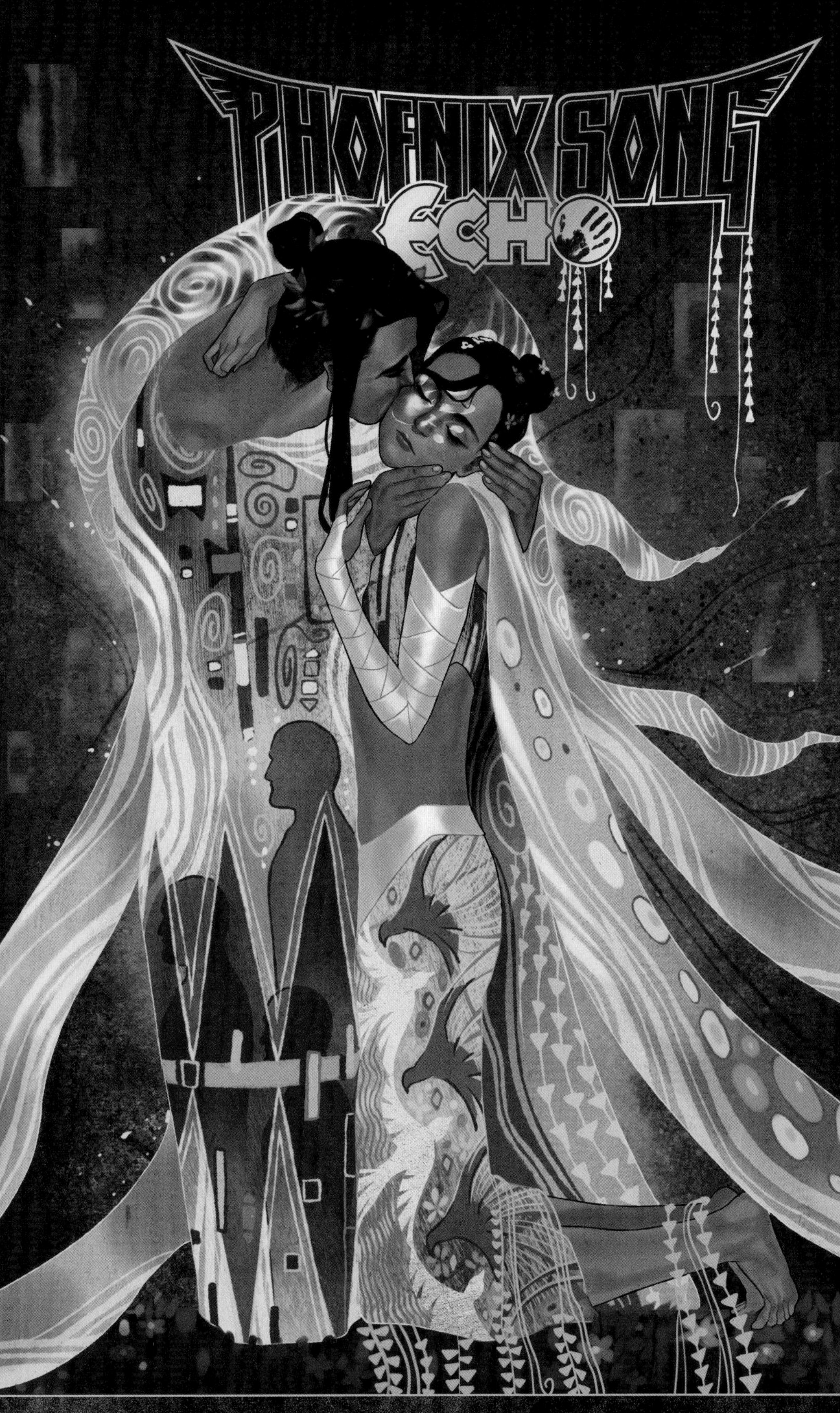
PHOENIX SONG
ECHO

#1 VARIANT BY **OSCAR VEGA**

3

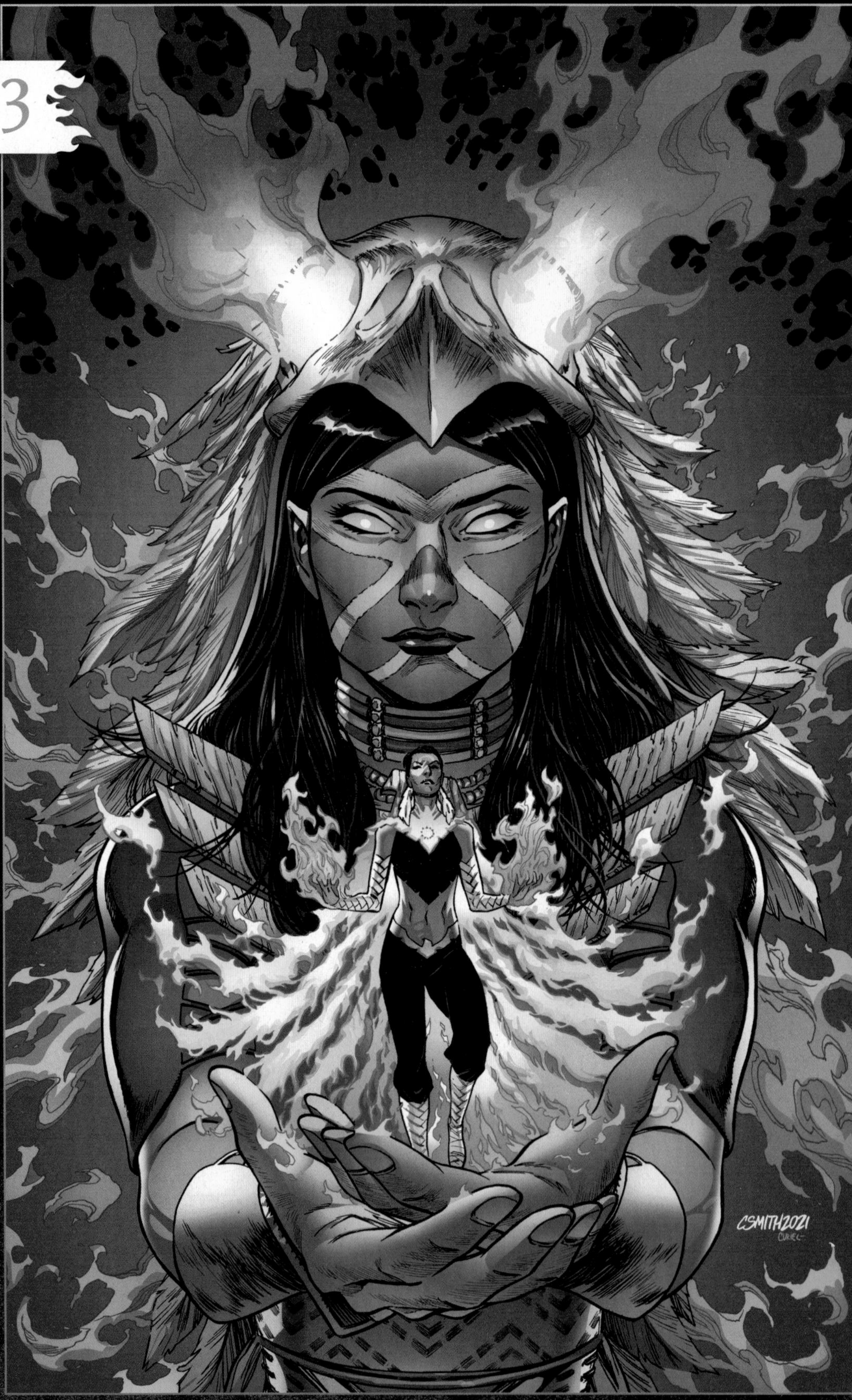
CSMITH2021

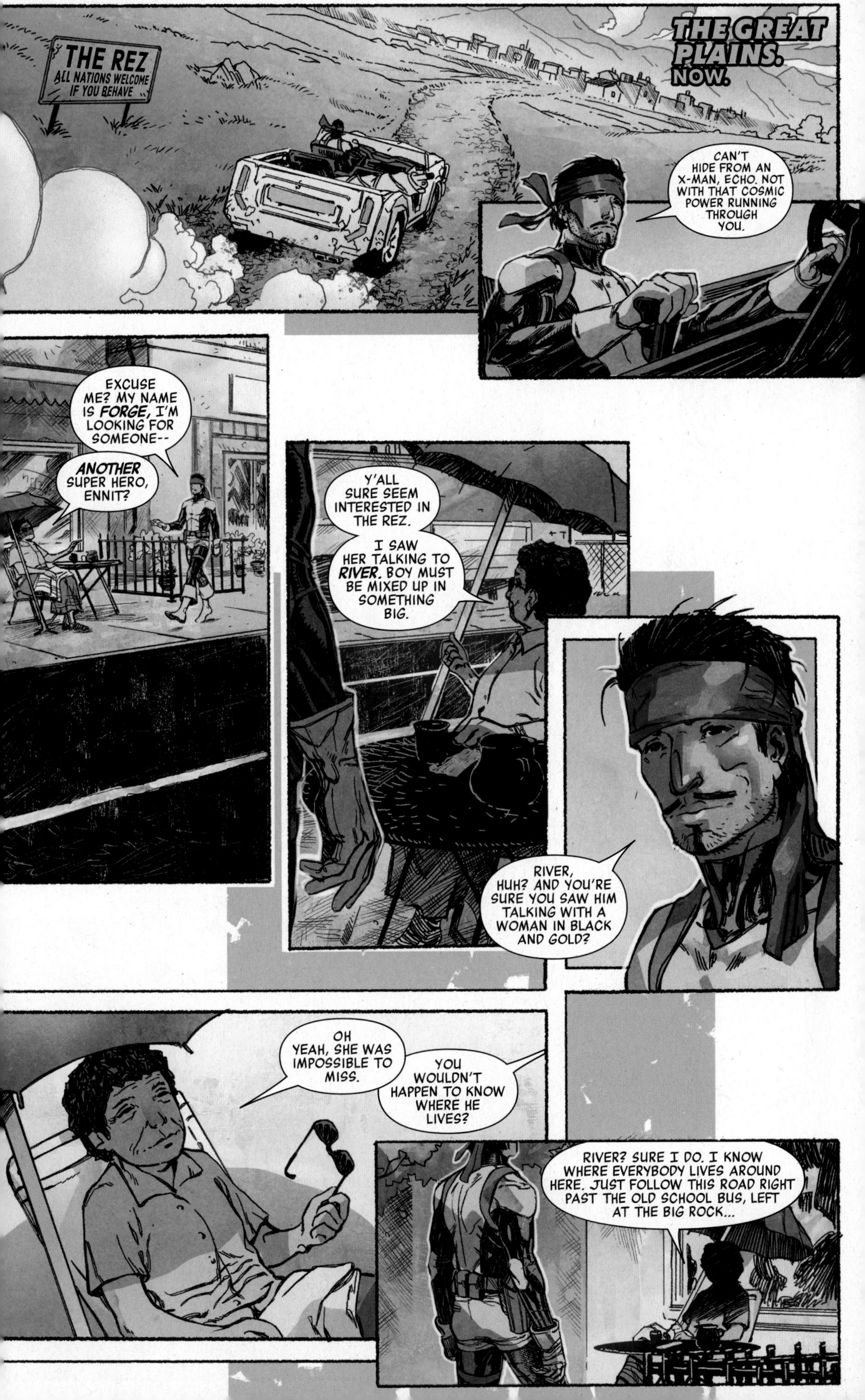
THE REZ
ALL NATIONS WELCOME IF YOU BEHAVE
THE GREAT PLAINS. NOW.
CAN'T HIDE FROM AN X-MAN, ECHO. NOT WITH THAT COSMIC POWER RUNNING THROUGH YOU.
EXCUSE ME? MY NAME IS FORGE, I'M LOOKING FOR SOMEONE--
ANOTHER SUPER HERO, ENNIT?
Y'ALL SURE SEEM INTERESTED IN THE REZ.
I SAW HER TALKING TO RIVER. BOY MUST BE MIXED UP IN SOMETHING BIG.
RIVER, HUH? AND YOU'RE SURE YOU SAW HIM TALKING WITH A WOMAN IN BLACK AND GOLD?
OH YEAH, SHE WAS IMPOSSIBLE TO MISS.
YOU WOULDN'T HAPPEN TO KNOW WHERE HE LIVES?
RIVER? SURE I DO. I KNOW WHERE EVERYBODY LIVES AROUND HERE. JUST FOLLOW THIS ROAD RIGHT PAST THE OLD SCHOOL BUS, LEFT AT THE BIG ROCK...

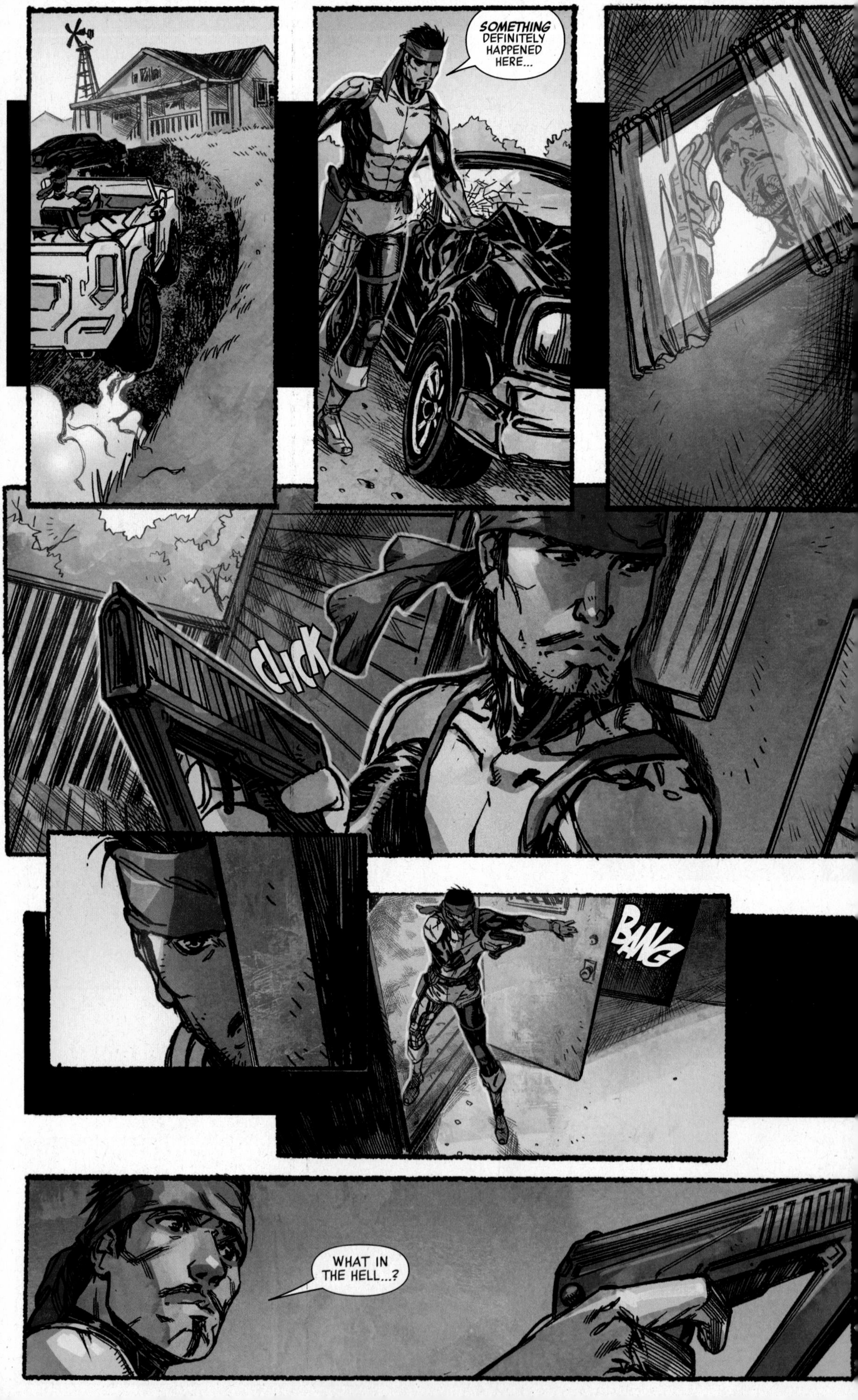
SOMETHING DEFINITELY HAPPENED HERE...
CLICK
BANG
WHAT IN THE HELL...?

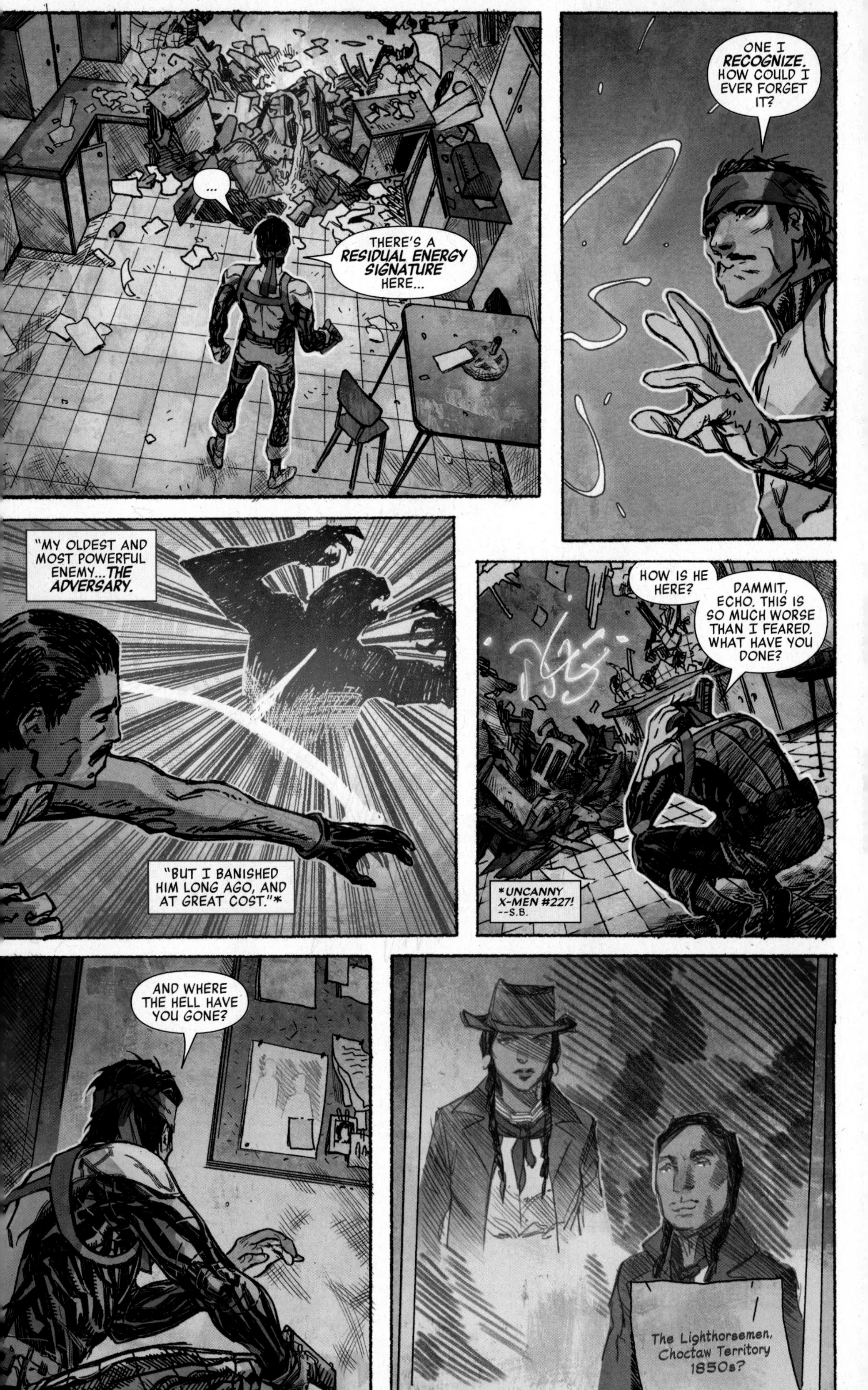
...
THERE'S A RESIDUAL ENERGY SIGNATURE HERE...
ONE I RECOGNIZE. HOW COULD I EVER FORGET IT?
"MY OLDEST AND MOST POWERFUL ENEMY...THE ADVERSARY.
"BUT I BANISHED HIM LONG AGO, AND AT GREAT COST."*
HOW IS HE HERE?
DAMMIT, ECHO. THIS IS SO MUCH WORSE THAN I FEARED. WHAT HAVE YOU DONE?
*UNCANNY X-MEN #227! --S.B.
AND WHERE THE HELL HAVE YOU GONE?
The Lighthorsemen, Choctaw Territory 1850s?

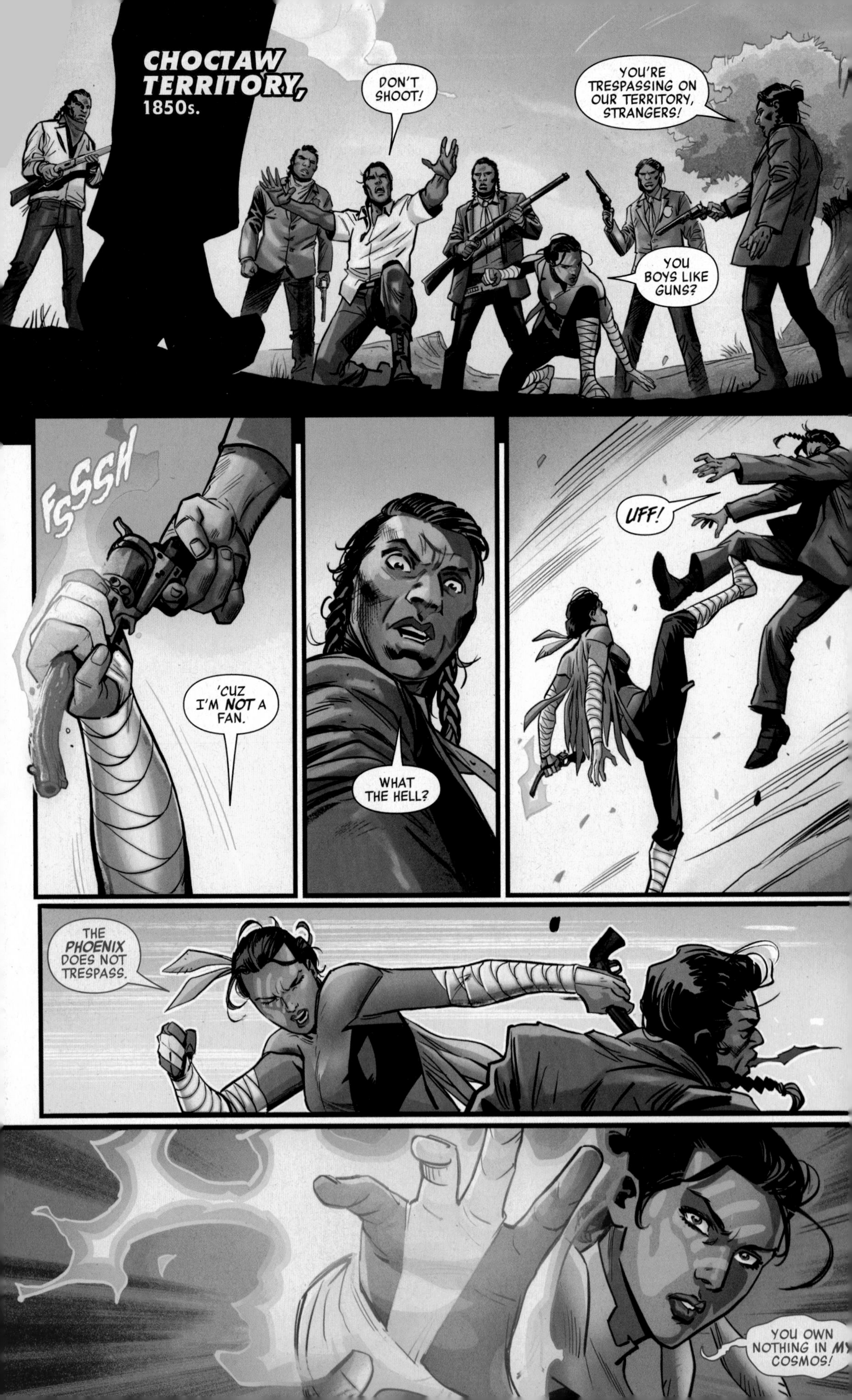
CHOCTAW TERRITORY, 1850s.
DON'T SHOOT!
YOU'RE TRESPASSING ON OUR TERRITORY, STRANGERS!
YOU BOYS LIKE GUNS?
FSSSH
'CUZ I'M NOT A FAN.
WHAT THE HELL?
UFF!
THE PHOENIX DOES NOT TRESPASS.
YOU OWN NOTHING IN MY COSMOS!

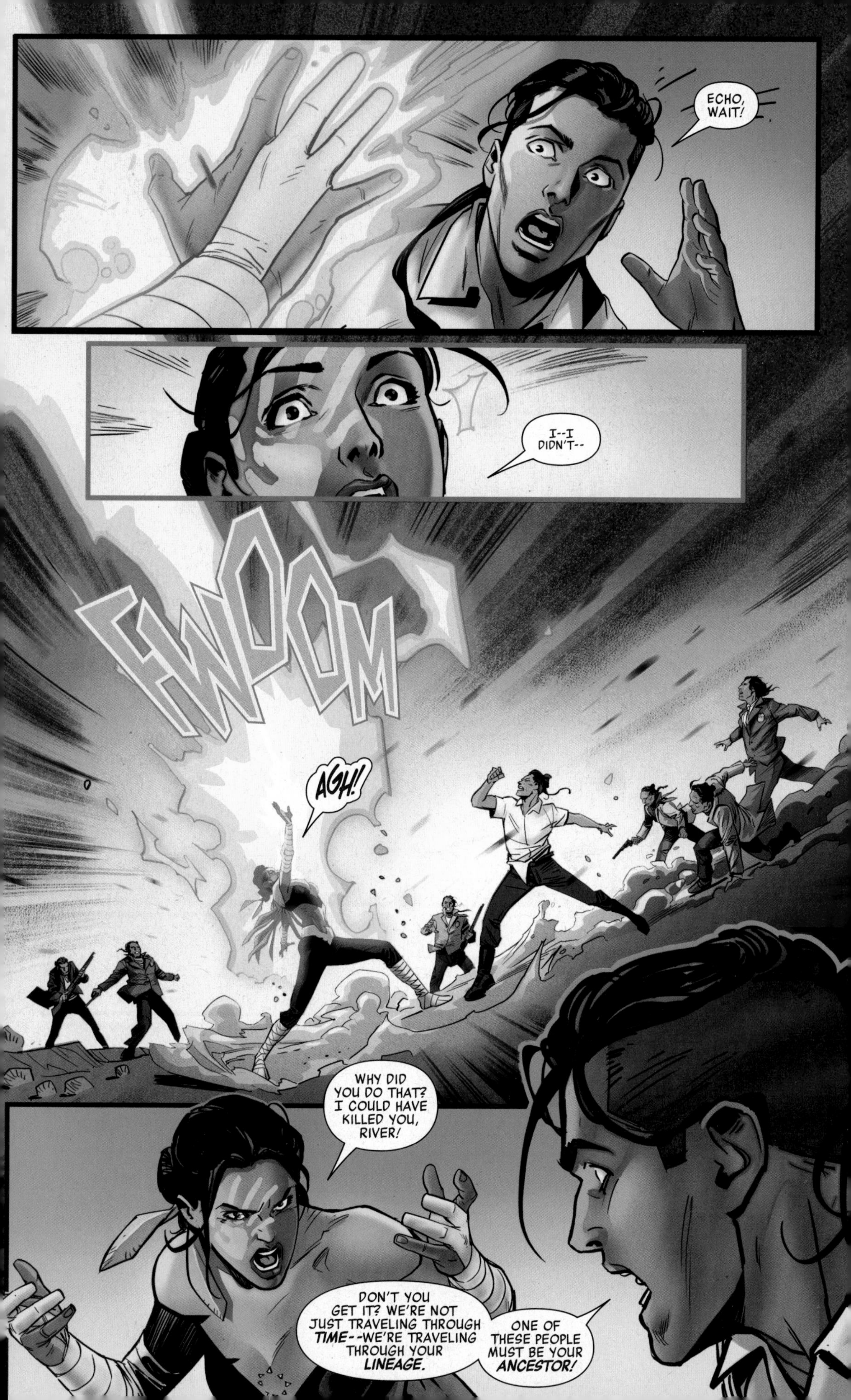
ECHO, WAIT!
I--I DIDN'T--
FWOOM
AGH!
WHY DID YOU DO THAT? I COULD HAVE KILLED YOU, RIVER!
DON'T YOU GET IT? WE'RE NOT JUST TRAVELING THROUGH TIME--WE'RE TRAVELING THROUGH YOUR LINEAGE.
ONE OF THESE PEOPLE MUST BE YOUR ANCESTOR!

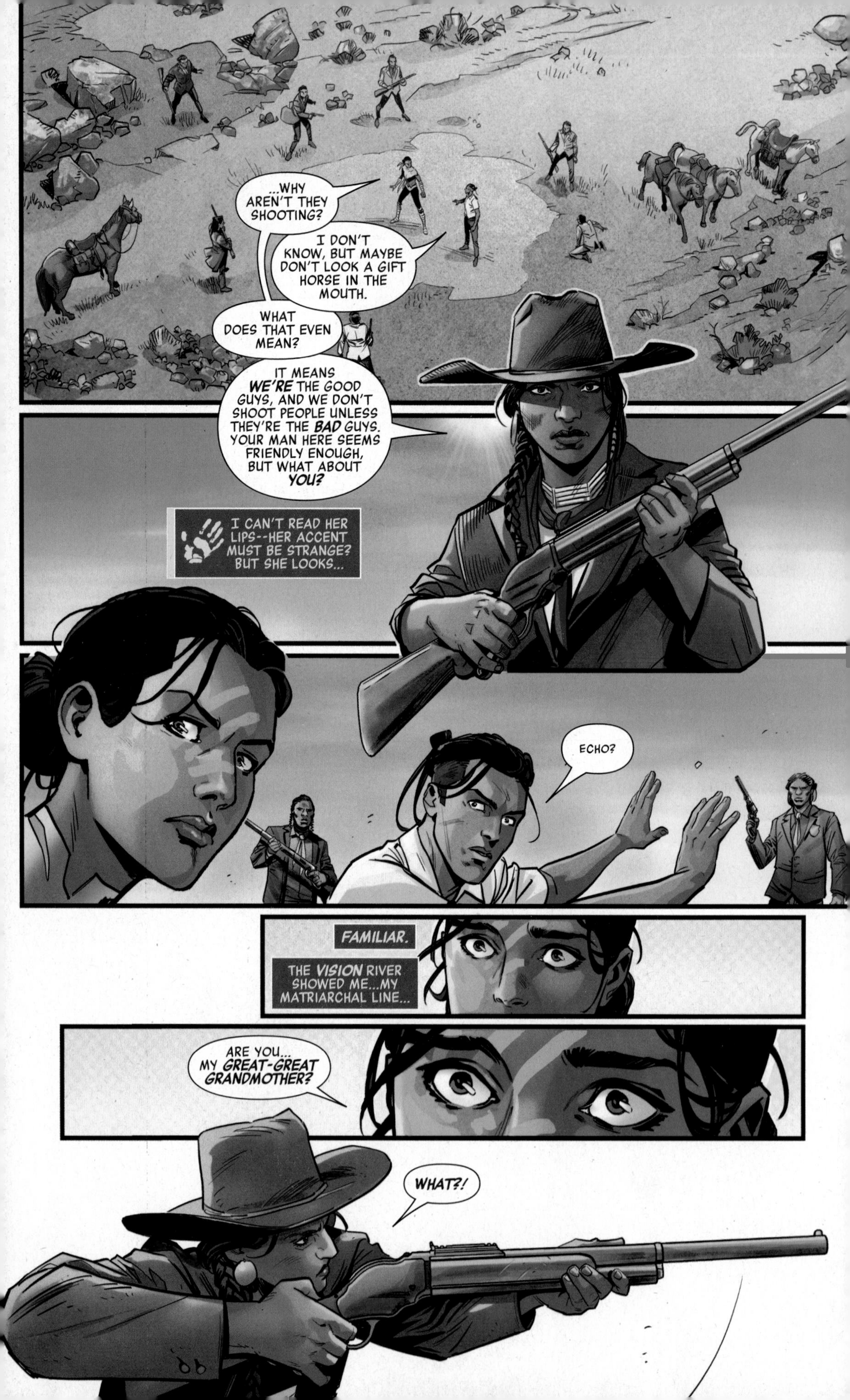
...WHY AREN'T THEY SHOOTING?
I DON'T KNOW, BUT MAYBE DON'T LOOK A GIFT HORSE IN THE MOUTH.
WHAT DOES THAT EVEN MEAN?
IT MEANS *WE'RE* THE GOOD GUYS, AND WE DON'T SHOOT PEOPLE UNLESS THEY'RE THE *BAD* GUYS. YOUR MAN HERE SEEMS FRIENDLY ENOUGH, BUT WHAT ABOUT *YOU?*
I CAN'T READ HER LIPS--HER ACCENT MUST BE STRANGE? BUT SHE LOOKS...
ECHO?
FAMILIAR.
THE *VISION* RIVER SHOWED ME...MY MATRIARCHAL LINE...
ARE YOU... MY *GREAT-GREAT GRANDMOTHER?*
WHAT?!

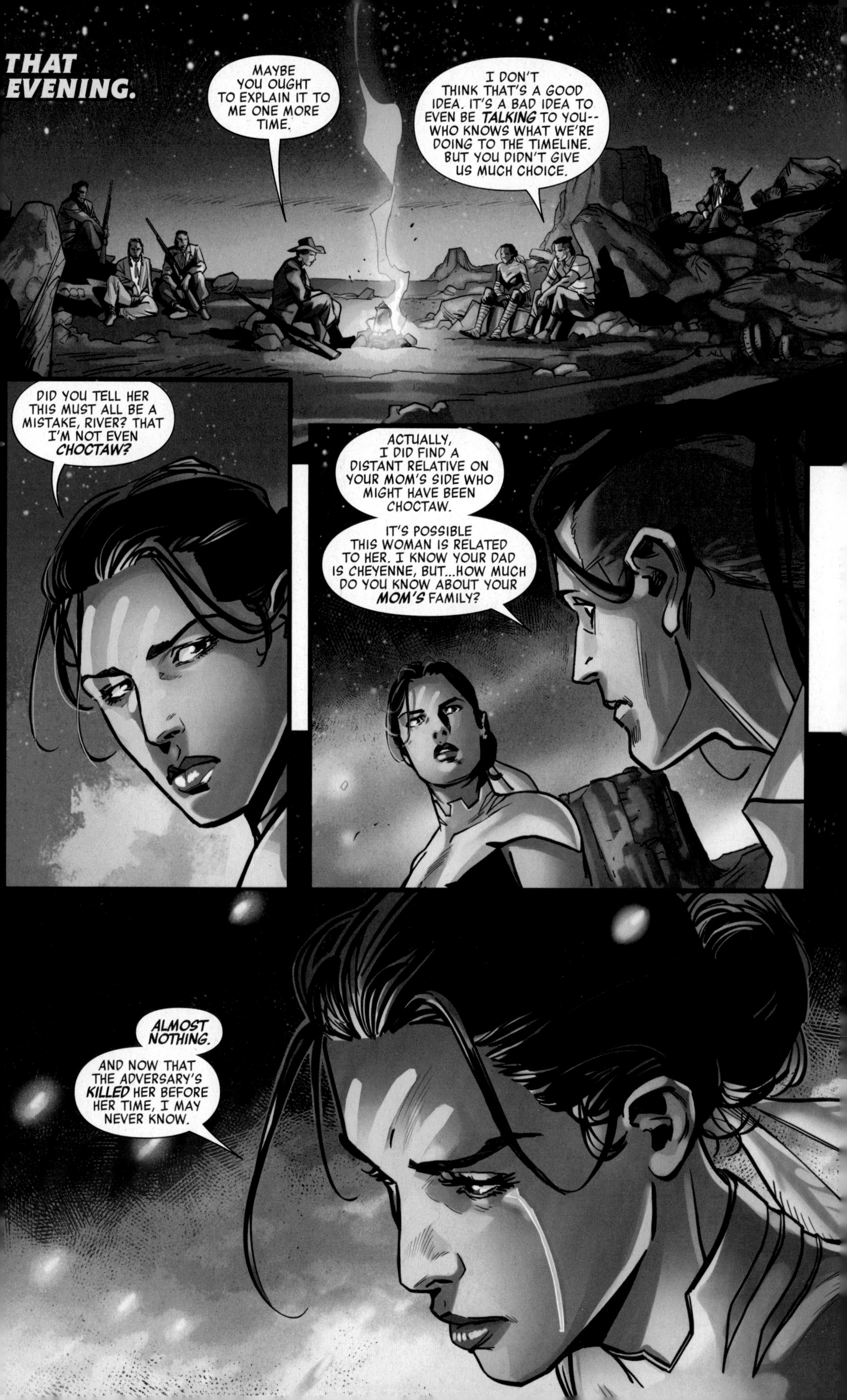
THAT EVENING.
MAYBE YOU OUGHT TO EXPLAIN IT TO ME ONE MORE TIME.
I DON'T THINK THAT'S A GOOD IDEA. IT'S A BAD IDEA TO EVEN BE TALKING TO YOU-- WHO KNOWS WHAT WE'RE DOING TO THE TIMELINE. BUT YOU DIDN'T GIVE US MUCH CHOICE.
DID YOU TELL HER THIS MUST ALL BE A MISTAKE, RIVER? THAT I'M NOT EVEN CHOCTAW?
ACTUALLY, I DID FIND A DISTANT RELATIVE ON YOUR MOM'S SIDE WHO MIGHT HAVE BEEN CHOCTAW.
IT'S POSSIBLE THIS WOMAN IS RELATED TO HER. I KNOW YOUR DAD IS CHEYENNE, BUT...HOW MUCH DO YOU KNOW ABOUT YOUR MOM'S FAMILY?
ALMOST NOTHING.
AND NOW THAT THE ADVERSARY'S KILLED HER BEFORE HER TIME, I MAY NEVER KNOW.

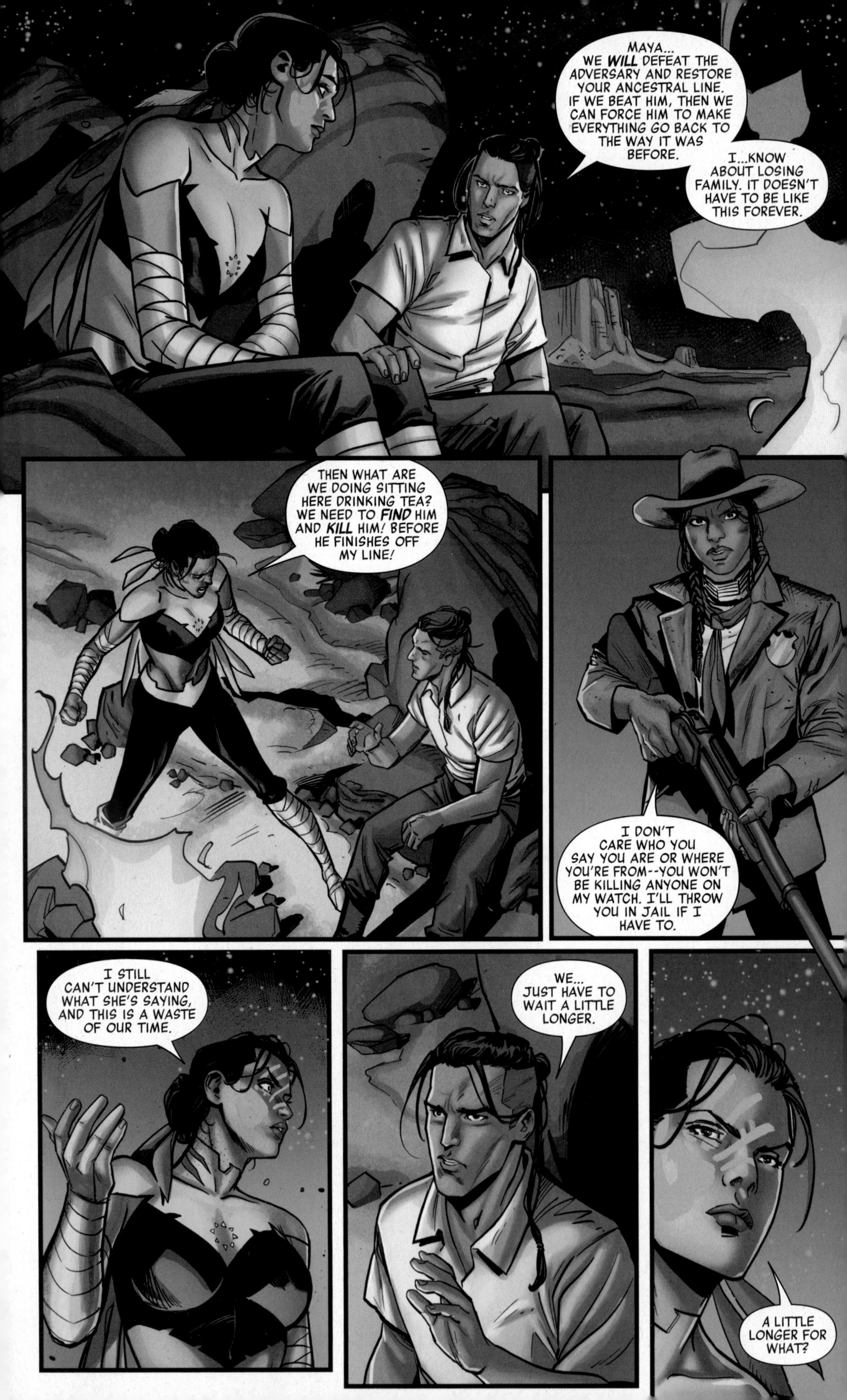
MAYA... WE WILL DEFEAT THE ADVERSARY AND RESTORE YOUR ANCESTRAL LINE. IF WE BEAT HIM, THEN WE CAN FORCE HIM TO MAKE EVERYTHING GO BACK TO THE WAY IT WAS BEFORE.
I...KNOW ABOUT LOSING FAMILY. IT DOESN'T HAVE TO BE LIKE THIS FOREVER.
THEN WHAT ARE WE DOING SITTING HERE DRINKING TEA? WE NEED TO FIND HIM AND KILL HIM! BEFORE HE FINISHES OFF MY LINE!
I DON'T CARE WHO YOU SAY YOU ARE OR WHERE YOU'RE FROM--YOU WON'T BE KILLING ANYONE ON MY WATCH. I'LL THROW YOU IN JAIL IF I HAVE TO.
I STILL CAN'T UNDERSTAND WHAT SHE'S SAYING, AND THIS IS A WASTE OF OUR TIME.
WE... JUST HAVE TO WAIT A LITTLE LONGER.
A LITTLE LONGER FOR WHAT?

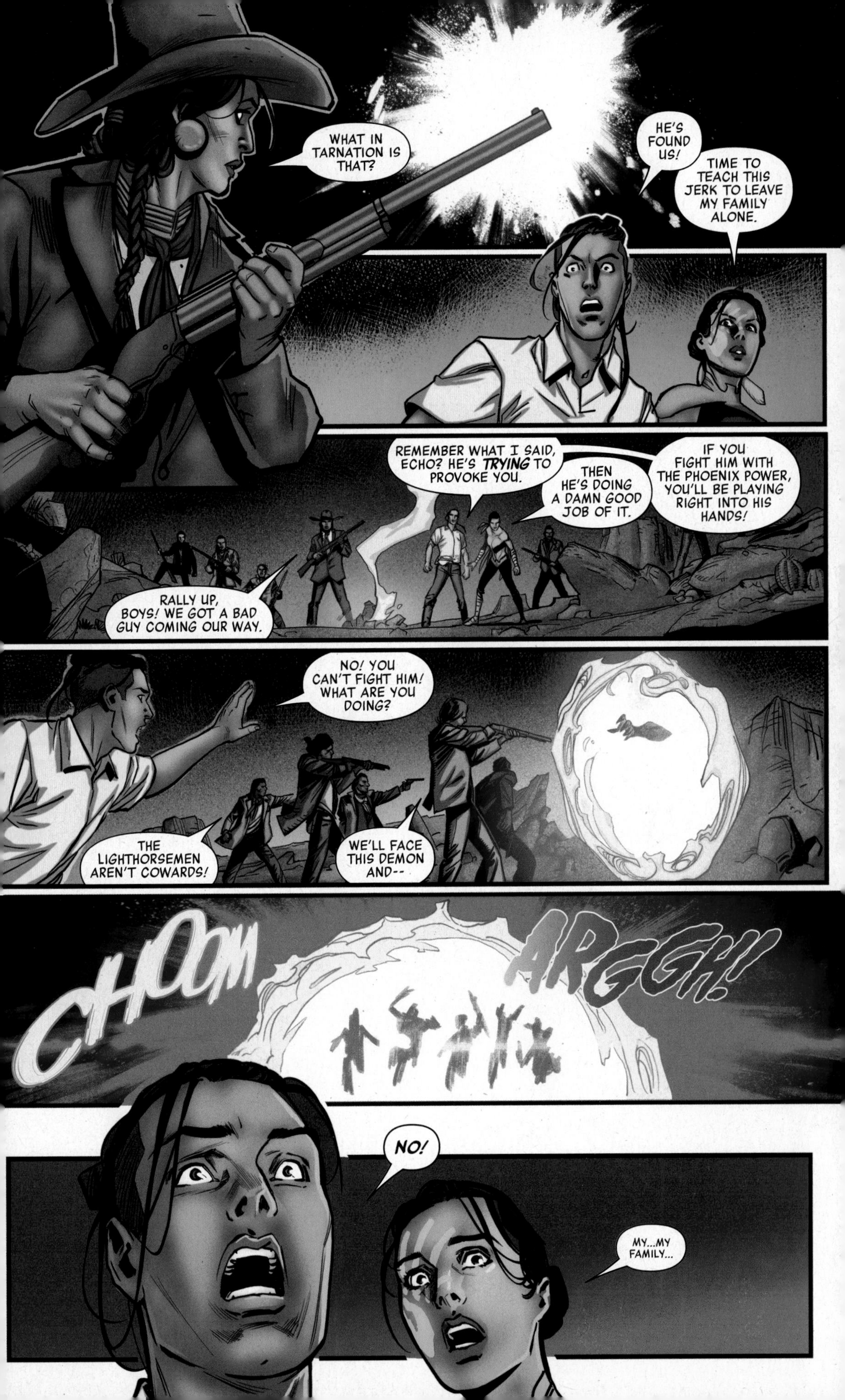
WHAT IN TARNATION IS THAT?
HE'S FOUND US!
TIME TO TEACH THIS JERK TO LEAVE MY FAMILY ALONE.
REMEMBER WHAT I SAID, ECHO? HE'S TRYING TO PROVOKE YOU.
THEN HE'S DOING A DAMN GOOD JOB OF IT.
IF YOU FIGHT HIM WITH THE PHOENIX POWER, YOU'LL BE PLAYING RIGHT INTO HIS HANDS!
RALLY UP, BOYS! WE GOT A BAD GUY COMING OUR WAY.
NO! YOU CAN'T FIGHT HIM! WHAT ARE YOU DOING?
THE LIGHTHORSEMEN AREN'T COWARDS!
WE'LL FACE THIS DEMON AND--
CHOOM
ARGGH!
NO!
MY...MY FAMILY...

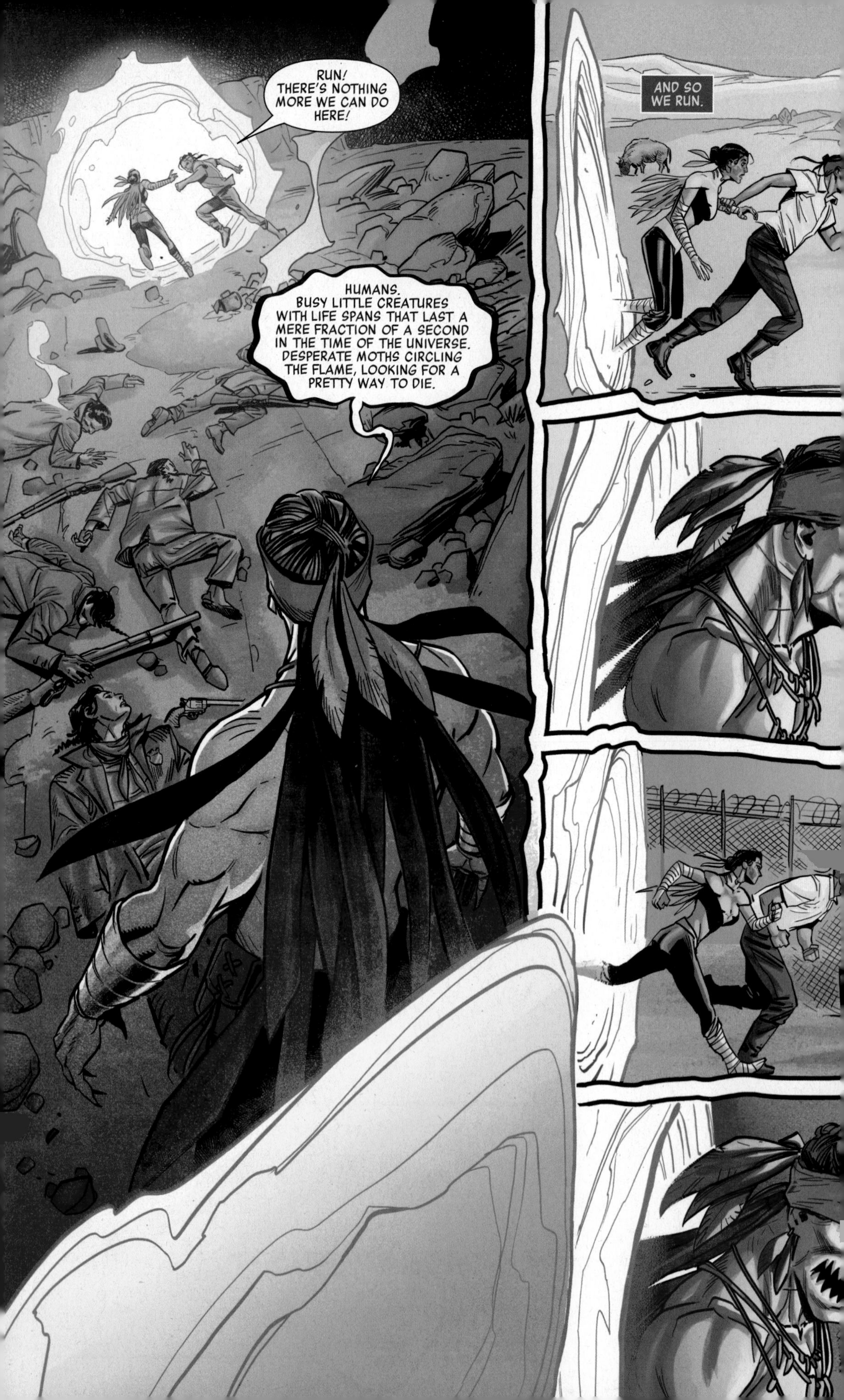
RUN! THERE'S NOTHING MORE WE CAN DO HERE!
HUMANS. BUSY LITTLE CREATURES WITH LIFE SPANS THAT LAST A MERE FRACTION OF A SECOND IN THE TIME OF THE UNIVERSE. DESPERATE MOTHS CIRCLING THE FLAME, LOOKING FOR A PRETTY WAY TO DIE.
AND SO WE RUN.

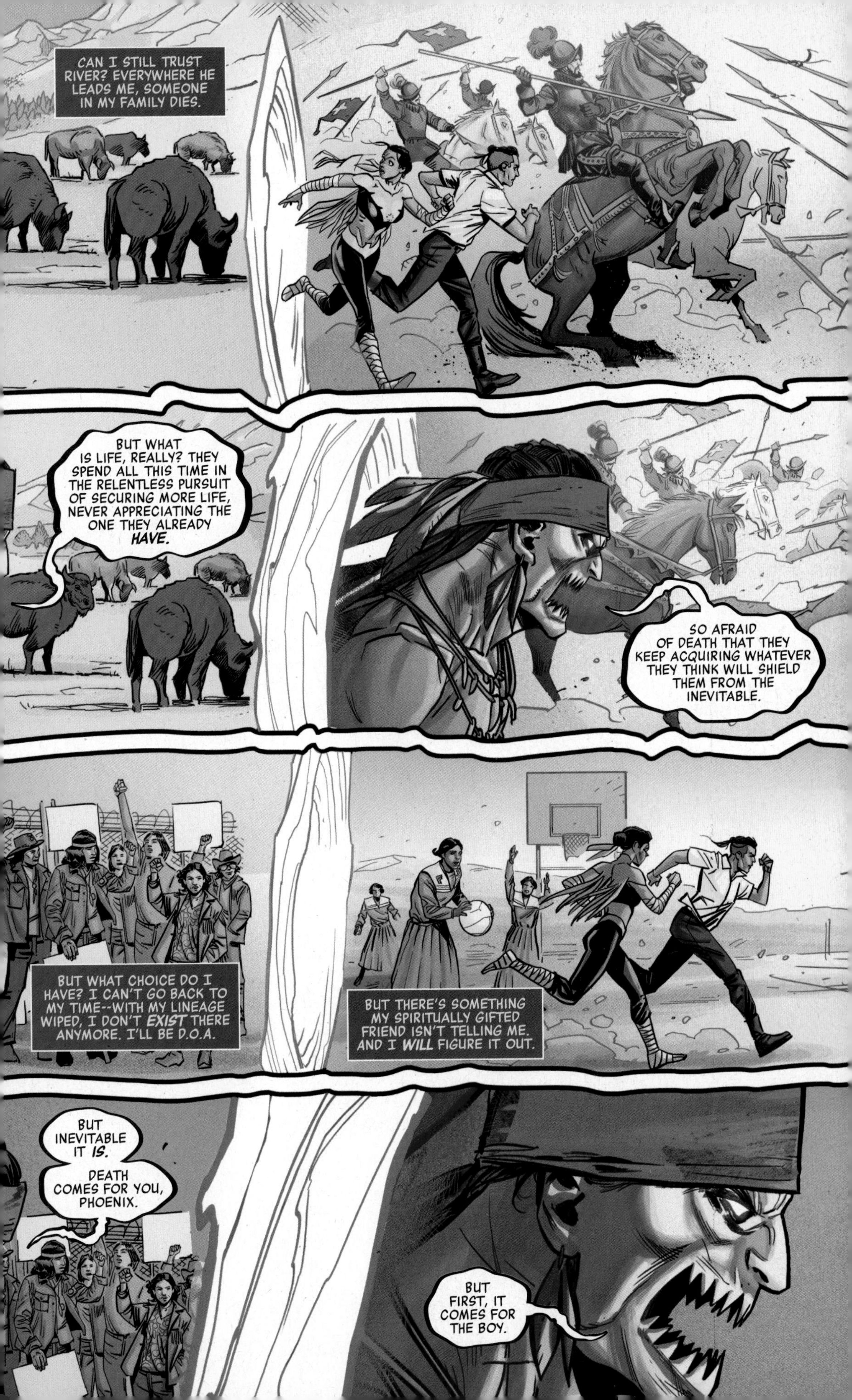
CAN I STILL TRUST RIVER? EVERYWHERE HE LEADS ME, SOMEONE IN MY FAMILY DIES.
BUT WHAT IS LIFE, REALLY? THEY SPEND ALL THIS TIME IN THE RELENTLESS PURSUIT OF SECURING MORE LIFE, NEVER APPRECIATING THE ONE THEY ALREADY *HAVE.*
SO AFRAID OF DEATH THAT THEY KEEP ACQUIRING WHATEVER THEY THINK WILL SHIELD THEM FROM THE INEVITABLE.
BUT WHAT CHOICE DO I HAVE? I CAN'T GO BACK TO MY TIME--WITH MY LINEAGE WIPED, I DON'T *EXIST* THERE ANYMORE. I'LL BE D.O.A.
BUT THERE'S SOMETHING MY SPIRITUALLY GIFTED FRIEND ISN'T TELLING ME. AND I *WILL* FIGURE IT OUT.
BUT INEVITABLE IT *IS.*
DEATH COMES FOR YOU, PHOENIX.
BUT FIRST, IT COMES FOR THE BOY.

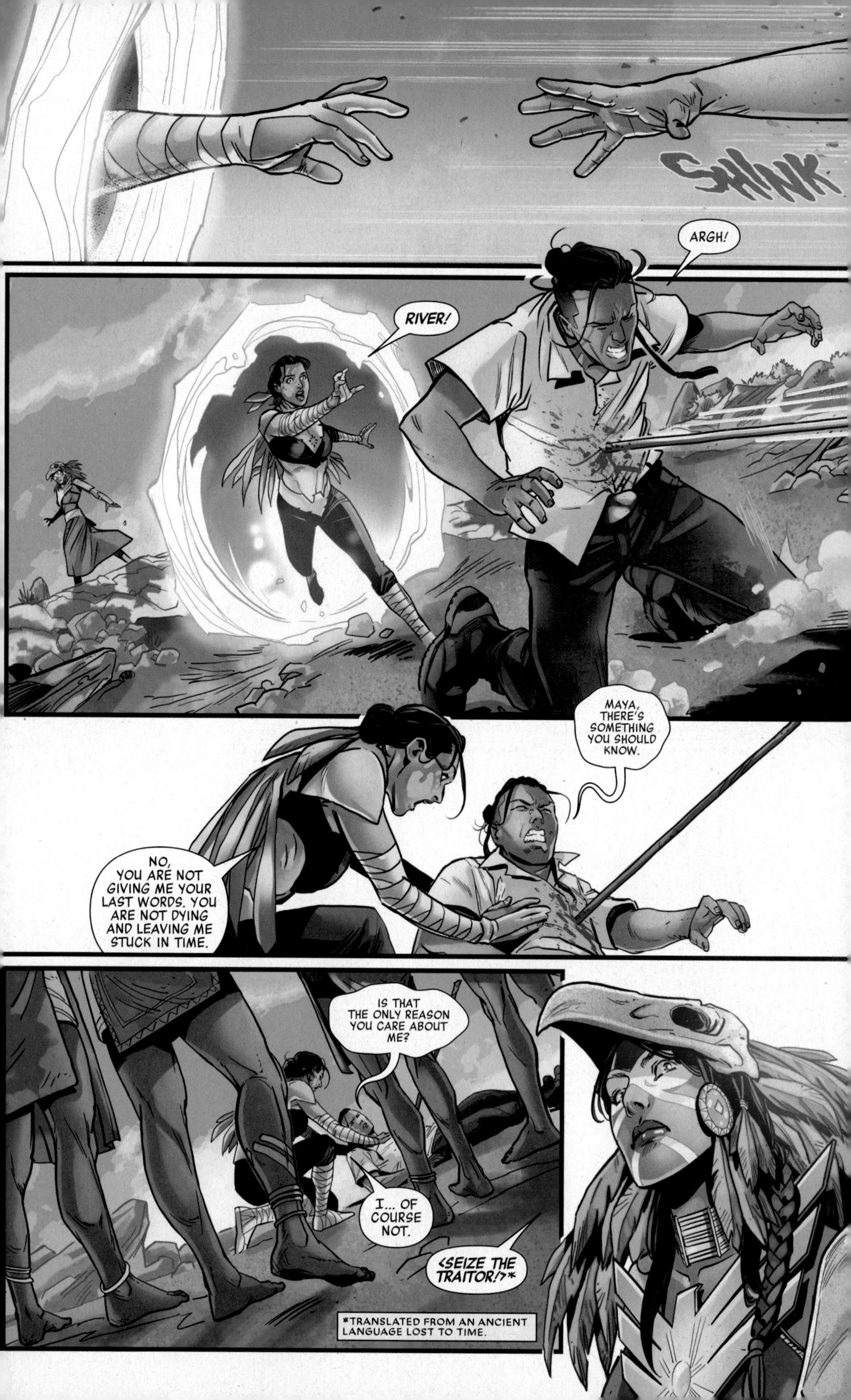
SHINK
ARGH!
RIVER!
MAYA, THERE'S SOMETHING YOU SHOULD KNOW.
NO, YOU ARE NOT GIVING ME YOUR LAST WORDS. YOU ARE NOT DYING AND LEAVING ME STUCK IN TIME.
IS THAT THE ONLY REASON YOU CARE ABOUT ME?
I... OF COURSE NOT.
<SEIZE THE TRAITOR!>*
*TRANSLATED FROM AN ANCIENT LANGUAGE LOST TO TIME.

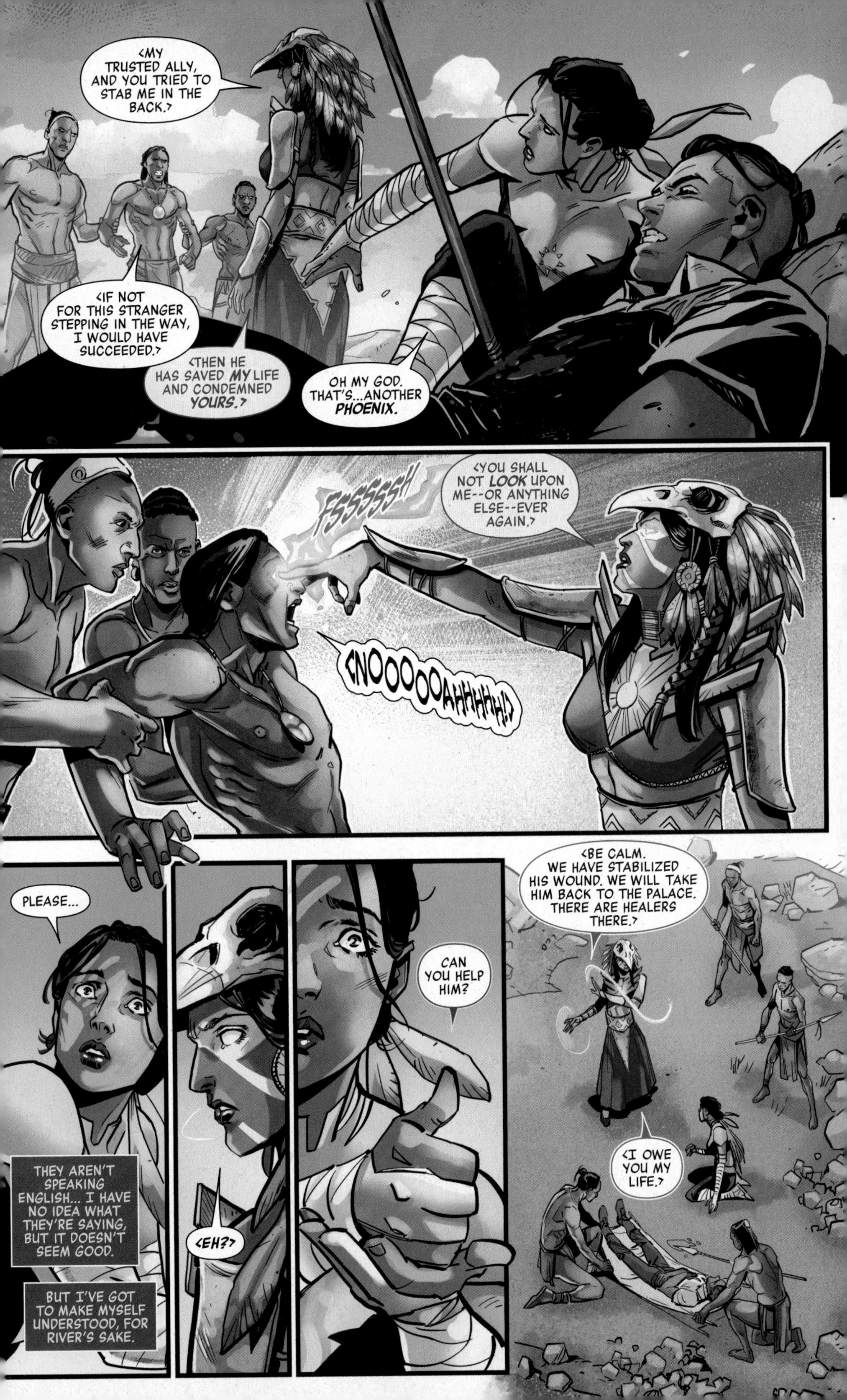
<MY TRUSTED ALLY, AND YOU TRIED TO STAB ME IN THE BACK.>
<IF NOT FOR THIS STRANGER STEPPING IN THE WAY, I WOULD HAVE SUCCEEDED.>
<THEN HE HAS SAVED MY LIFE AND CONDEMNED YOURS.>
OH MY GOD. THAT'S...ANOTHER PHOENIX.
FSSSSSSH
<YOU SHALL NOT LOOK UPON ME--OR ANYTHING ELSE--EVER AGAIN.>
<NOOOOOOAHHHHH!>
PLEASE...
THEY AREN'T SPEAKING ENGLISH... I HAVE NO IDEA WHAT THEY'RE SAYING, BUT IT DOESN'T SEEM GOOD.
BUT I'VE GOT TO MAKE MYSELF UNDERSTOOD, FOR RIVER'S SAKE.
<EH?>
CAN YOU HELP HIM?
<BE CALM. WE HAVE STABILIZED HIS WOUND. WE WILL TAKE HIM BACK TO THE PALACE. THERE ARE HEALERS THERE.>
<I OWE YOU MY LIFE.>

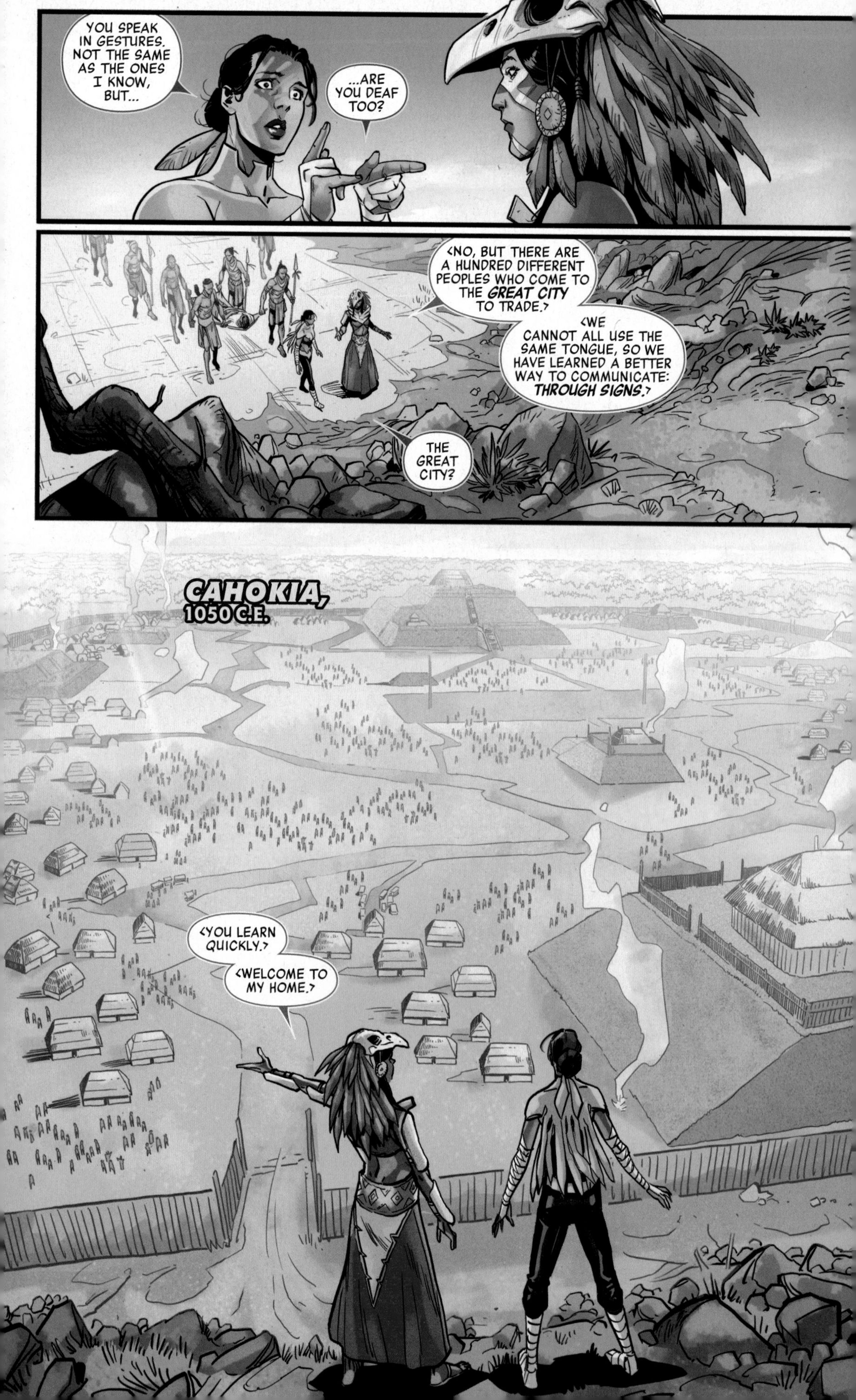
YOU SPEAK IN GESTURES. NOT THE SAME AS THE ONES I KNOW, BUT...
...ARE YOU DEAF TOO?
<NO, BUT THERE ARE A HUNDRED DIFFERENT PEOPLES WHO COME TO THE GREAT CITY TO TRADE.>
<WE CANNOT ALL USE THE SAME TONGUE, SO WE HAVE LEARNED A BETTER WAY TO COMMUNICATE: THROUGH SIGNS.>
THE GREAT CITY?
CAHOKIA, 1050 C.E.
<YOU LEARN QUICKLY.>
<WELCOME TO MY HOME.>

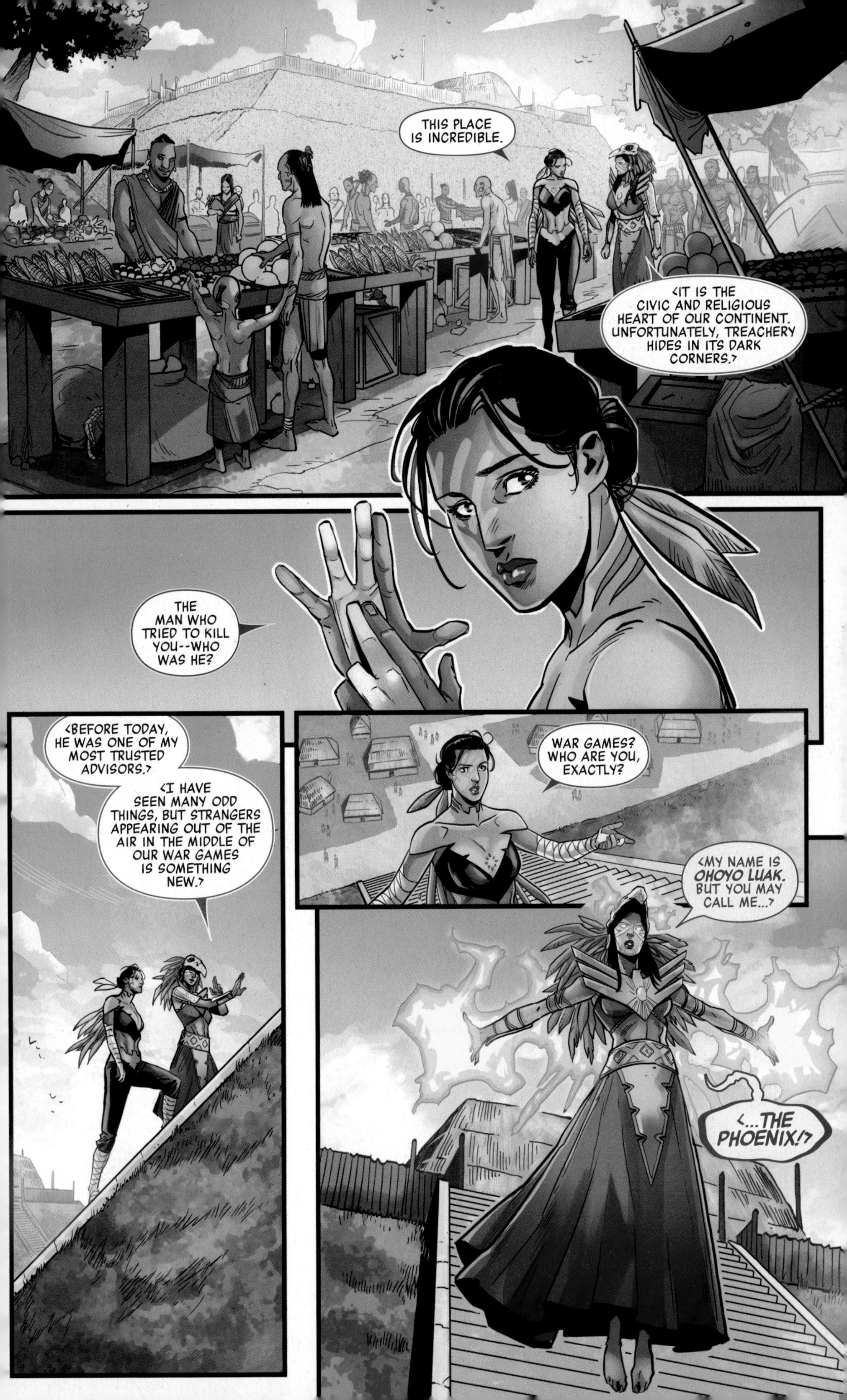
THIS PLACE IS INCREDIBLE.
<IT IS THE CIVIC AND RELIGIOUS HEART OF OUR CONTINENT. UNFORTUNATELY, TREACHERY HIDES IN ITS DARK CORNERS.>
THE MAN WHO TRIED TO KILL YOU--WHO WAS HE?
<BEFORE TODAY, HE WAS ONE OF MY MOST TRUSTED ADVISORS.>
<I HAVE SEEN MANY ODD THINGS, BUT STRANGERS APPEARING OUT OF THE AIR IN THE MIDDLE OF OUR WAR GAMES IS SOMETHING NEW.>
WAR GAMES? WHO ARE YOU, EXACTLY?
<MY NAME IS *OHOYO LUAK.* BUT YOU MAY CALL ME...>
<...THE PHOENIX!>

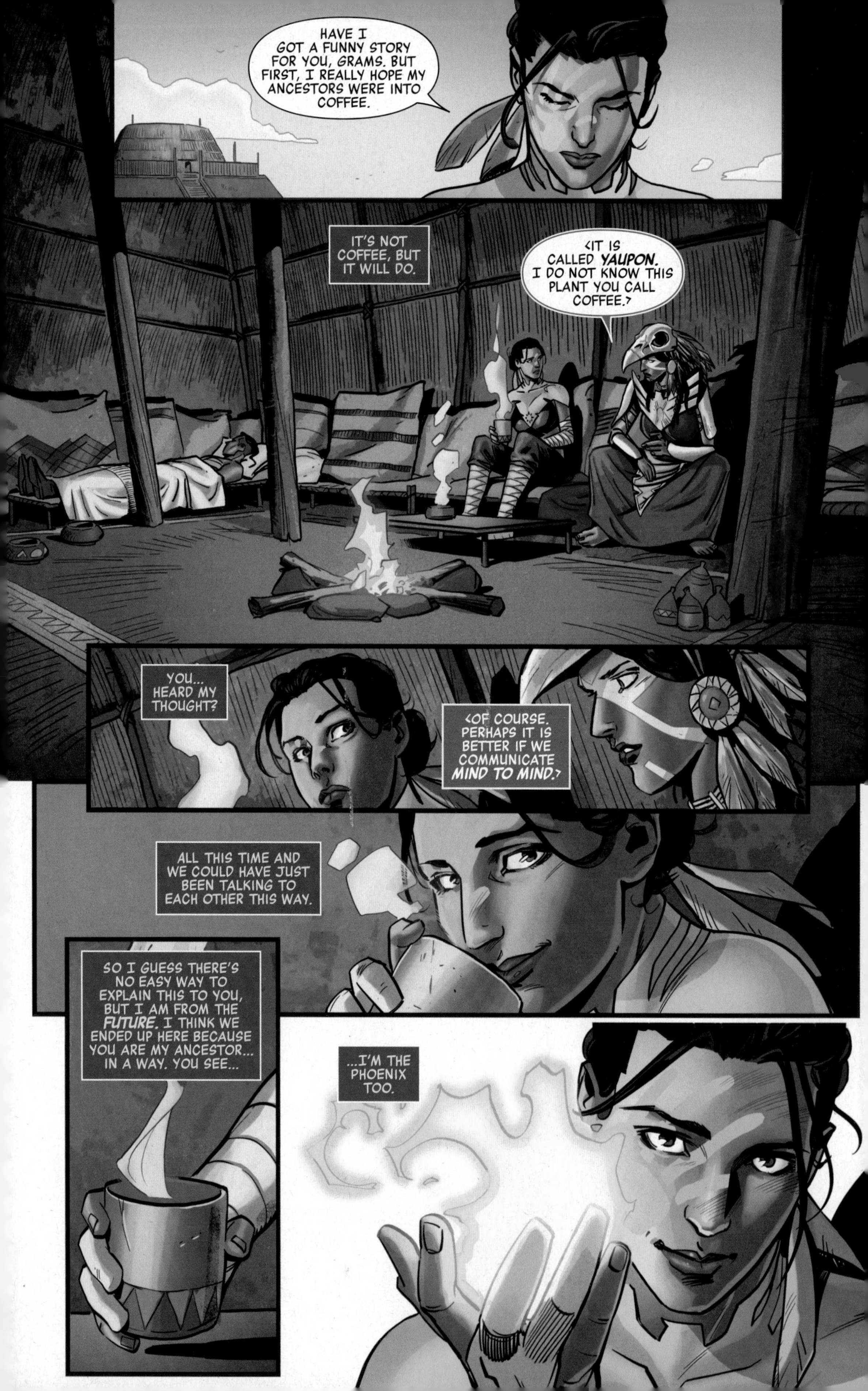
HAVE I GOT A FUNNY STORY FOR YOU, GRAMS. BUT FIRST, I REALLY HOPE MY ANCESTORS WERE INTO COFFEE.
IT'S NOT COFFEE, BUT IT WILL DO.
<IT IS CALLED YAUPON. I DO NOT KNOW THIS PLANT YOU CALL COFFEE.>
YOU... HEARD MY THOUGHT?
<OF COURSE. PERHAPS IT IS BETTER IF WE COMMUNICATE MIND TO MIND.>
ALL THIS TIME AND WE COULD HAVE JUST BEEN TALKING TO EACH OTHER THIS WAY.
SO I GUESS THERE'S NO EASY WAY TO EXPLAIN THIS TO YOU, BUT I AM FROM THE FUTURE. I THINK WE ENDED UP HERE BECAUSE YOU ARE MY ANCESTOR... IN A WAY. YOU SEE...
...I'M THE PHOENIX TOO.

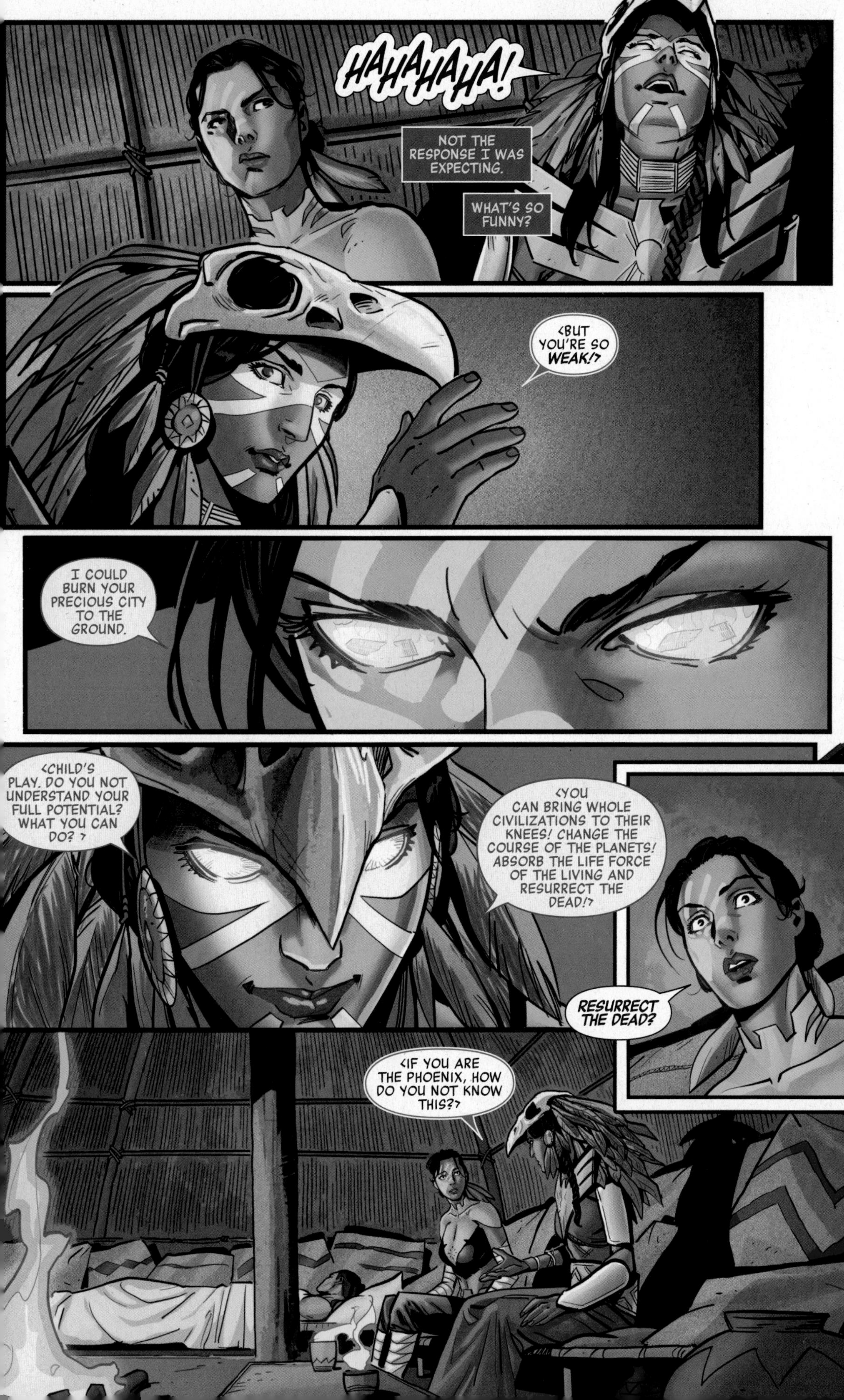
HAHAHAHA!
NOT THE RESPONSE I WAS EXPECTING.
WHAT'S SO FUNNY?
<BUT YOU'RE SO WEAK!>
I COULD BURN YOUR PRECIOUS CITY TO THE GROUND.
<CHILD'S PLAY. DO YOU NOT UNDERSTAND YOUR FULL POTENTIAL? WHAT YOU CAN DO? >
<YOU CAN BRING WHOLE CIVILIZATIONS TO THEIR KNEES! CHANGE THE COURSE OF THE PLANETS! ABSORB THE LIFE FORCE OF THE LIVING AND RESURRECT THE DEAD!>
RESURRECT THE DEAD?
<IF YOU ARE THE PHOENIX, HOW DO YOU NOT KNOW THIS?>

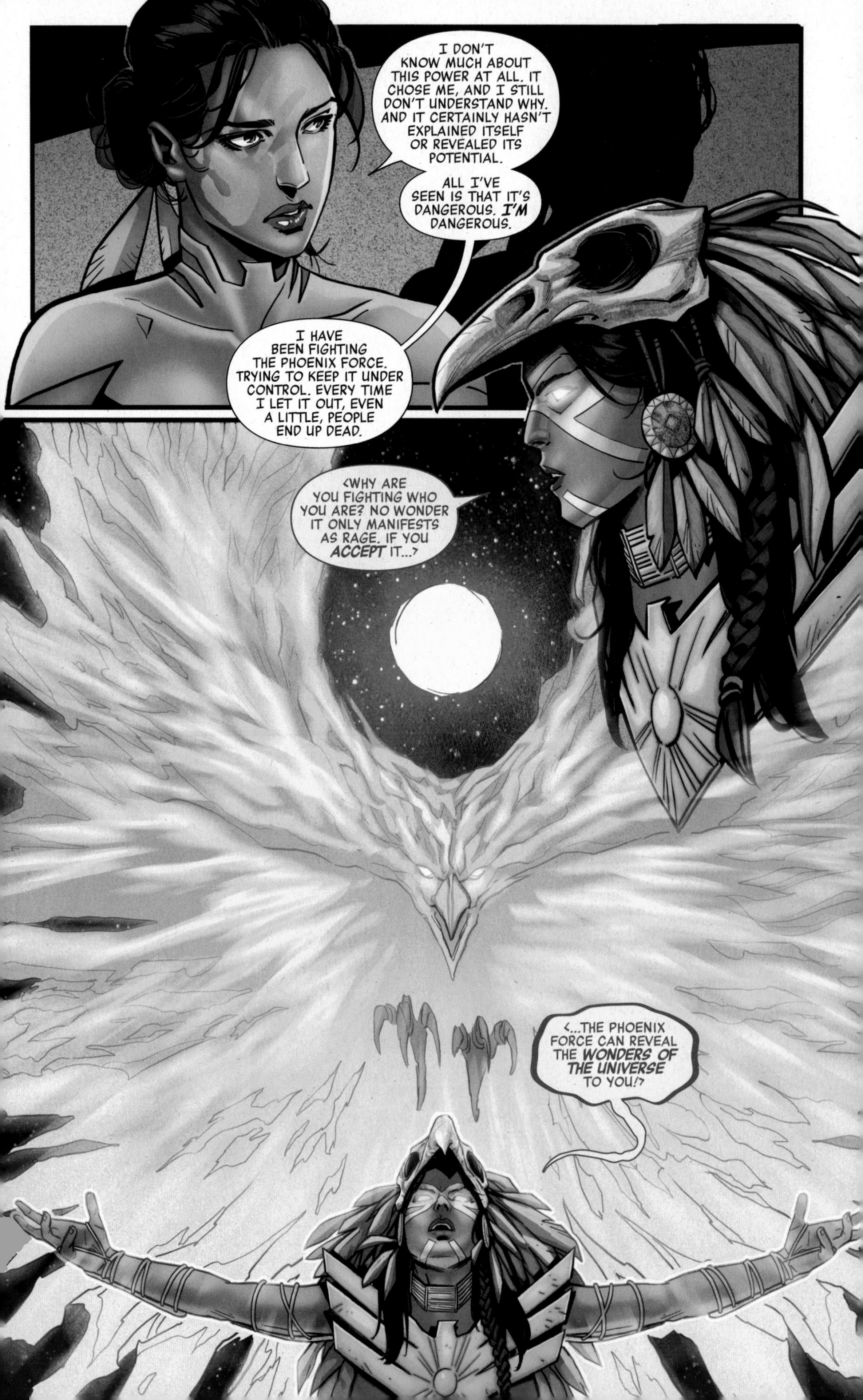
I DON'T KNOW MUCH ABOUT THIS POWER AT ALL. IT CHOSE ME, AND I STILL DON'T UNDERSTAND WHY. AND IT CERTAINLY HASN'T EXPLAINED ITSELF OR REVEALED ITS POTENTIAL.
ALL I'VE SEEN IS THAT IT'S DANGEROUS. I'M DANGEROUS.
I HAVE BEEN FIGHTING THE PHOENIX FORCE. TRYING TO KEEP IT UNDER CONTROL. EVERY TIME I LET IT OUT, EVEN A LITTLE, PEOPLE END UP DEAD.
<WHY ARE YOU FIGHTING WHO YOU ARE? NO WONDER IT ONLY MANIFESTS AS RAGE. IF YOU ACCEPT IT...>
<...THE PHOENIX FORCE CAN REVEAL THE WONDERS OF THE UNIVERSE TO YOU!>

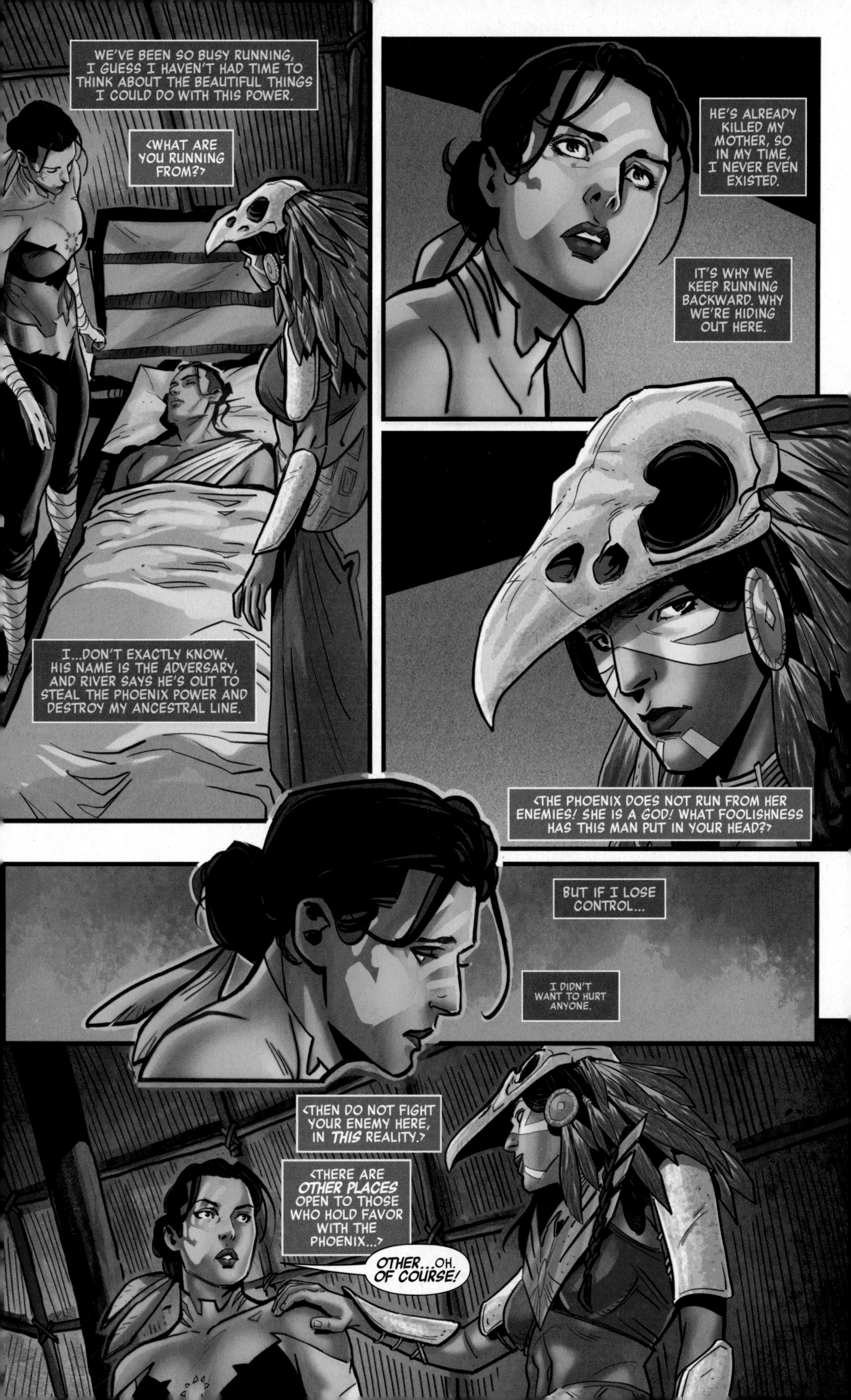
WE'VE BEEN SO BUSY RUNNING, I GUESS I HAVEN'T HAD TIME TO THINK ABOUT THE BEAUTIFUL THINGS I COULD DO WITH THIS POWER.
<WHAT ARE YOU RUNNING FROM?>
I...DON'T EXACTLY KNOW. HIS NAME IS THE ADVERSARY, AND RIVER SAYS HE'S OUT TO STEAL THE PHOENIX POWER AND DESTROY MY ANCESTRAL LINE.
HE'S ALREADY KILLED MY MOTHER, SO IN MY TIME, I NEVER EVEN EXISTED.
IT'S WHY WE KEEP RUNNING BACKWARD. WHY WE'RE HIDING OUT HERE.
<THE PHOENIX DOES NOT RUN FROM HER ENEMIES! SHE IS A GOD! WHAT FOOLISHNESS HAS THIS MAN PUT IN YOUR HEAD?>
BUT IF I LOSE CONTROL...
I DIDN'T WANT TO HURT ANYONE.
<THEN DO NOT FIGHT YOUR ENEMY HERE, IN *THIS* REALITY.>
<THERE ARE *OTHER PLACES* OPEN TO THOSE WHO HOLD FAVOR WITH THE PHOENIX...>
OTHER...OH. *OF COURSE!*

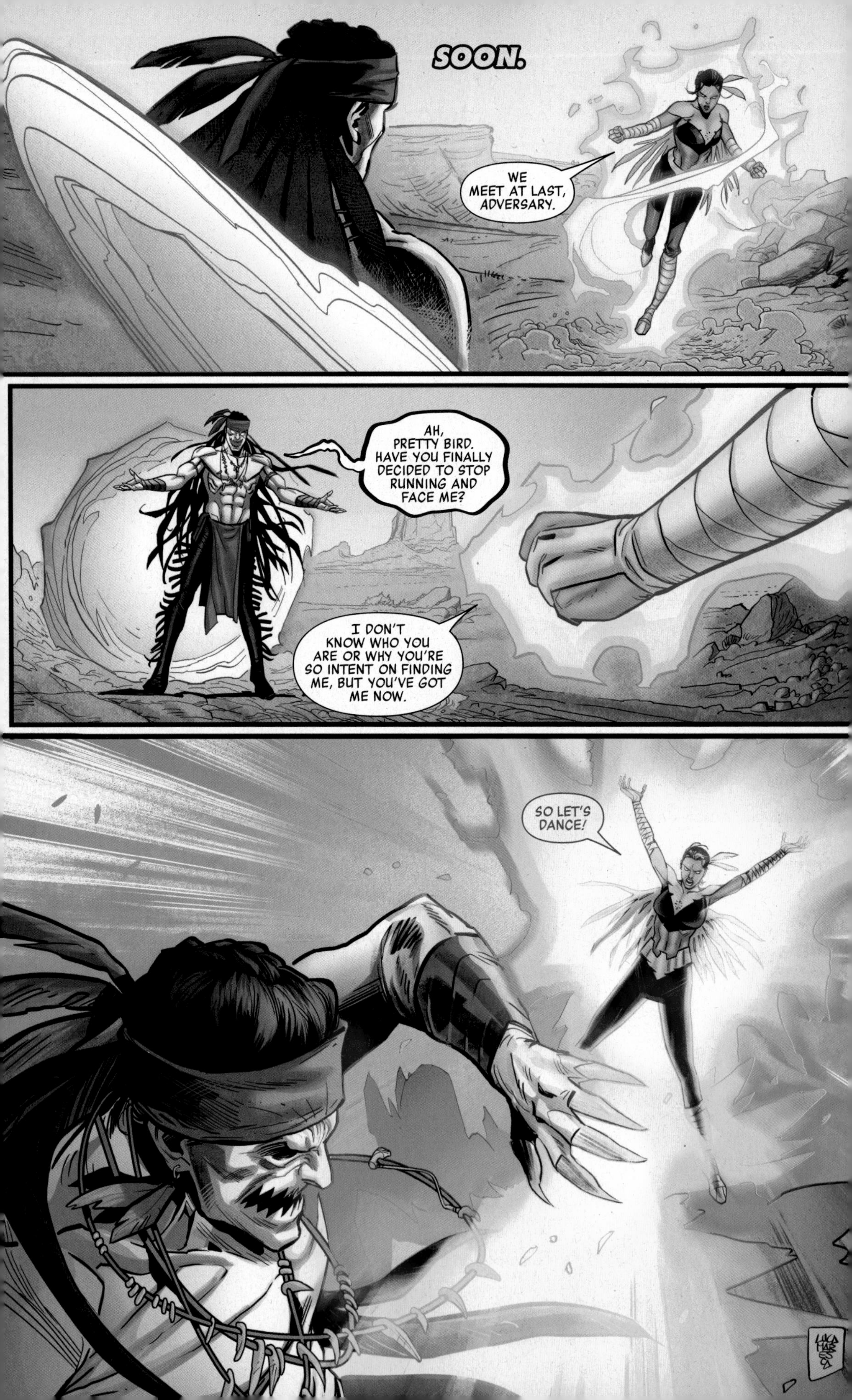
SOON.
WE MEET AT LAST, ADVERSARY.
AH, PRETTY BIRD. HAVE YOU FINALLY DECIDED TO STOP RUNNING AND FACE ME?
I DON'T KNOW WHO YOU ARE OR WHY YOU'RE SO INTENT ON FINDING ME, BUT YOU'VE GOT ME NOW.
SO LET'S DANCE!

4

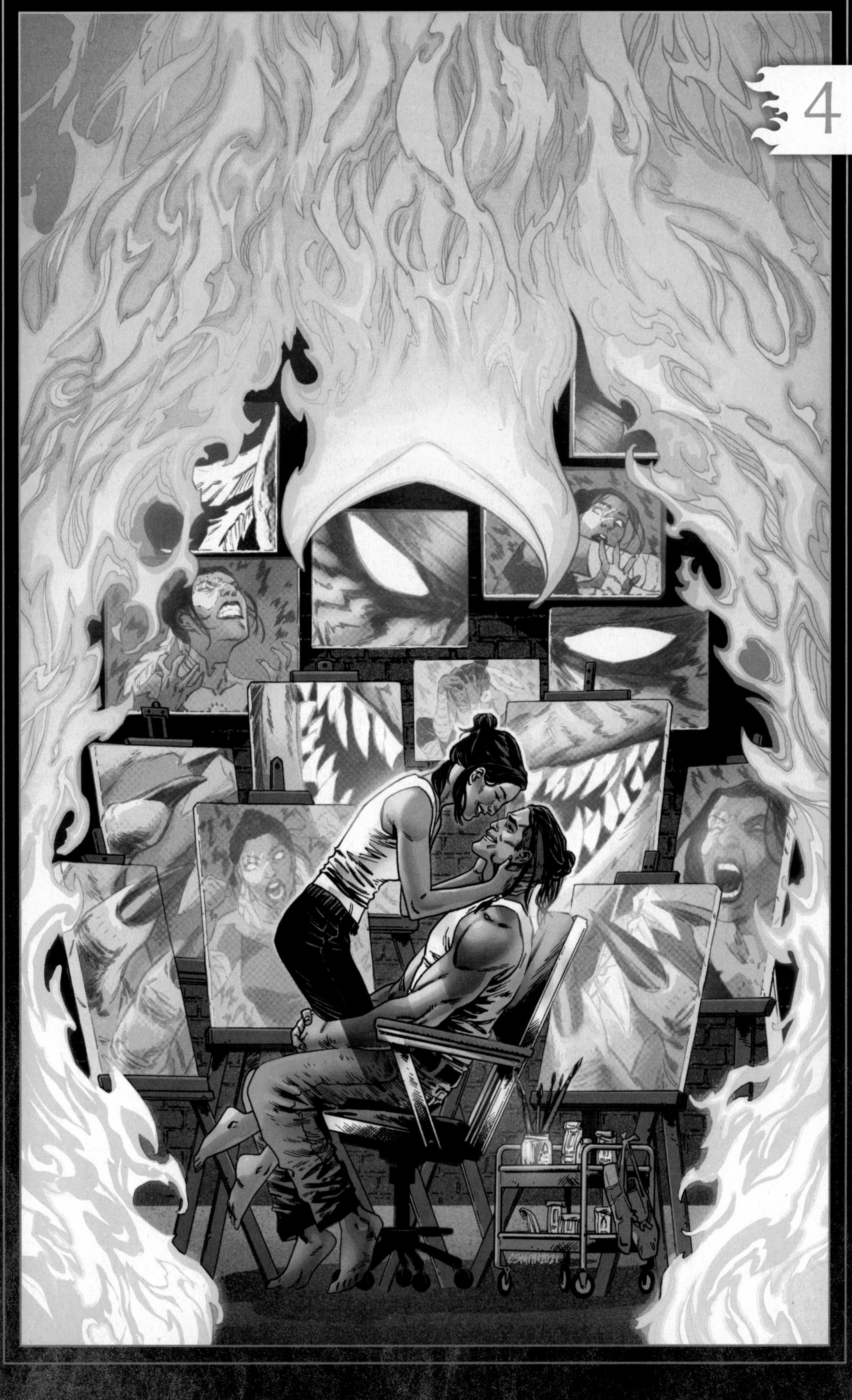

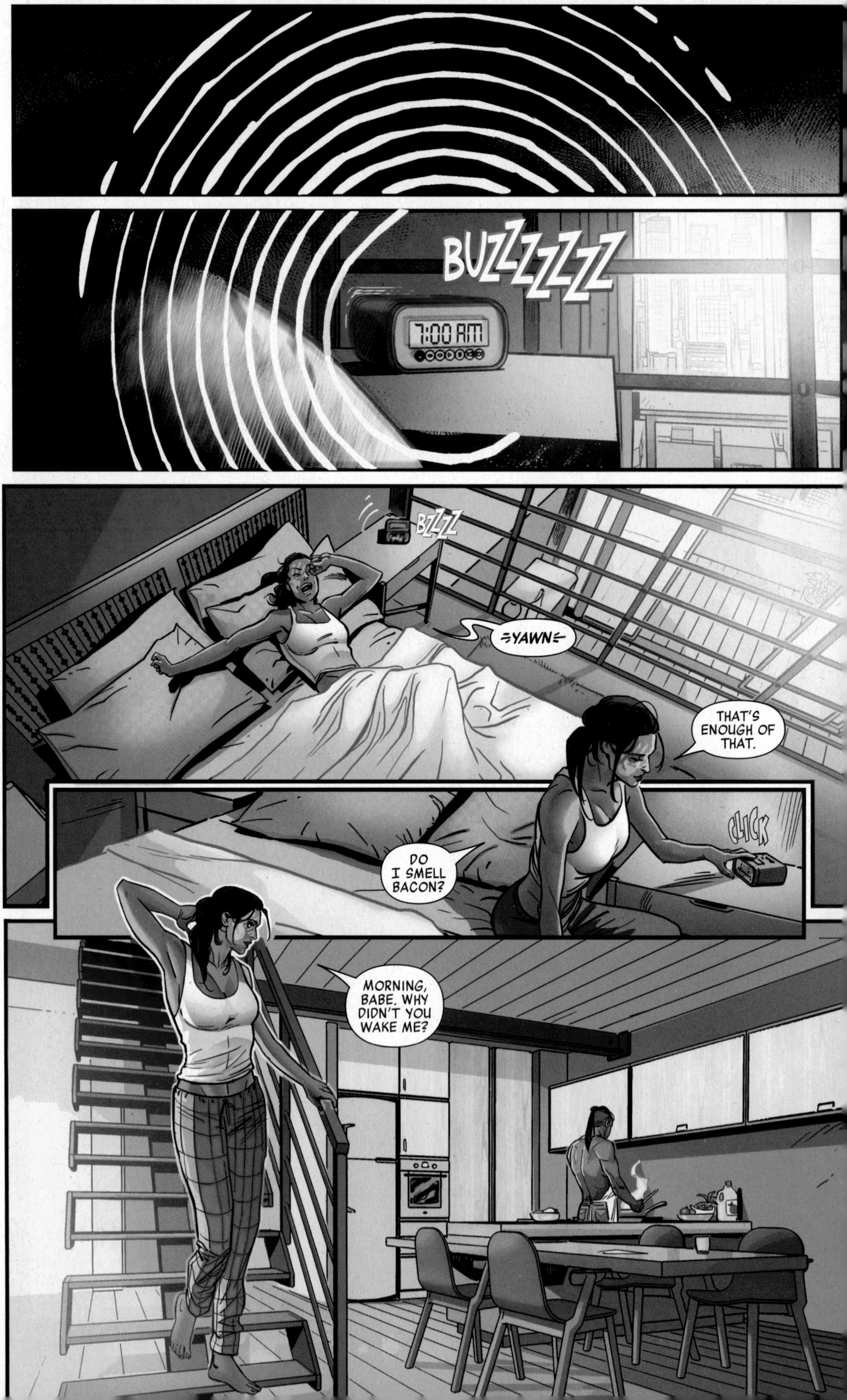
BUZZZZZZZ
7:00 AM
BZZZZ
YAWN
THAT'S ENOUGH OF THAT.
CLICK
DO I SMELL BACON?
MORNING, BABE. WHY DIDN'T YOU WAKE ME?

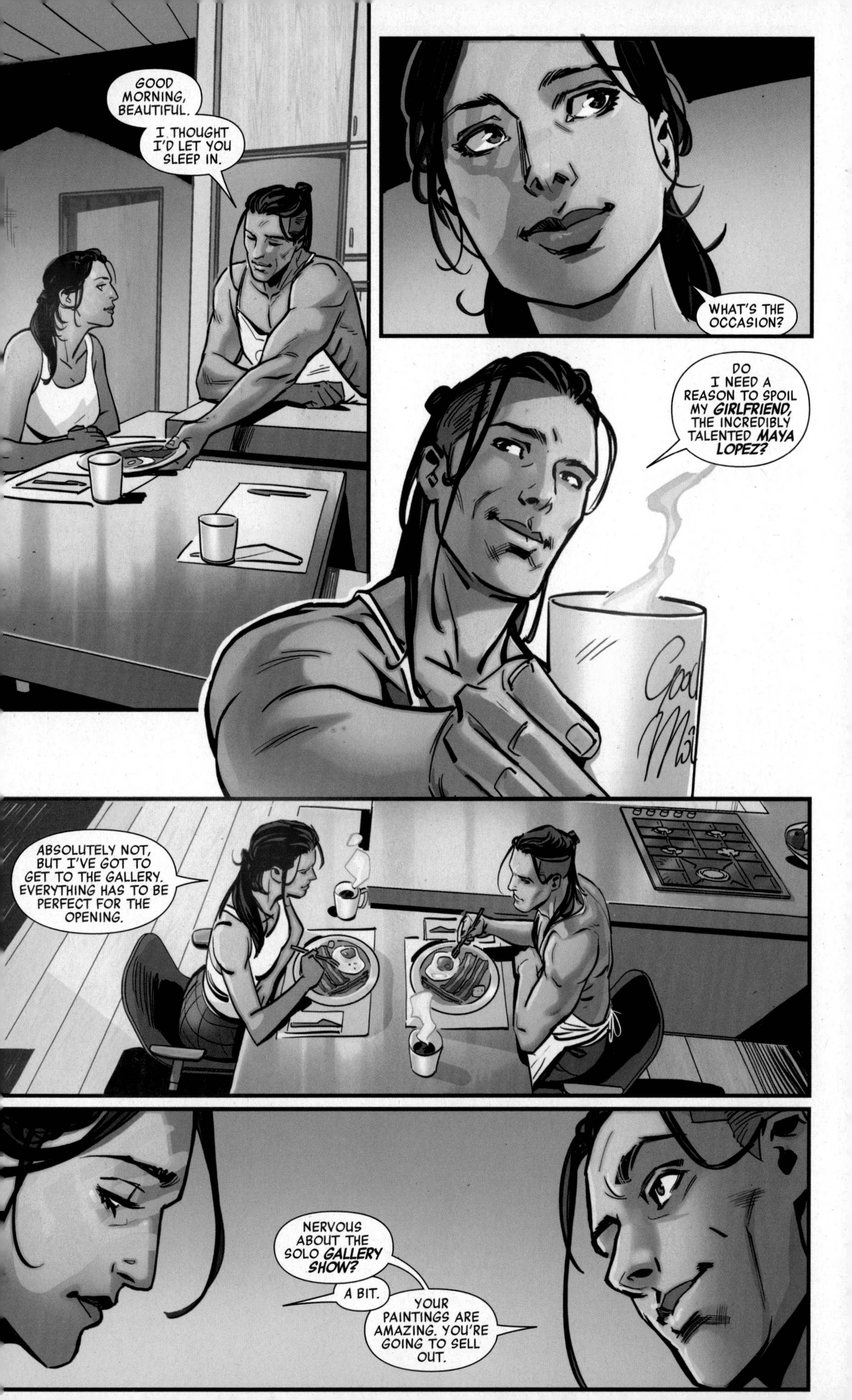
GOOD MORNING, BEAUTIFUL.
I THOUGHT I'D LET YOU SLEEP IN.
WHAT'S THE OCCASION?
DO I NEED A REASON TO SPOIL MY GIRLFRIEND, THE INCREDIBLY TALENTED MAYA LOPEZ?
ABSOLUTELY NOT, BUT I'VE GOT TO GET TO THE GALLERY. EVERYTHING HAS TO BE PERFECT FOR THE OPENING.
NERVOUS ABOUT THE SOLO GALLERY SHOW?
A BIT.
YOUR PAINTINGS ARE AMAZING. YOU'RE GOING TO SELL OUT.

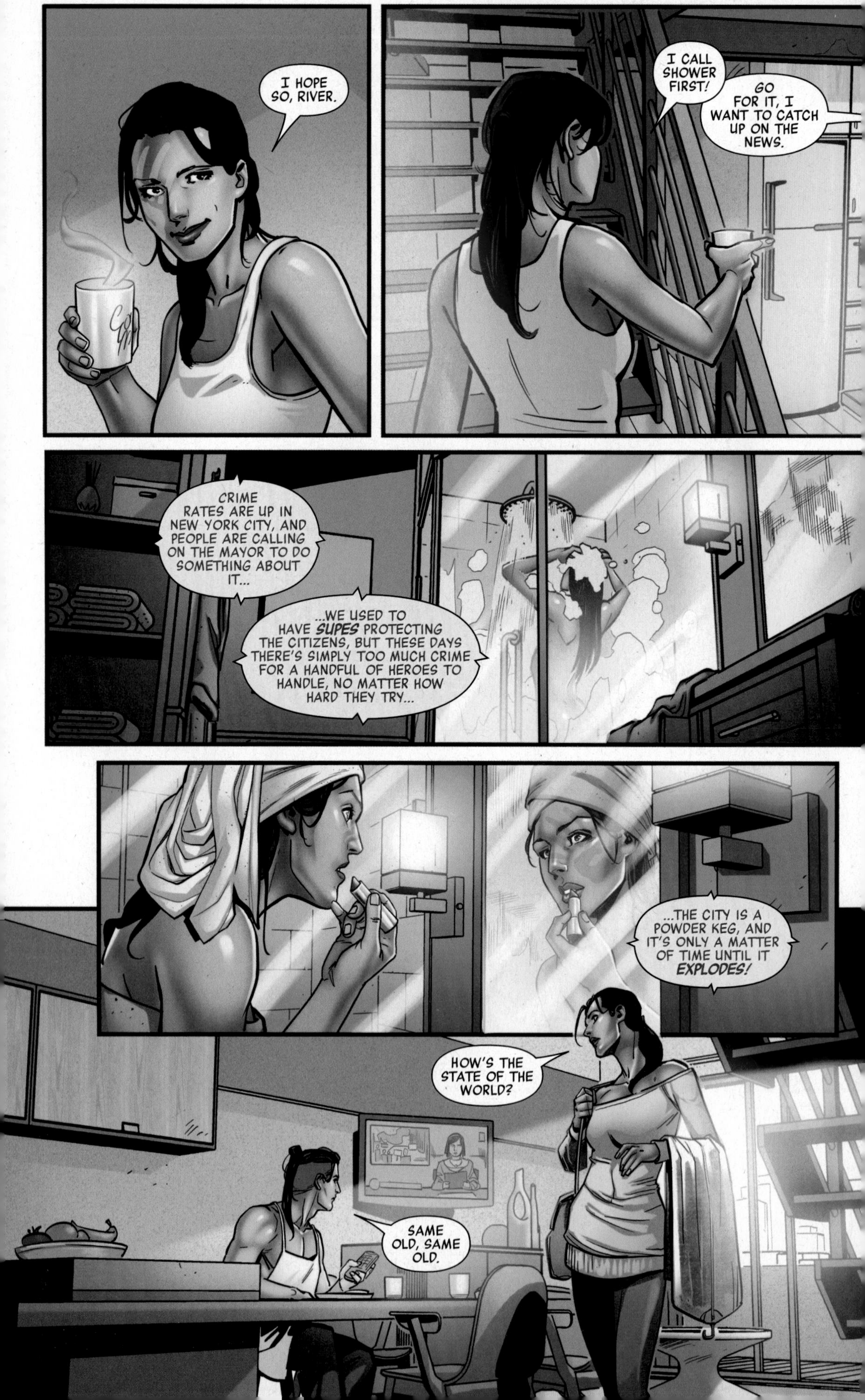
I HOPE SO, RIVER.
I CALL SHOWER FIRST!
GO FOR IT, I WANT TO CATCH UP ON THE NEWS.
CRIME RATES ARE UP IN NEW YORK CITY, AND PEOPLE ARE CALLING ON THE MAYOR TO DO SOMETHING ABOUT IT...
...WE USED TO HAVE SUPES PROTECTING THE CITIZENS, BUT THESE DAYS THERE'S SIMPLY TOO MUCH CRIME FOR A HANDFUL OF HEROES TO HANDLE, NO MATTER HOW HARD THEY TRY...
...THE CITY IS A POWDER KEG, AND IT'S ONLY A MATTER OF TIME UNTIL IT EXPLODES!
HOW'S THE STATE OF THE WORLD?
SAME OLD, SAME OLD.

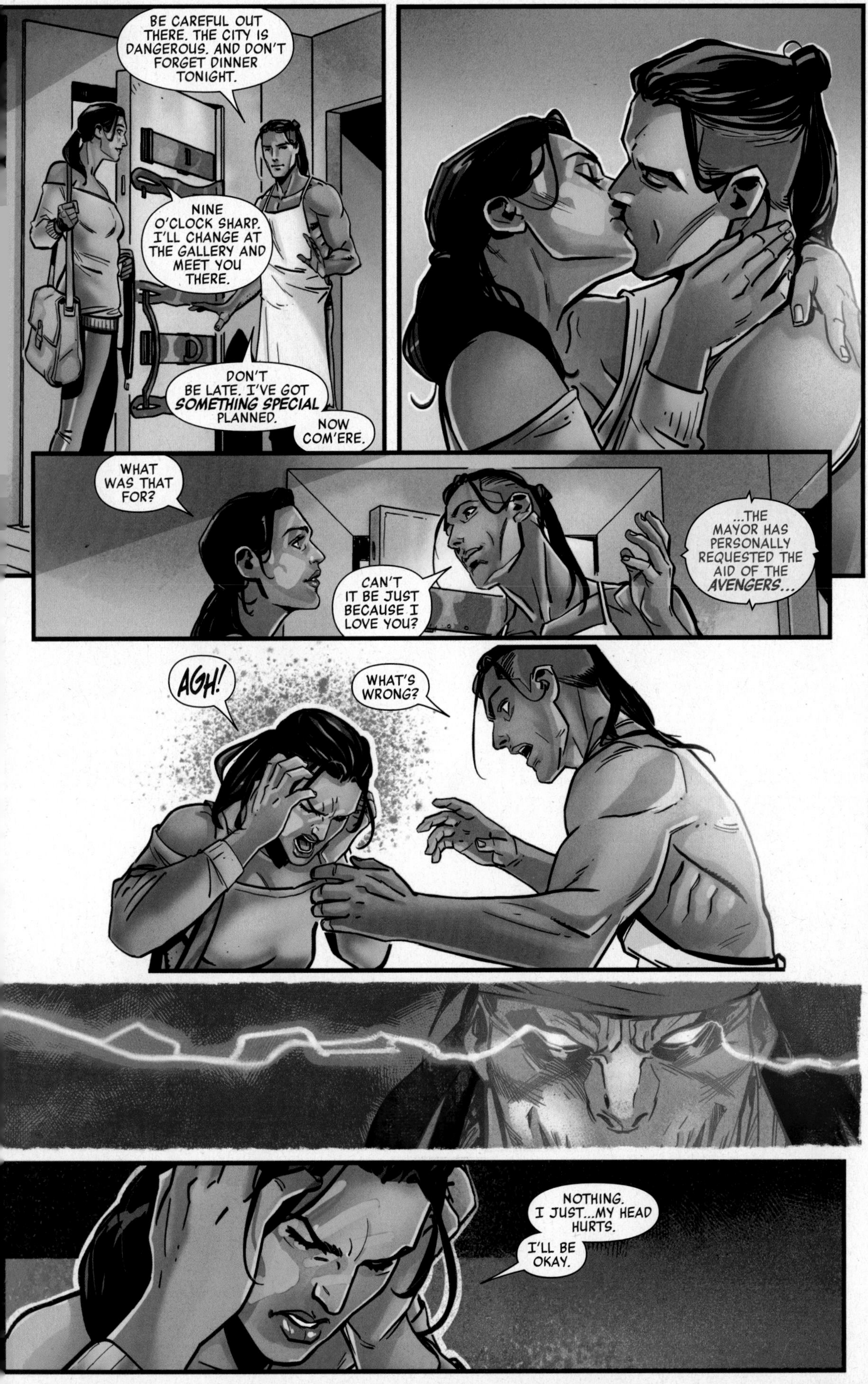
BE CAREFUL OUT THERE. THE CITY IS DANGEROUS. AND DON'T FORGET DINNER TONIGHT.
NINE O'CLOCK SHARP. I'LL CHANGE AT THE GALLERY AND MEET YOU THERE.
DON'T BE LATE. I'VE GOT *SOMETHING SPECIAL* PLANNED.
NOW COM'ERE.
WHAT WAS THAT FOR?
CAN'T IT BE JUST BECAUSE I LOVE YOU?
...THE MAYOR HAS PERSONALLY REQUESTED THE AID OF THE *AVENGERS...*
AGH!
WHAT'S WRONG?
NOTHING. I JUST...MY HEAD HURTS.
I'LL BE OKAY.

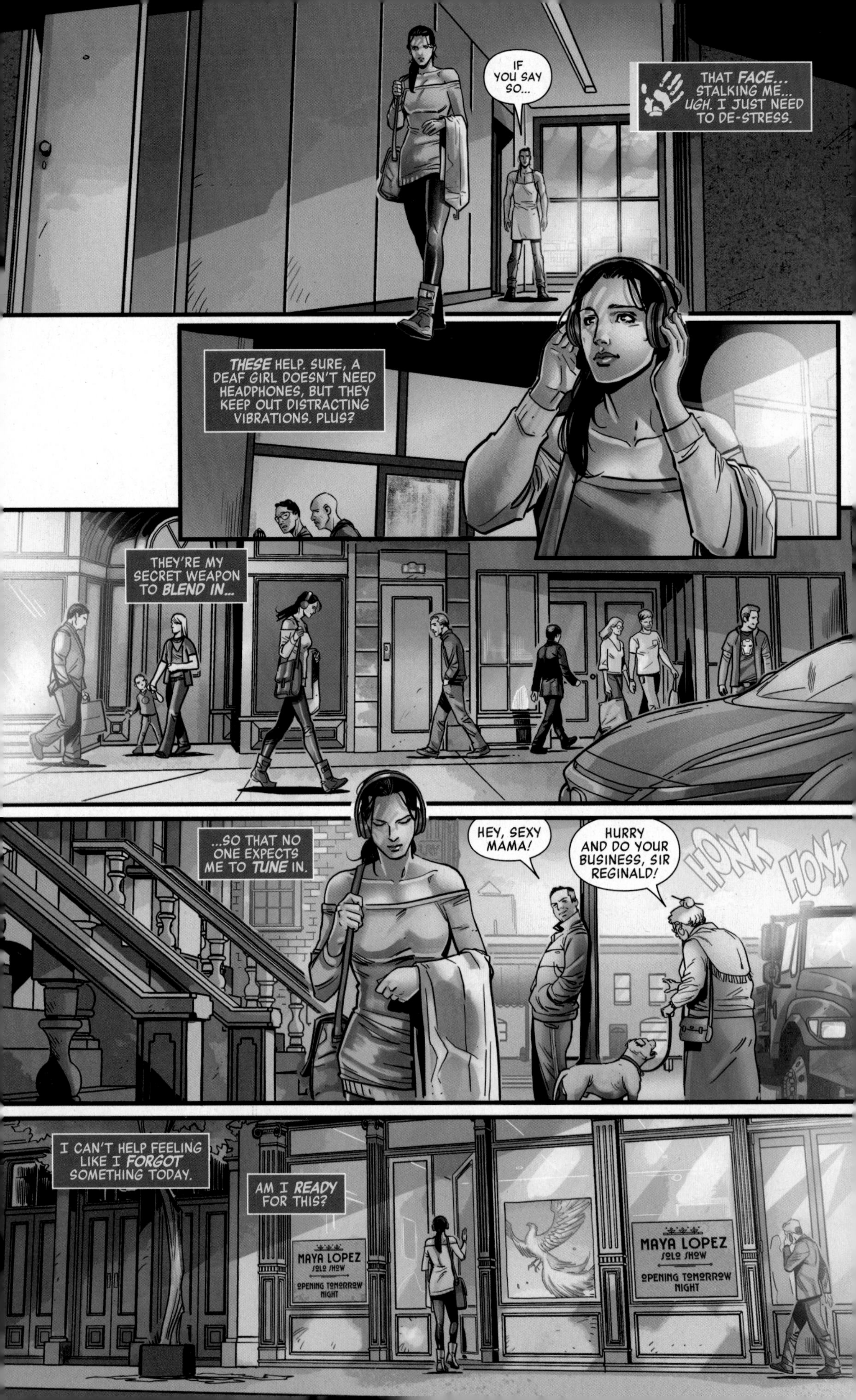
IF YOU SAY SO...
THAT FACE... STALKING ME... UGH. I JUST NEED TO DE-STRESS.
THESE HELP. SURE, A DEAF GIRL DOESN'T NEED HEADPHONES, BUT THEY KEEP OUT DISTRACTING VIBRATIONS. PLUS?
THEY'RE MY SECRET WEAPON TO BLEND IN...
...SO THAT NO ONE EXPECTS ME TO TUNE IN.
HEY, SEXY MAMA!
HURRY AND DO YOUR BUSINESS, SIR REGINALD!
HONK HONK
I CAN'T HELP FEELING LIKE I FORGOT SOMETHING TODAY.
AM I READY FOR THIS?
MAYA LOPEZ SOLO SHOW OPENING TOMORROW NIGHT
MAYA LOPEZ SOLO SHOW OPENING TOMORROW NIGHT

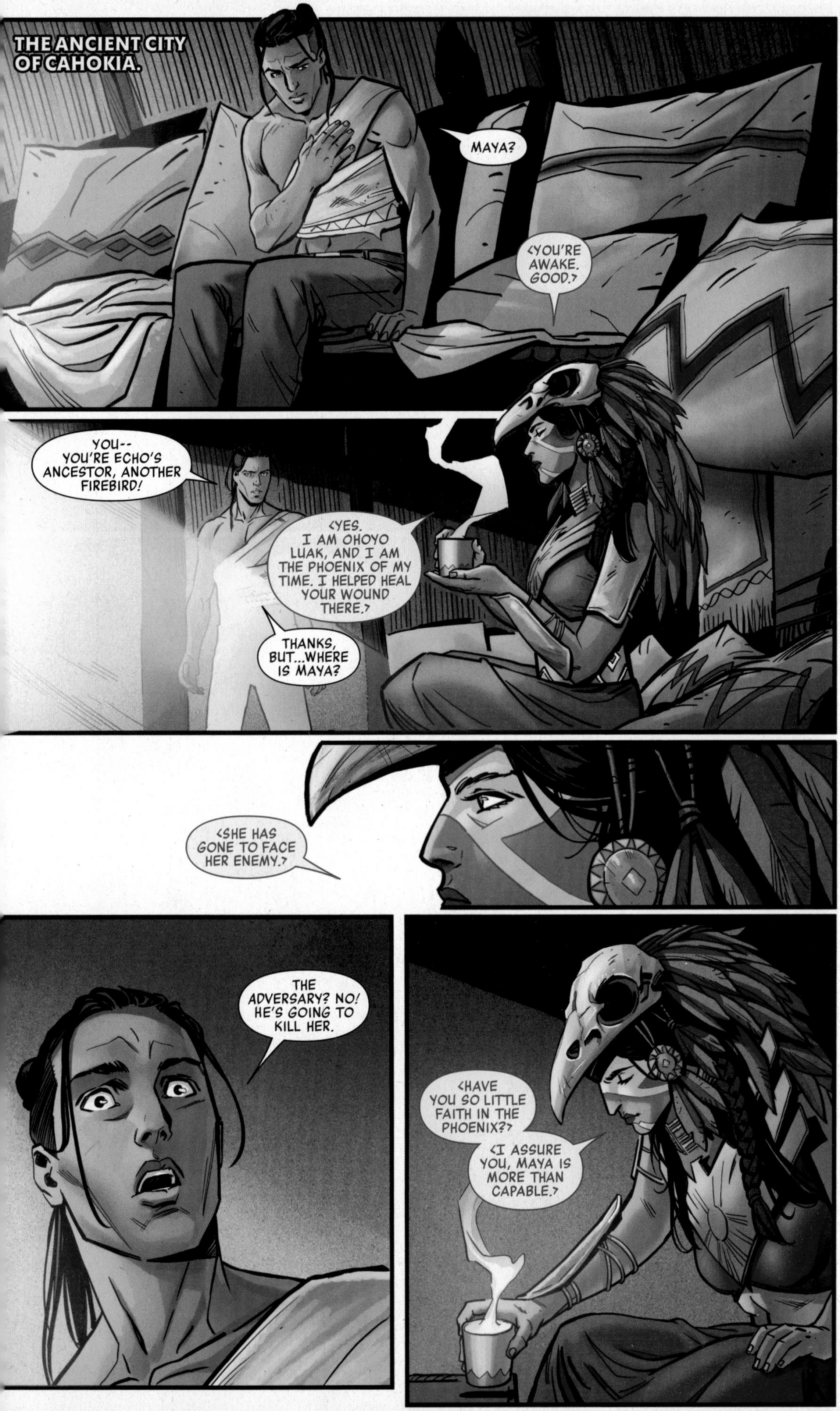
THE ANCIENT CITY OF CAHOKIA.
MAYA?
<YOU'RE AWAKE. GOOD.>
YOU-- YOU'RE ECHO'S ANCESTOR, ANOTHER FIREBIRD!
<YES. I AM OHOYO LUAK, AND I AM THE PHOENIX OF MY TIME. I HELPED HEAL YOUR WOUND THERE.>
THANKS, BUT...WHERE IS MAYA?
<SHE HAS GONE TO FACE HER ENEMY.>
THE ADVERSARY? NO! HE'S GOING TO KILL HER.
<HAVE YOU SO LITTLE FAITH IN THE PHOENIX?>
<I ASSURE YOU, MAYA IS MORE THAN CAPABLE.>

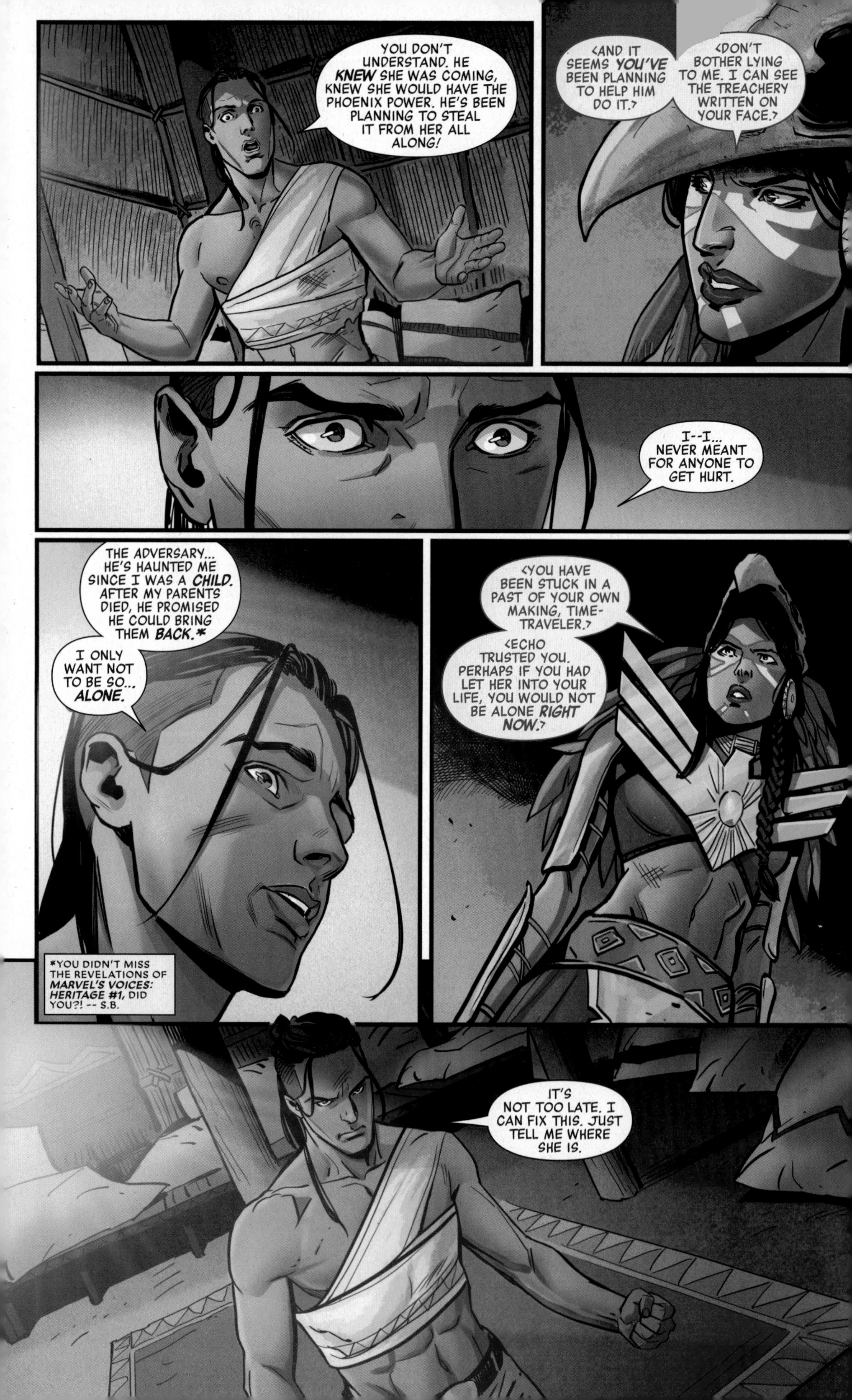
YOU DON'T UNDERSTAND. HE KNEW SHE WAS COMING, KNEW SHE WOULD HAVE THE PHOENIX POWER. HE'S BEEN PLANNING TO STEAL IT FROM HER ALL ALONG!
<AND IT SEEMS YOU'VE BEEN PLANNING TO HELP HIM DO IT.>
<DON'T BOTHER LYING TO ME. I CAN SEE THE TREACHERY WRITTEN ON YOUR FACE.>
I--I... NEVER MEANT FOR ANYONE TO GET HURT.
THE ADVERSARY... HE'S HAUNTED ME SINCE I WAS A CHILD. AFTER MY PARENTS DIED, HE PROMISED HE COULD BRING THEM BACK.*
I ONLY WANT NOT TO BE SO... ALONE.
*YOU DIDN'T MISS THE REVELATIONS OF MARVEL'S VOICES: HERITAGE #1, DID YOU?! -- S.B.
<YOU HAVE BEEN STUCK IN A PAST OF YOUR OWN MAKING, TIME-TRAVELER.>
<ECHO TRUSTED YOU. PERHAPS IF YOU HAD LET HER INTO YOUR LIFE, YOU WOULD NOT BE ALONE RIGHT NOW.>
IT'S NOT TOO LATE. I CAN FIX THIS. JUST TELL ME WHERE SHE IS.

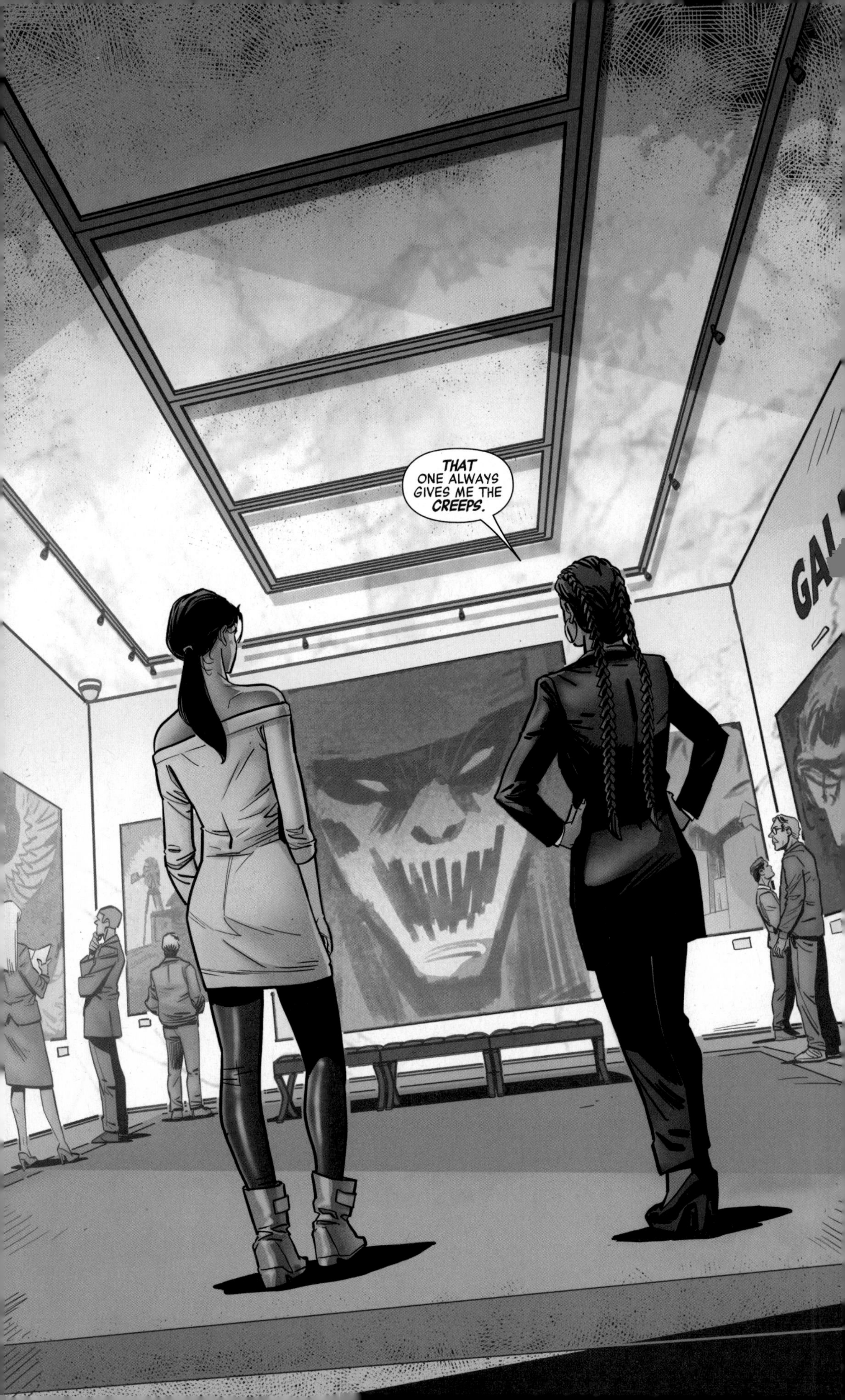
THAT ONE ALWAYS GIVES ME THE CREEPS.

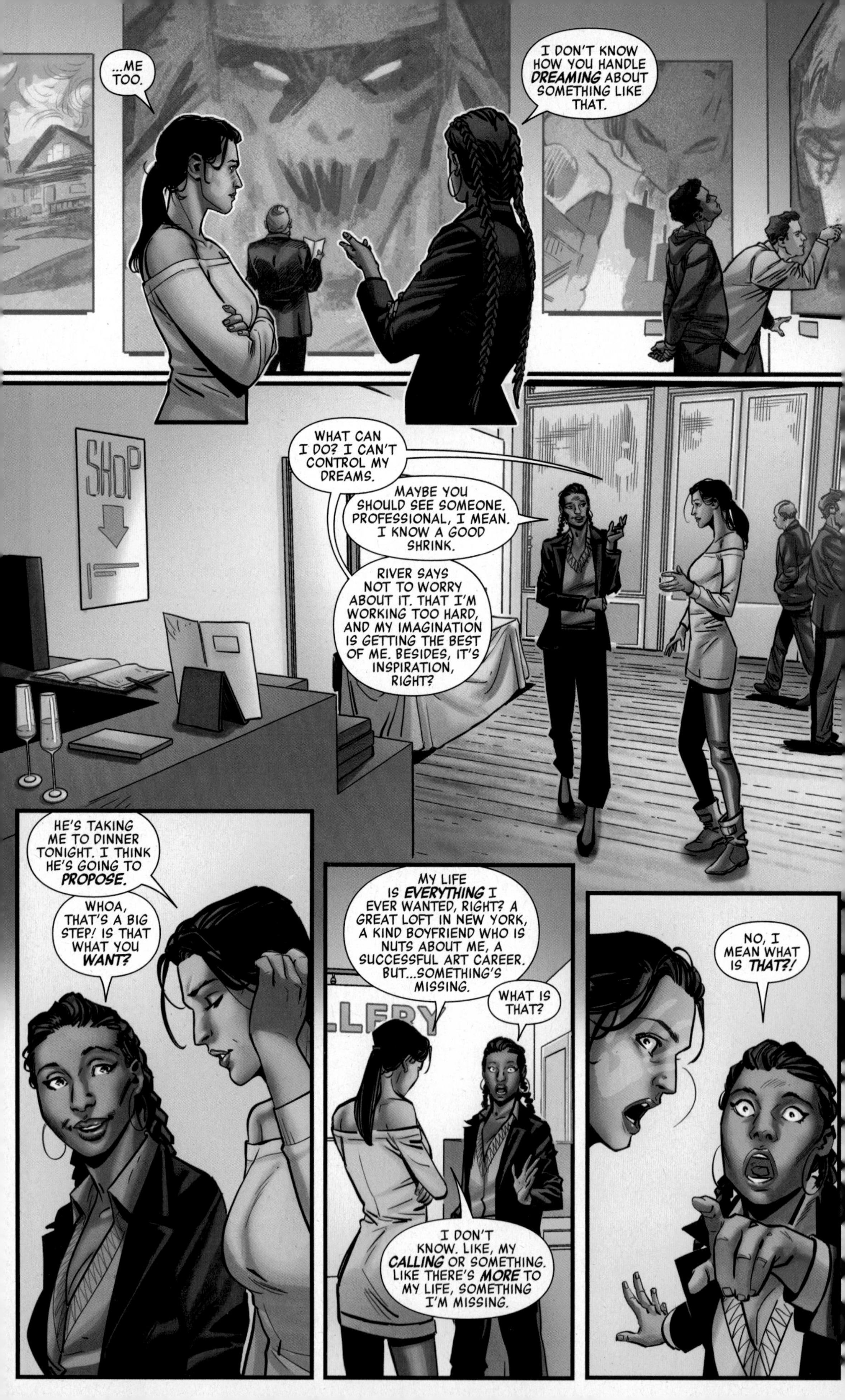

...ME TOO.
I DON'T KNOW HOW YOU HANDLE DREAMING ABOUT SOMETHING LIKE THAT.
SHOP
WHAT CAN I DO? I CAN'T CONTROL MY DREAMS.
MAYBE YOU SHOULD SEE SOMEONE. PROFESSIONAL, I MEAN. I KNOW A GOOD SHRINK.
RIVER SAYS NOT TO WORRY ABOUT IT. THAT I'M WORKING TOO HARD, AND MY IMAGINATION IS GETTING THE BEST OF ME. BESIDES, IT'S INSPIRATION, RIGHT?
HE'S TAKING ME TO DINNER TONIGHT. I THINK HE'S GOING TO PROPOSE.
WHOA, THAT'S A BIG STEP! IS THAT WHAT YOU WANT?
MY LIFE IS EVERYTHING I EVER WANTED, RIGHT? A GREAT LOFT IN NEW YORK, A KIND BOYFRIEND WHO IS NUTS ABOUT ME, A SUCCESSFUL ART CAREER. BUT...SOMETHING'S MISSING.
WHAT IS THAT?
I DON'T KNOW. LIKE, MY CALLING OR SOMETHING. LIKE THERE'S MORE TO MY LIFE, SOMETHING I'M MISSING.
NO, I MEAN WHAT IS THAT?!

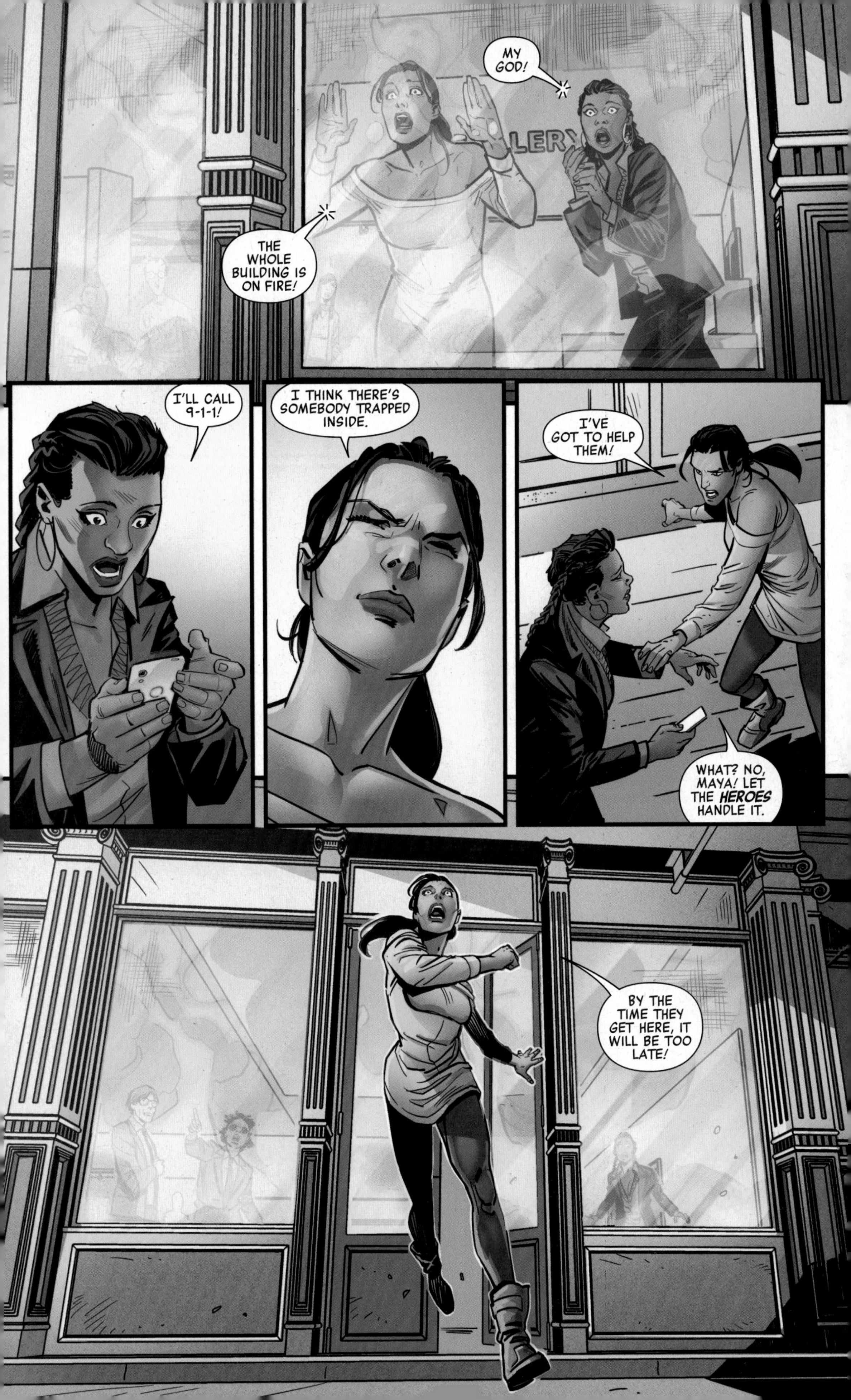
MY GOD!
THE WHOLE BUILDING IS ON FIRE!
LERY
I'LL CALL 9-1-1!
I THINK THERE'S SOMEBODY TRAPPED INSIDE.
I'VE GOT TO HELP THEM!
WHAT? NO, MAYA! LET THE HEROES HANDLE IT.
BY THE TIME THEY GET HERE, IT WILL BE TOO LATE!

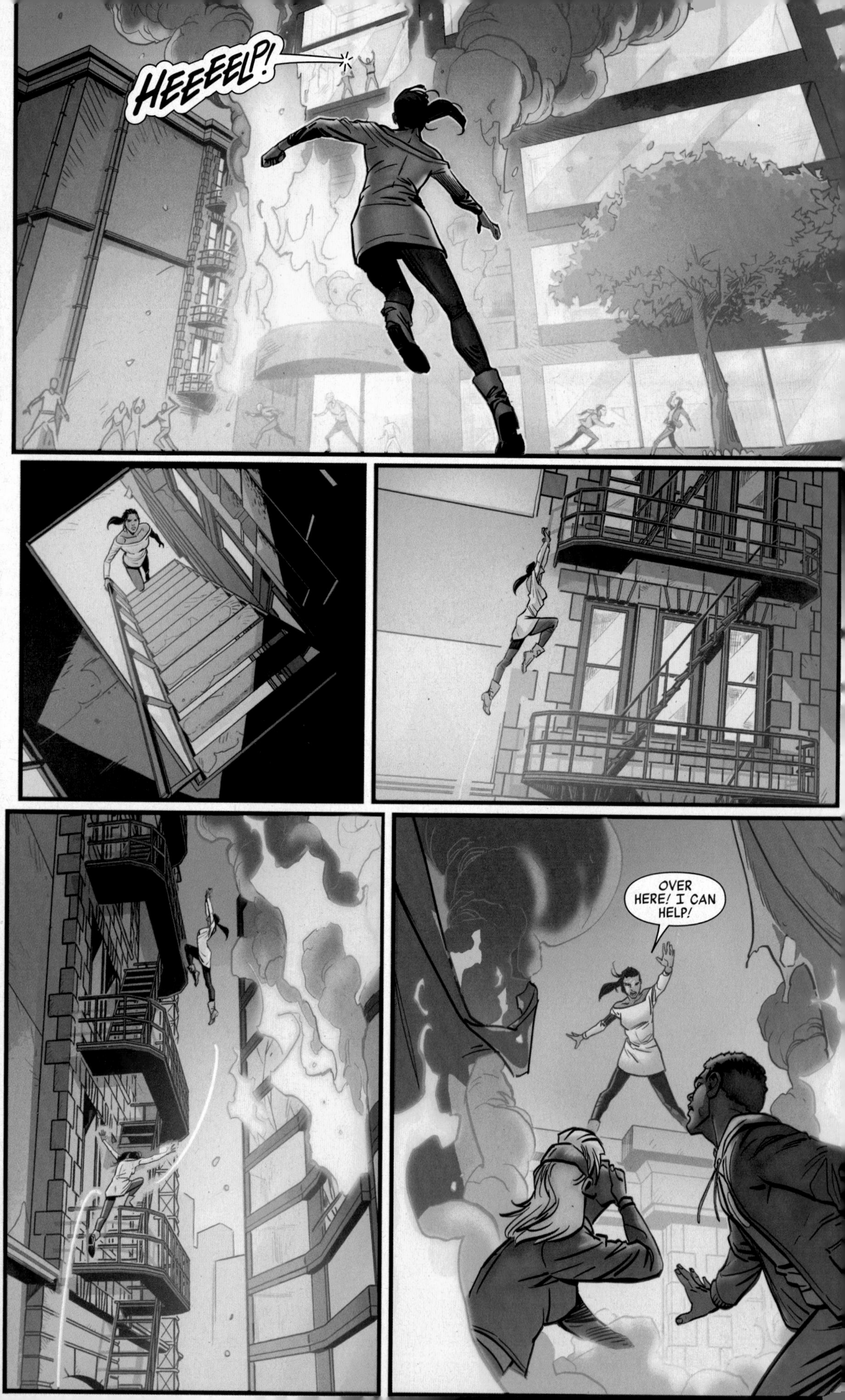
HEEEELP!
OVER HERE! I CAN HELP!

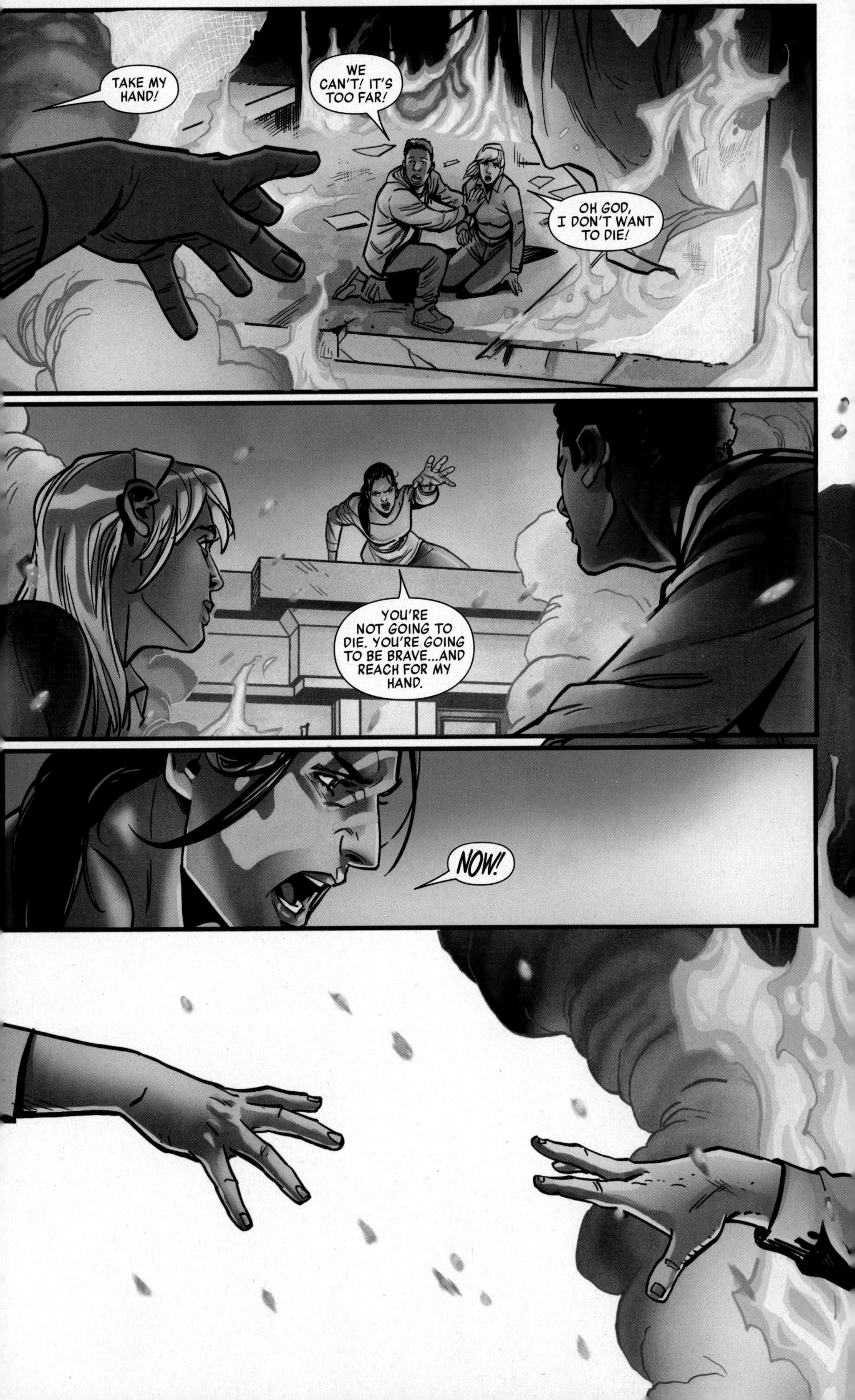
TAKE MY HAND!
WE CAN'T! IT'S TOO FAR!
OH GOD, I DON'T WANT TO DIE!
YOU'RE NOT GOING TO DIE. YOU'RE GOING TO BE BRAVE...AND REACH FOR MY HAND.
NOW!

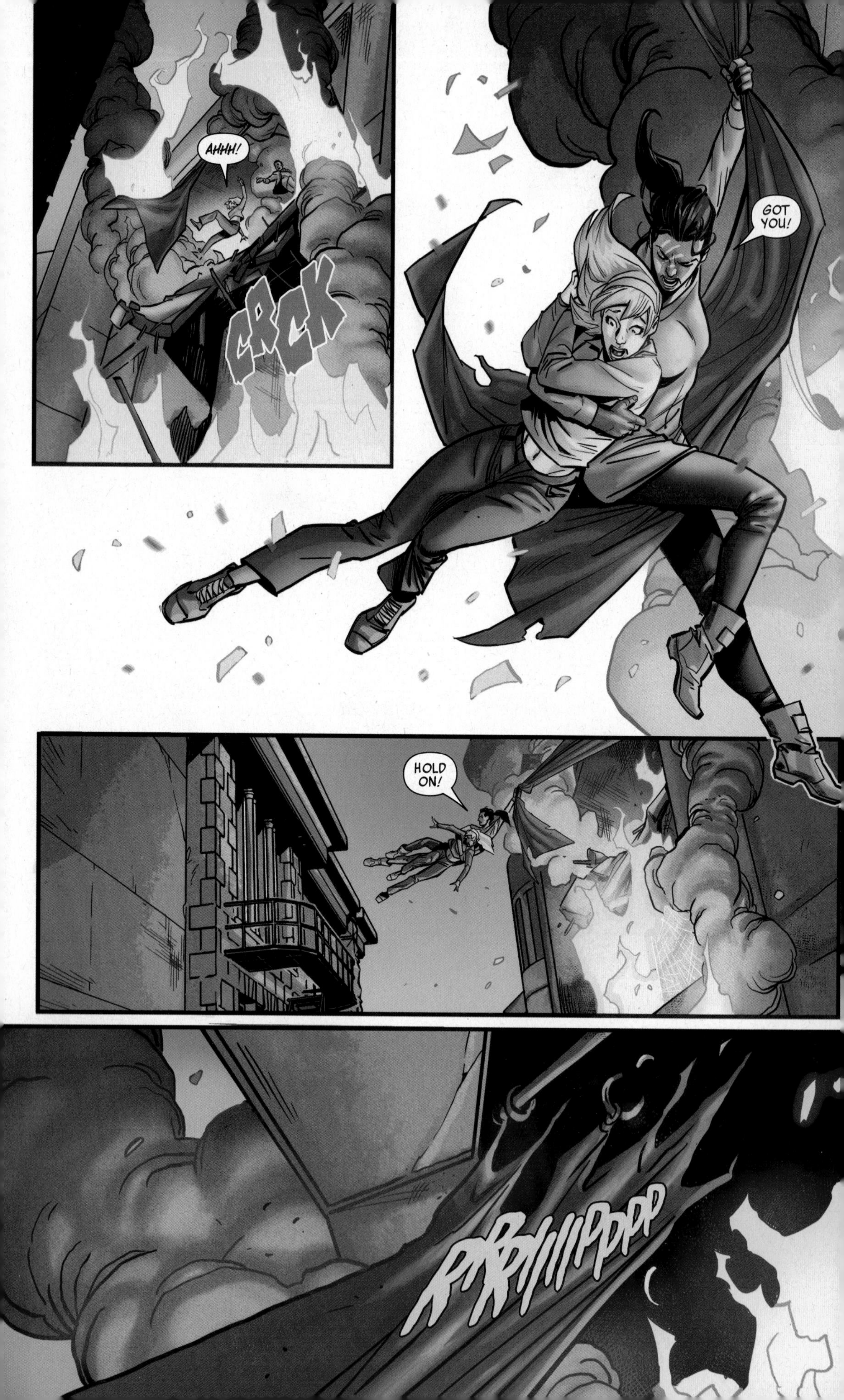
AHHH!
CRCK
GOT YOU!
HOLD ON!
RRRIIIPPPP

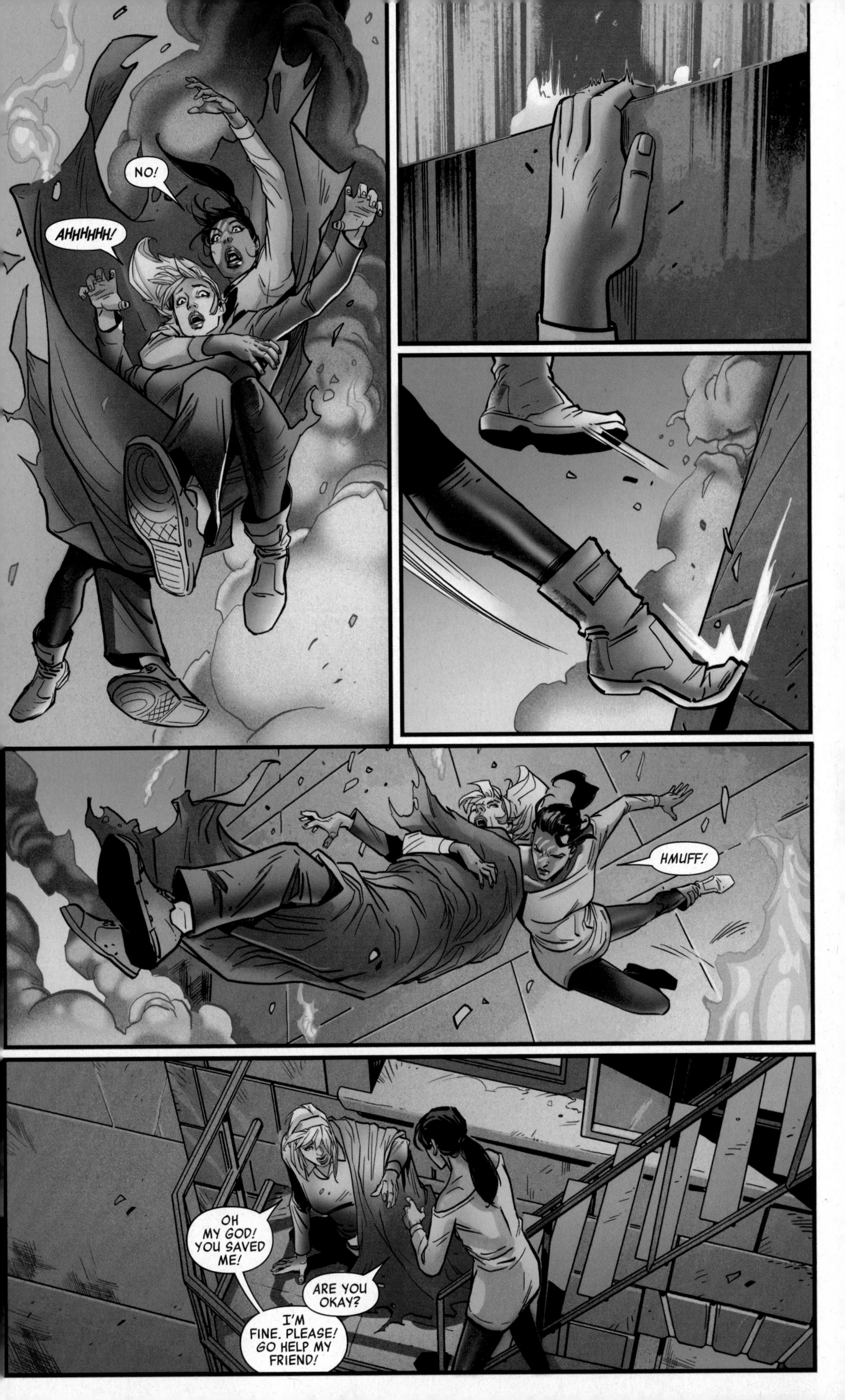
NO!
AHHHHHH!
HMUFF!
OH MY GOD! YOU SAVED ME!
ARE YOU OKAY?
I'M FINE. PLEASE! GO HELP MY FRIEND!

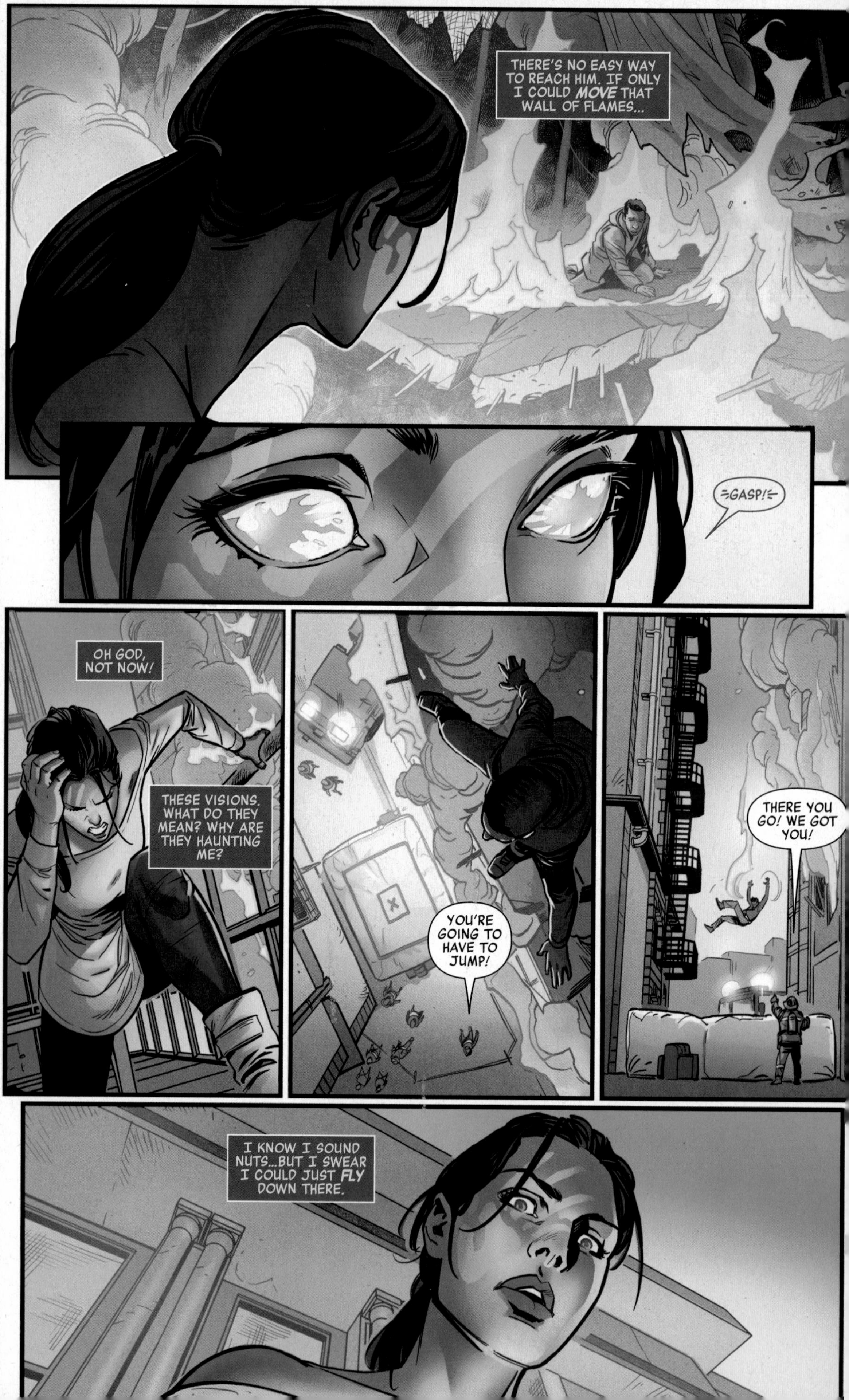
THERE'S NO EASY WAY TO REACH HIM. IF ONLY I COULD MOVE THAT WALL OF FLAMES...
GASP!
OH GOD, NOT NOW!
THESE VISIONS. WHAT DO THEY MEAN? WHY ARE THEY HAUNTING ME?
YOU'RE GOING TO HAVE TO JUMP!
THERE YOU GO! WE GOT YOU!
I KNOW I SOUND NUTS...BUT I SWEAR I COULD JUST FLY DOWN THERE.

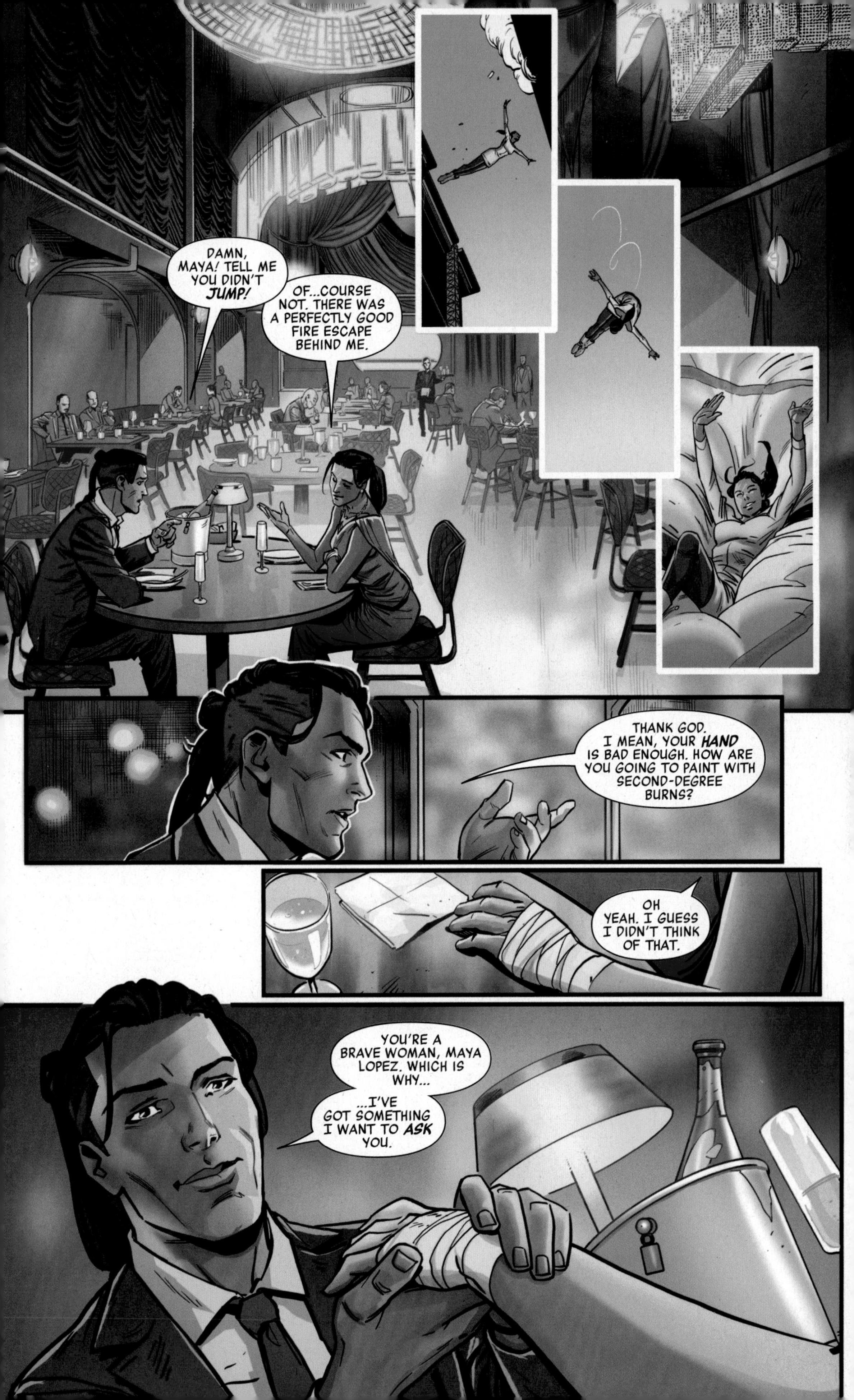
DAMN, MAYA! TELL ME YOU DIDN'T JUMP!
OF...COURSE NOT. THERE WAS A PERFECTLY GOOD FIRE ESCAPE BEHIND ME.
THANK GOD. I MEAN, YOUR HAND IS BAD ENOUGH. HOW ARE YOU GOING TO PAINT WITH SECOND-DEGREE BURNS?
OH YEAH. I GUESS I DIDN'T THINK OF THAT.
YOU'RE A BRAVE WOMAN, MAYA LOPEZ. WHICH IS WHY...
...I'VE GOT SOMETHING I WANT TO ASK YOU.

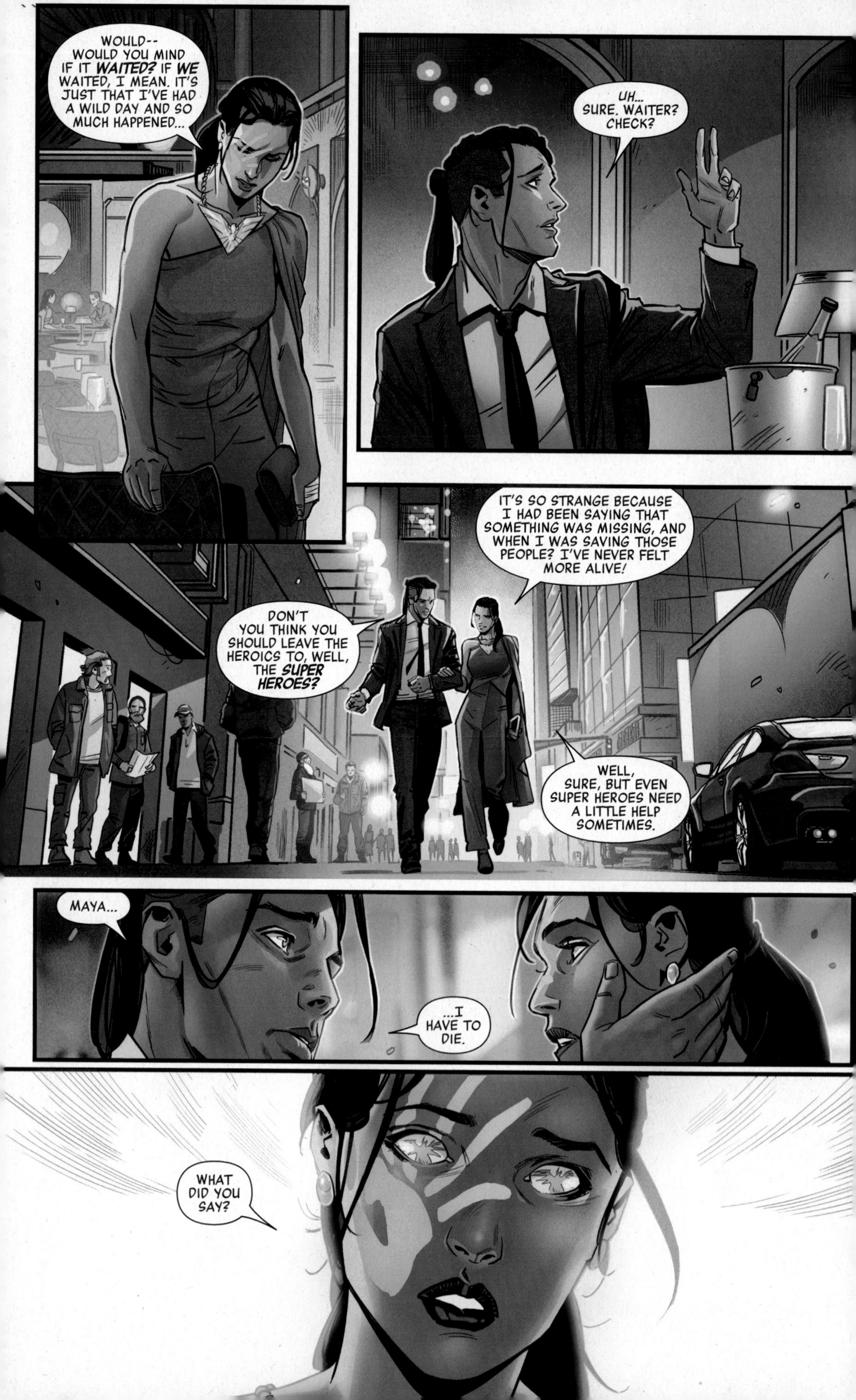
WOULD-- WOULD YOU MIND IF IT WAITED? IF WE WAITED, I MEAN. IT'S JUST THAT I'VE HAD A WILD DAY AND SO MUCH HAPPENED...
UH... SURE. WAITER? CHECK?
IT'S SO STRANGE BECAUSE I HAD BEEN SAYING THAT SOMETHING WAS MISSING, AND WHEN I WAS SAVING THOSE PEOPLE? I'VE NEVER FELT MORE ALIVE!
DON'T YOU THINK YOU SHOULD LEAVE THE HEROICS TO, WELL, THE SUPER HEROES?
WELL, SURE, BUT EVEN SUPER HEROES NEED A LITTLE HELP SOMETIMES.
MAYA...
...I HAVE TO DIE.
WHAT DID YOU SAY?

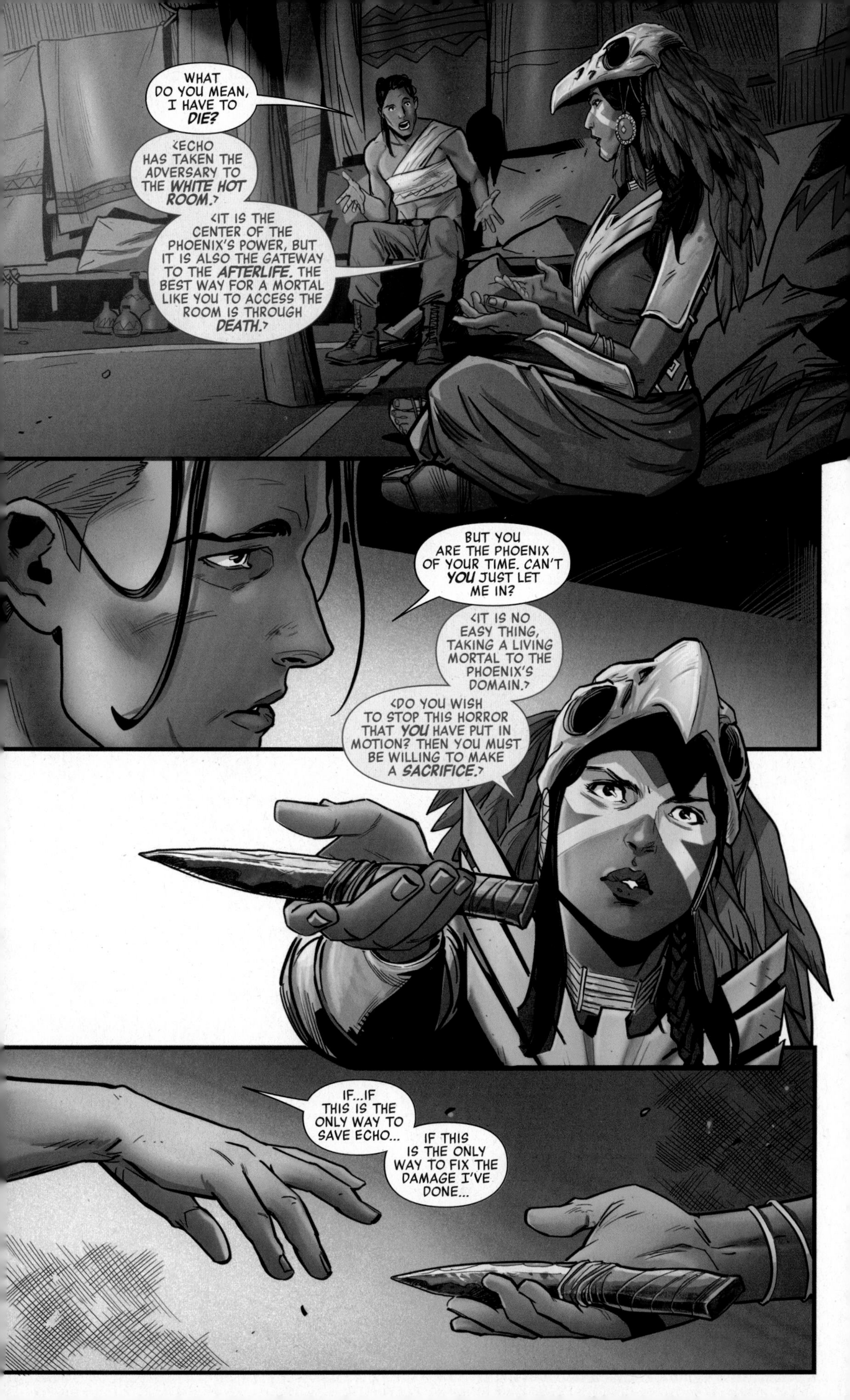
WHAT DO YOU MEAN, I HAVE TO DIE?
<ECHO HAS TAKEN THE ADVERSARY TO THE WHITE HOT ROOM.>
<IT IS THE CENTER OF THE PHOENIX'S POWER, BUT IT IS ALSO THE GATEWAY TO THE AFTERLIFE. THE BEST WAY FOR A MORTAL LIKE YOU TO ACCESS THE ROOM IS THROUGH DEATH.>
BUT YOU ARE THE PHOENIX OF YOUR TIME. CAN'T YOU JUST LET ME IN?
<IT IS NO EASY THING, TAKING A LIVING MORTAL TO THE PHOENIX'S DOMAIN.>
<DO YOU WISH TO STOP THIS HORROR THAT YOU HAVE PUT IN MOTION? THEN YOU MUST BE WILLING TO MAKE A SACRIFICE.>
IF...IF THIS IS THE ONLY WAY TO SAVE ECHO...
IF THIS IS THE ONLY WAY TO FIX THE DAMAGE I'VE DONE...

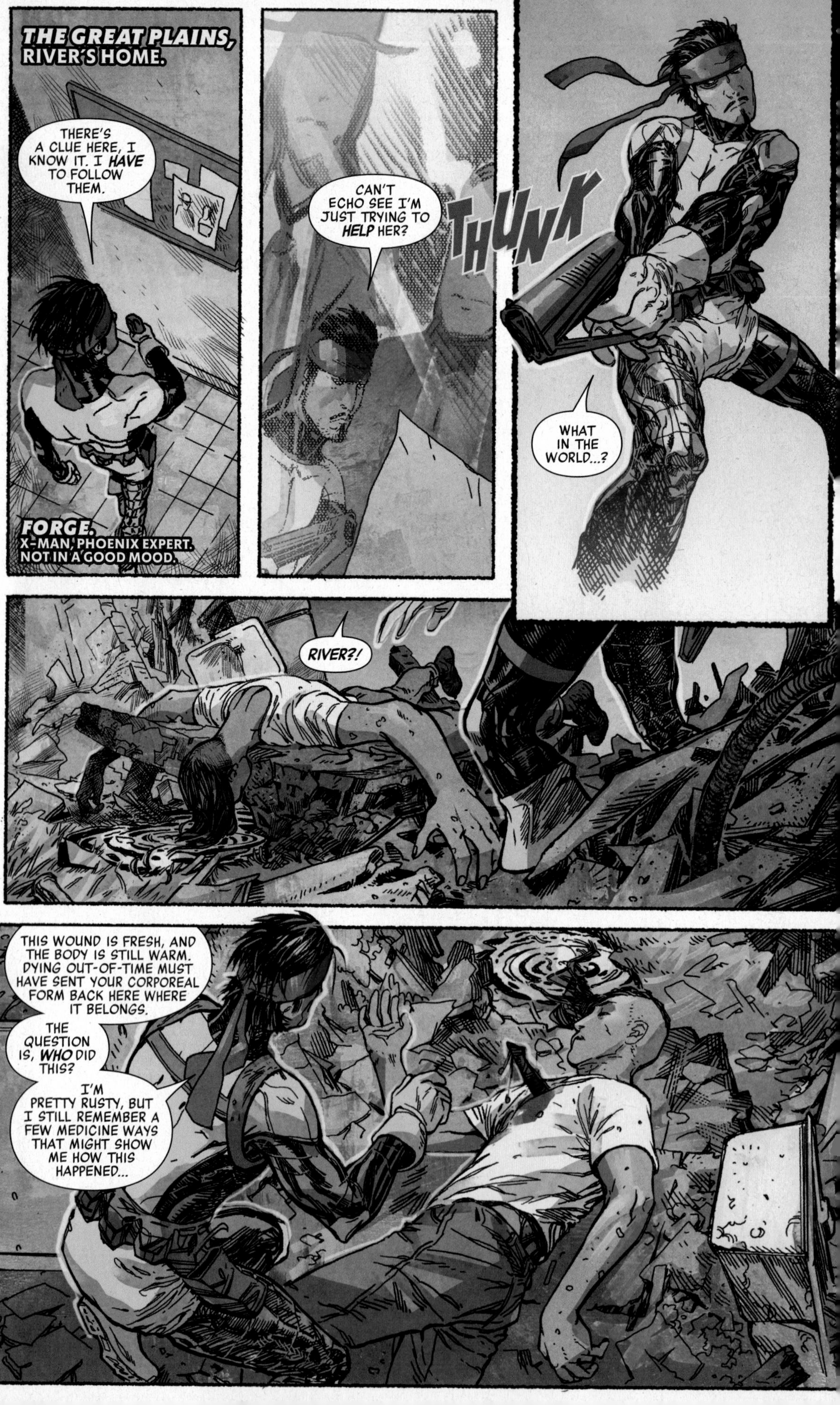
THE GREAT PLAINS, RIVER'S HOME.
THERE'S A CLUE HERE, I KNOW IT. I HAVE TO FOLLOW THEM.
FORGE. X-MAN, PHOENIX EXPERT. NOT IN A GOOD MOOD.
CAN'T ECHO SEE I'M JUST TRYING TO HELP HER?
THUNK
WHAT IN THE WORLD...?
RIVER?!
THIS WOUND IS FRESH, AND THE BODY IS STILL WARM. DYING OUT-OF-TIME MUST HAVE SENT YOUR CORPOREAL FORM BACK HERE WHERE IT BELONGS.
THE QUESTION IS, WHO DID THIS?
I'M PRETTY RUSTY, BUT I STILL REMEMBER A FEW MEDICINE WAYS THAT MIGHT SHOW ME HOW THIS HAPPENED...

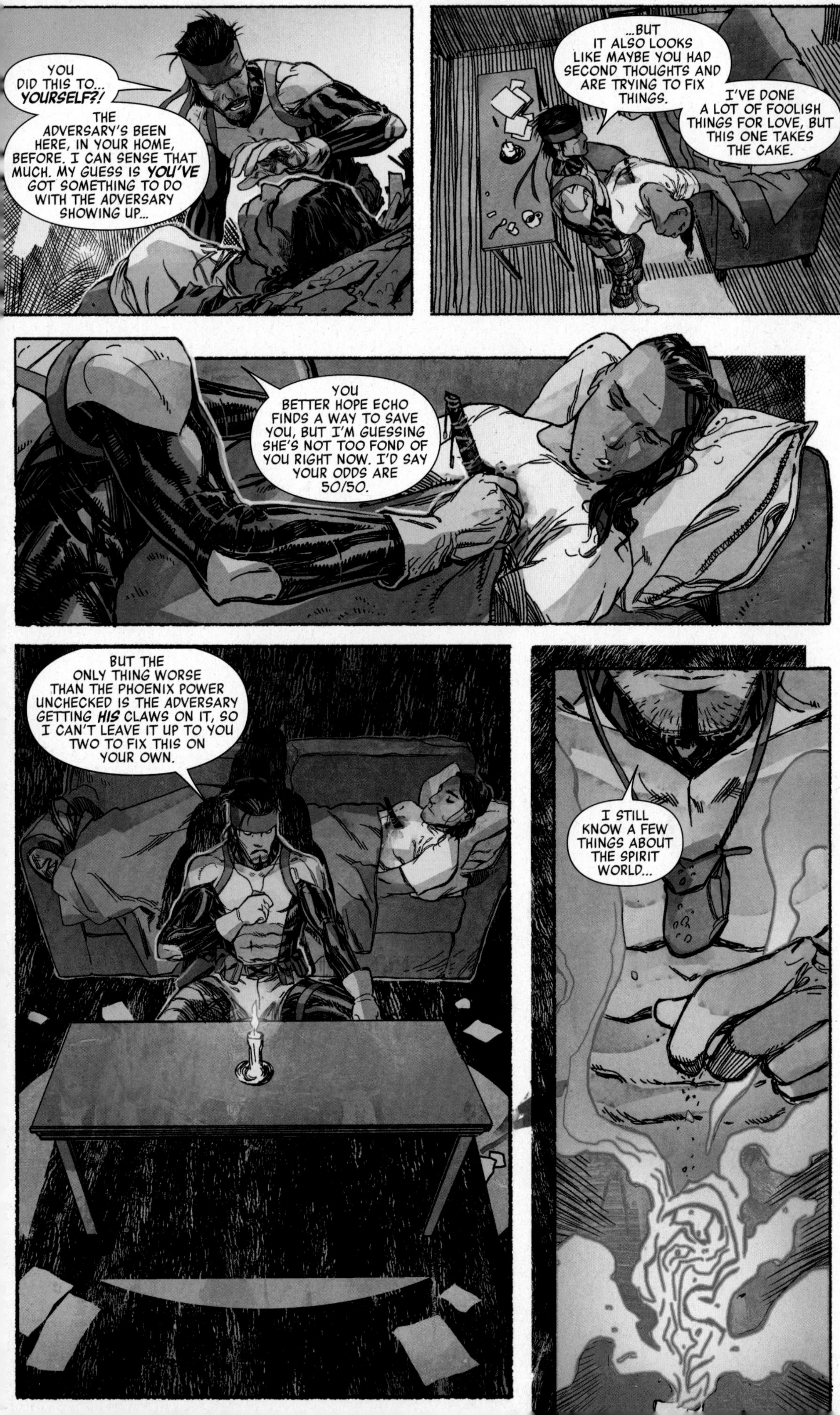
YOU DID THIS TO... YOURSELF?!
THE ADVERSARY'S BEEN HERE, IN YOUR HOME, BEFORE. I CAN SENSE THAT MUCH. MY GUESS IS YOU'VE GOT SOMETHING TO DO WITH THE ADVERSARY SHOWING UP...
...BUT IT ALSO LOOKS LIKE MAYBE YOU HAD SECOND THOUGHTS AND ARE TRYING TO FIX THINGS.
I'VE DONE A LOT OF FOOLISH THINGS FOR LOVE, BUT THIS ONE TAKES THE CAKE.
YOU BETTER HOPE ECHO FINDS A WAY TO SAVE YOU, BUT I'M GUESSING SHE'S NOT TOO FOND OF YOU RIGHT NOW. I'D SAY YOUR ODDS ARE 50/50.
BUT THE ONLY THING WORSE THAN THE PHOENIX POWER UNCHECKED IS THE ADVERSARY GETTING HIS CLAWS ON IT, SO I CAN'T LEAVE IT UP TO YOU TWO TO FIX THIS ON YOUR OWN.
I STILL KNOW A FEW THINGS ABOUT THE SPIRIT WORLD...

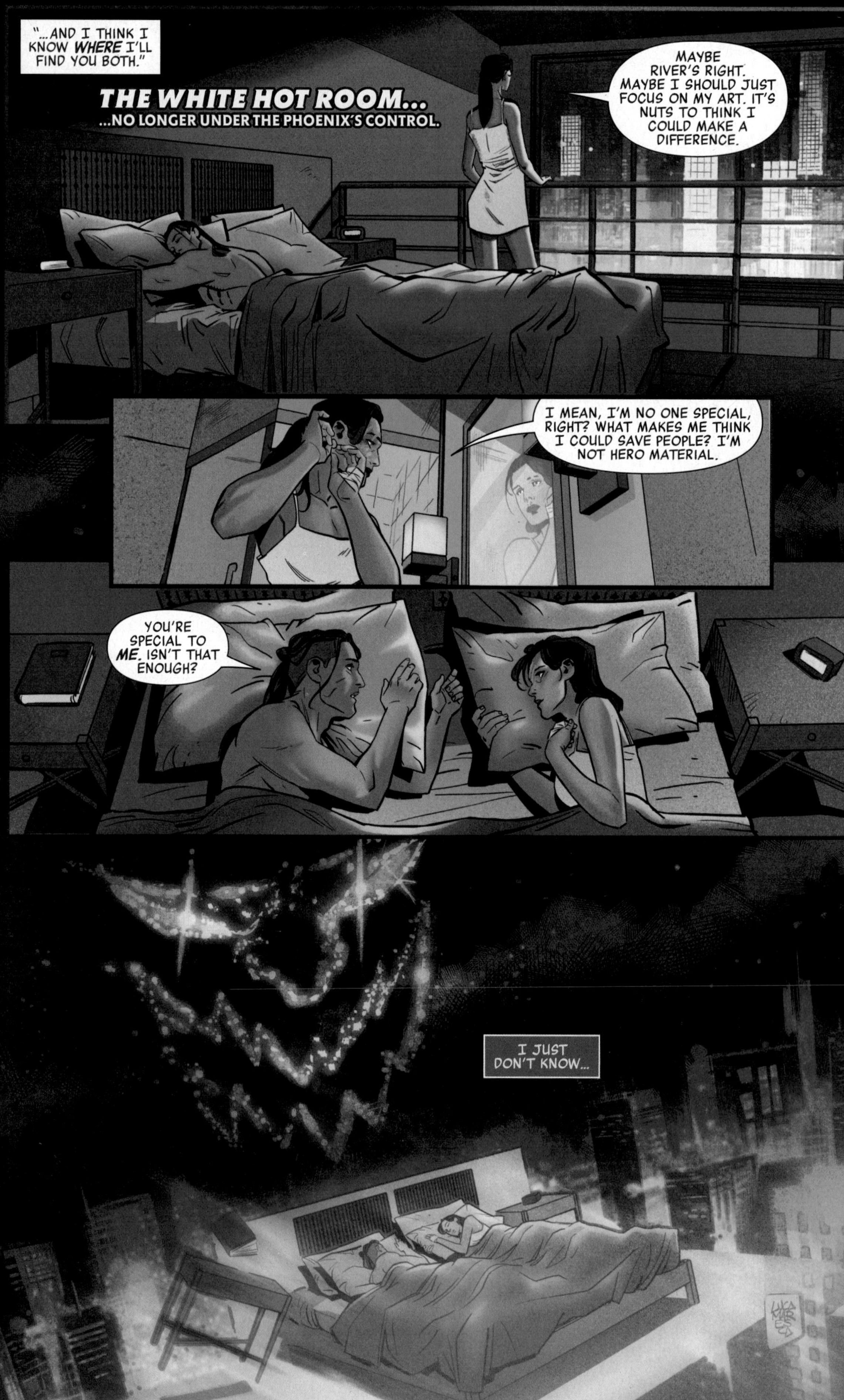
"...AND I THINK I KNOW WHERE I'LL FIND YOU BOTH."
THE WHITE HOT ROOM...
...NO LONGER UNDER THE PHOENIX'S CONTROL.
MAYBE RIVER'S RIGHT. MAYBE I SHOULD JUST FOCUS ON MY ART. IT'S NUTS TO THINK I COULD MAKE A DIFFERENCE.
I MEAN, I'M NO ONE SPECIAL, RIGHT? WHAT MAKES ME THINK I COULD SAVE PEOPLE? I'M NOT HERO MATERIAL.
YOU'RE SPECIAL TO ME. ISN'T THAT ENOUGH?
I JUST DON'T KNOW...

5

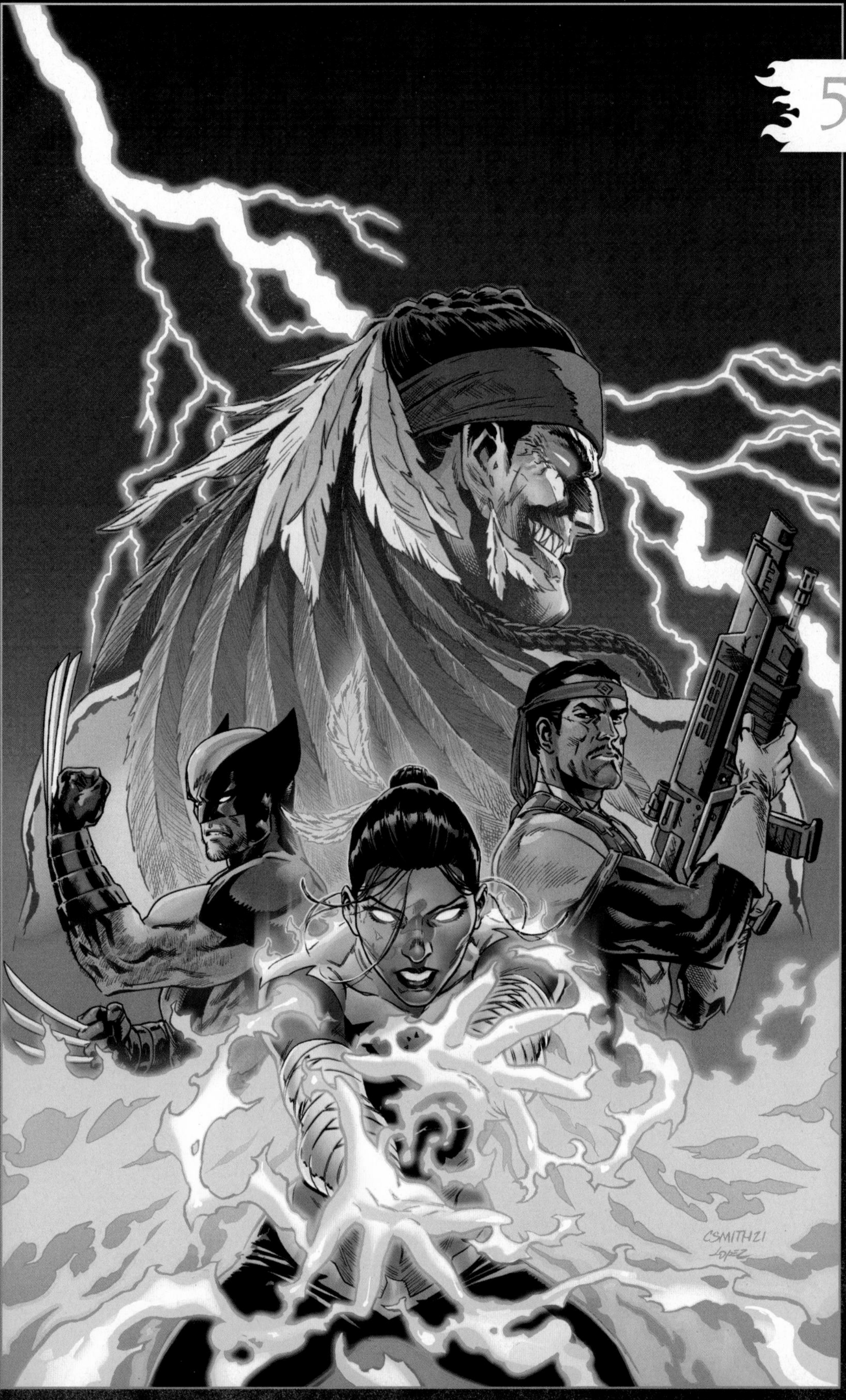
CSMITH21
LOPEZ

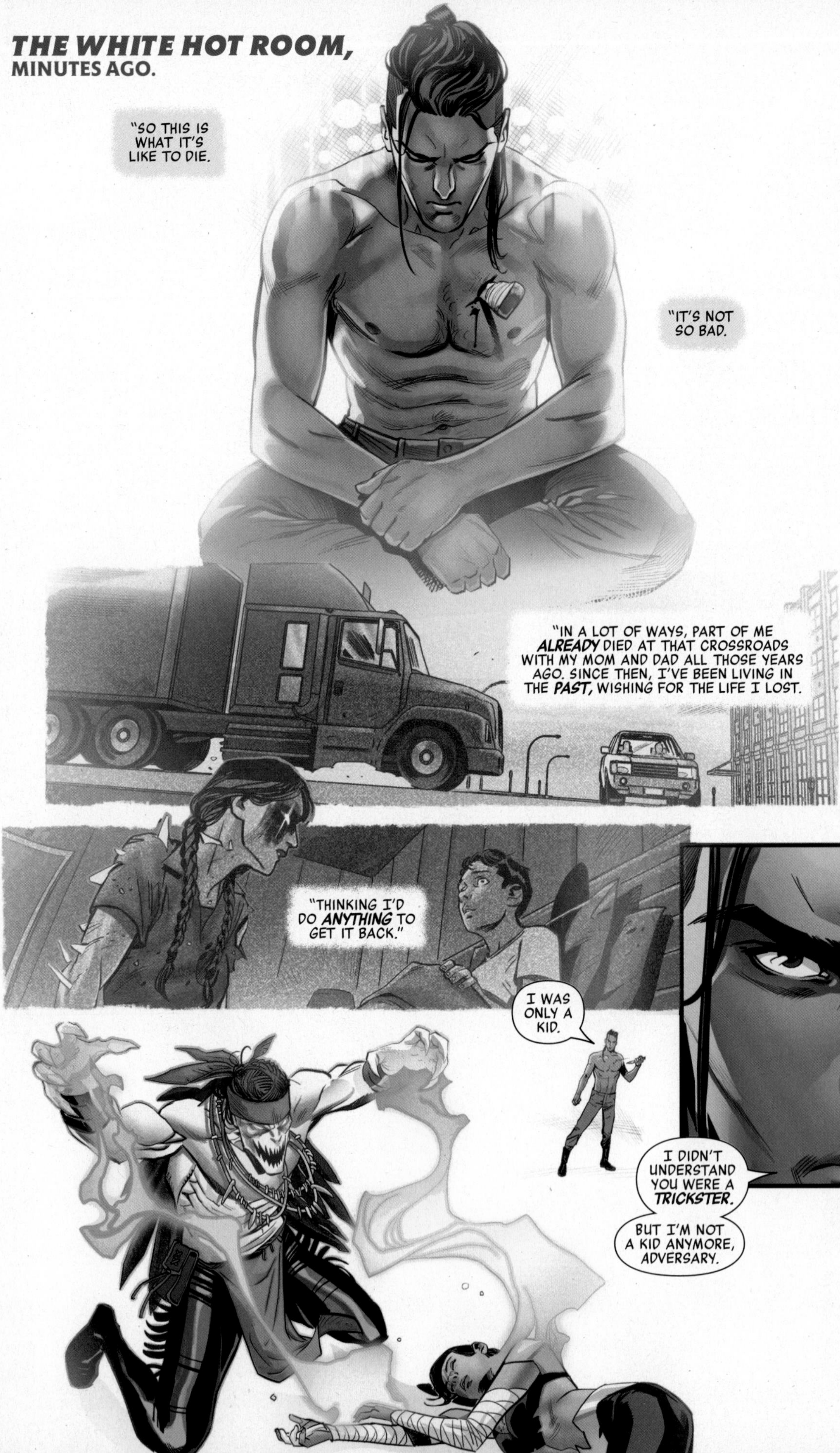
THE WHITE HOT ROOM, MINUTES AGO.
"SO THIS IS WHAT IT'S LIKE TO DIE.
"IT'S NOT SO BAD.
"IN A LOT OF WAYS, PART OF ME ALREADY DIED AT THAT CROSSROADS WITH MY MOM AND DAD ALL THOSE YEARS AGO. SINCE THEN, I'VE BEEN LIVING IN THE PAST, WISHING FOR THE LIFE I LOST.
"THINKING I'D DO ANYTHING TO GET IT BACK."
I WAS ONLY A KID.
I DIDN'T UNDERSTAND YOU WERE A TRICKSTER.
BUT I'M NOT A KID ANYMORE, ADVERSARY.

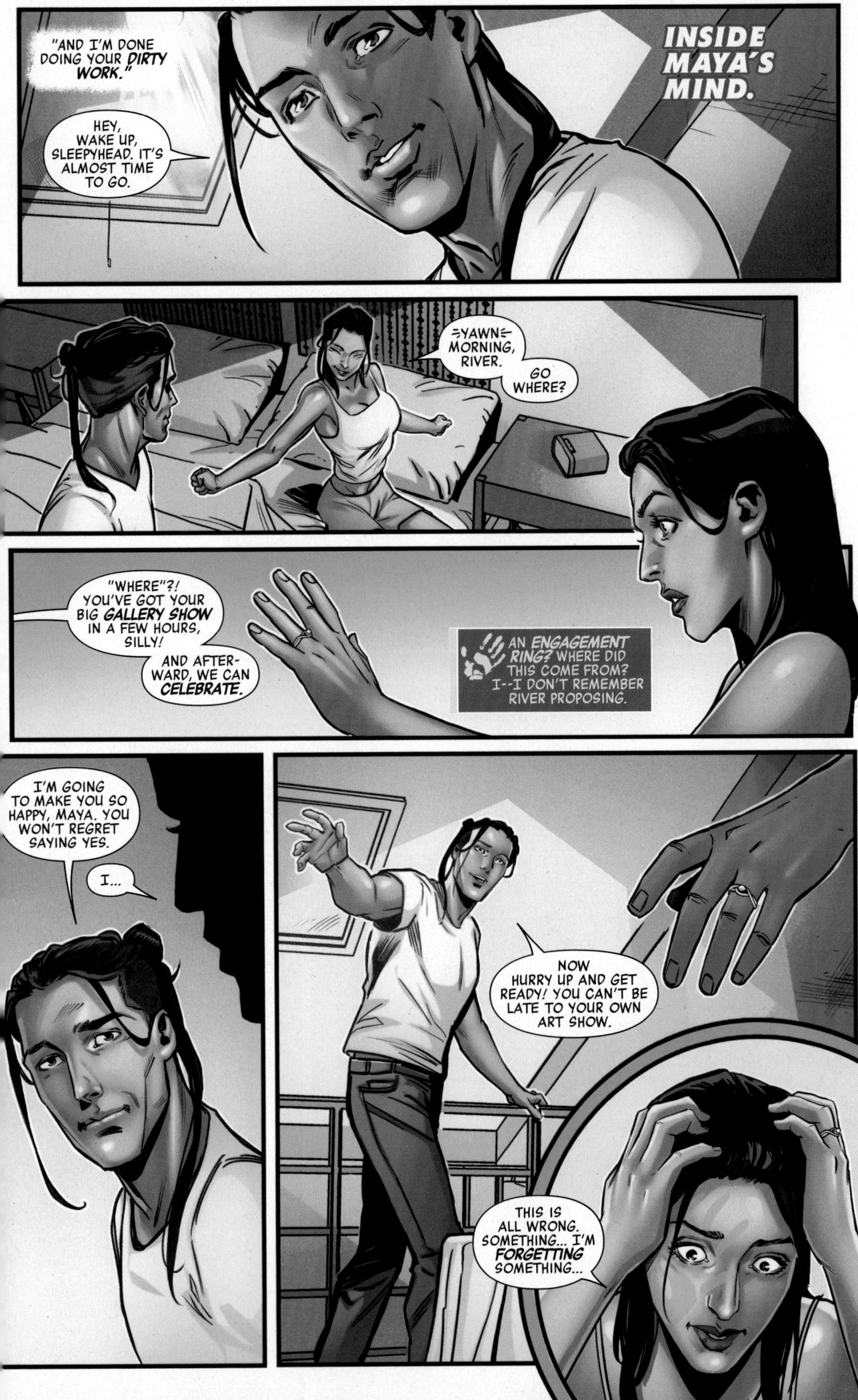
"AND I'M DONE DOING YOUR DIRTY WORK."
INSIDE MAYA'S MIND.
HEY, WAKE UP, SLEEPYHEAD. IT'S ALMOST TIME TO GO.
=YAWN= MORNING, RIVER.
GO WHERE?
"WHERE"?! YOU'VE GOT YOUR BIG GALLERY SHOW IN A FEW HOURS, SILLY!
AND AFTER-WARD, WE CAN CELEBRATE.
AN ENGAGEMENT RING? WHERE DID THIS COME FROM? I--I DON'T REMEMBER RIVER PROPOSING.
I'M GOING TO MAKE YOU SO HAPPY, MAYA. YOU WON'T REGRET SAYING YES.
I...
NOW HURRY UP AND GET READY! YOU CAN'T BE LATE TO YOUR OWN ART SHOW.
THIS IS ALL WRONG. SOMETHING... I'M FORGETTING SOMETHING...

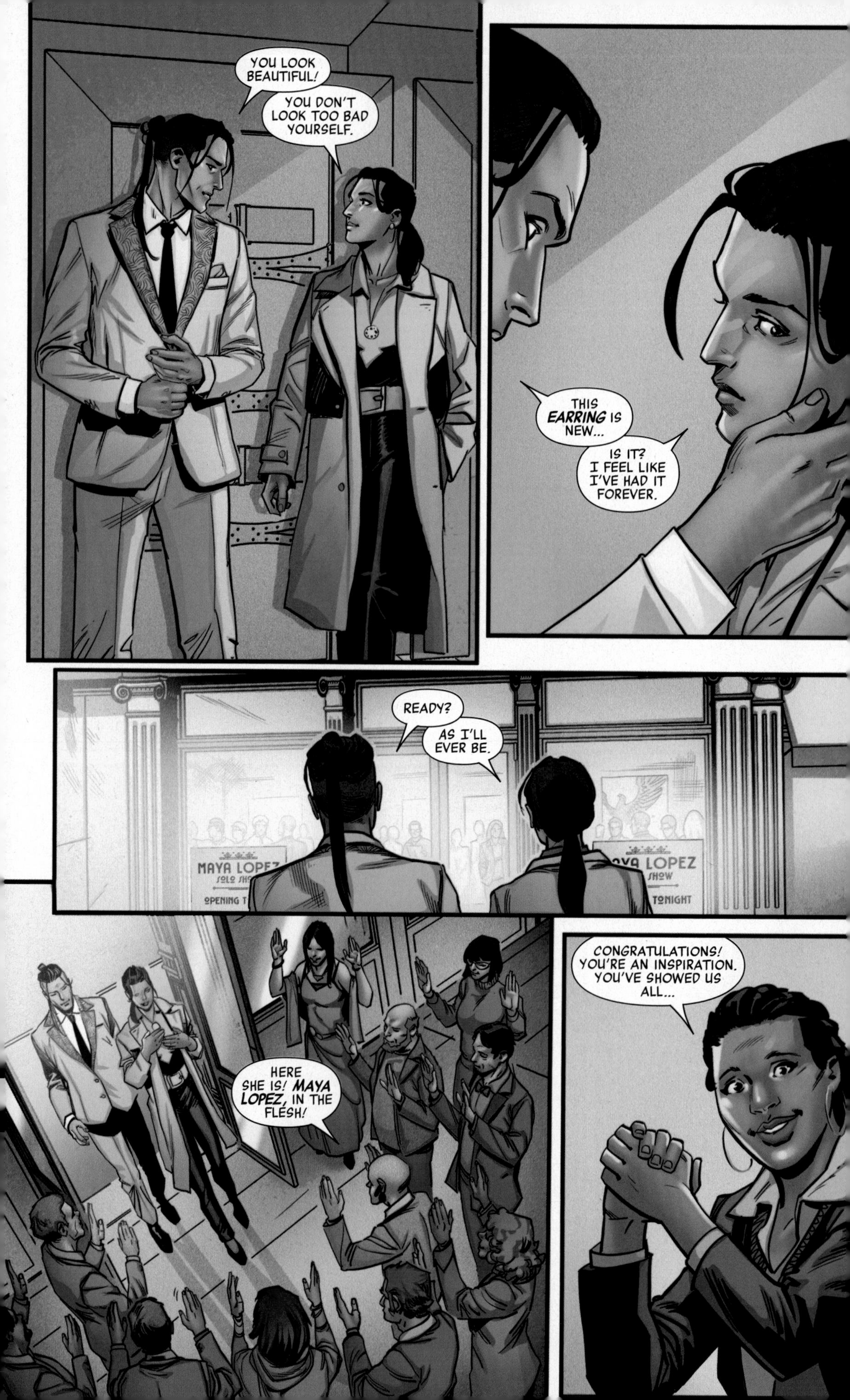
YOU LOOK BEAUTIFUL!
YOU DON'T LOOK TOO BAD YOURSELF.
THIS EARRING IS NEW...
IS IT? I FEEL LIKE I'VE HAD IT FOREVER.
READY?
AS I'LL EVER BE.
MAYA LOPEZ SOLO SHOW
OPENING T
MAYA LOPEZ SHOW
TONIGHT
HERE SHE IS! MAYA LOPEZ, IN THE FLESH!
CONGRATULATIONS! YOU'RE AN INSPIRATION. YOU'VE SHOWED US ALL...

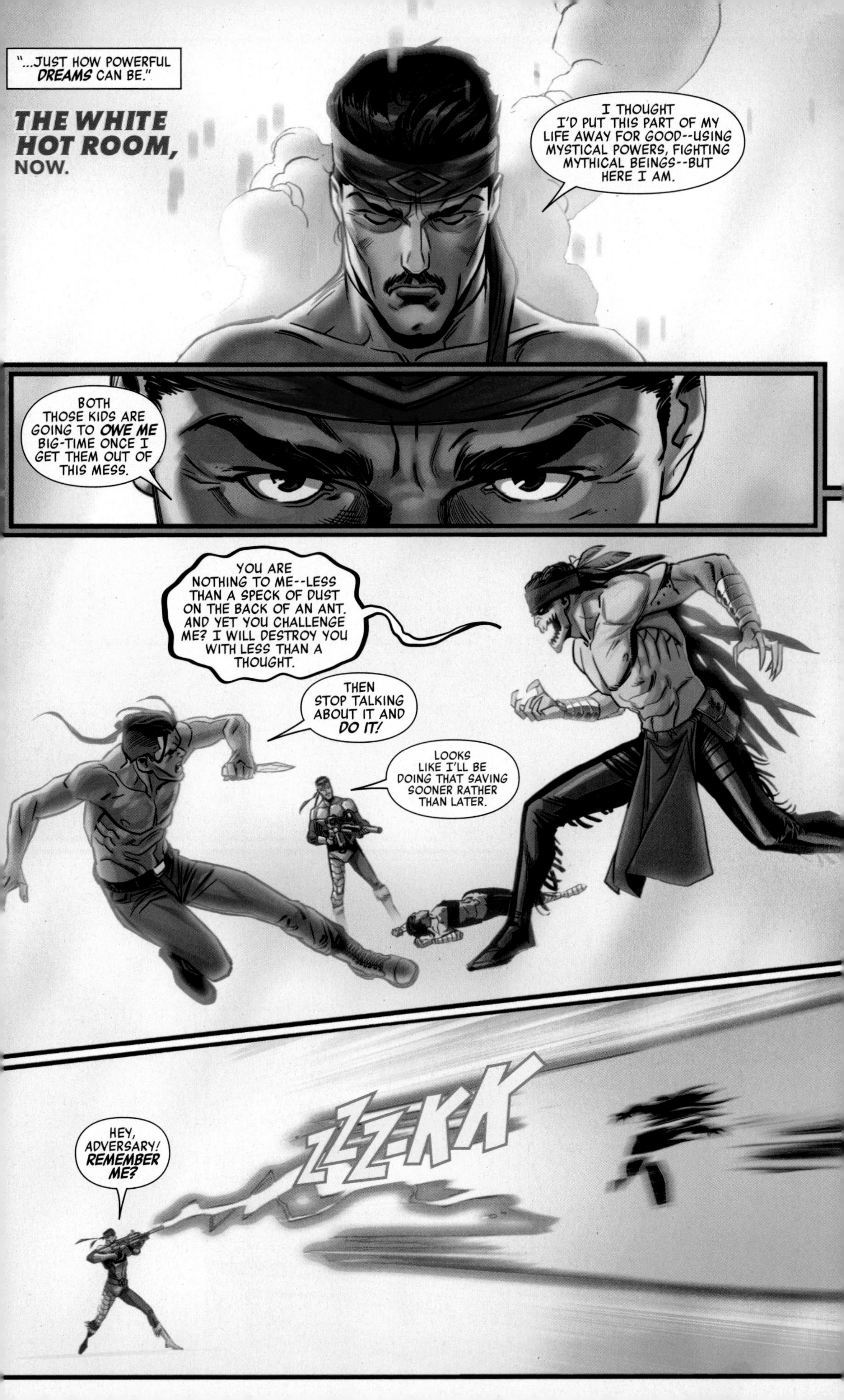
"...JUST HOW POWERFUL DREAMS CAN BE."
THE WHITE HOT ROOM, NOW.
I THOUGHT I'D PUT THIS PART OF MY LIFE AWAY FOR GOOD--USING MYSTICAL POWERS, FIGHTING MYTHICAL BEINGS--BUT HERE I AM.
BOTH THOSE KIDS ARE GOING TO OWE ME BIG-TIME ONCE I GET THEM OUT OF THIS MESS.
YOU ARE NOTHING TO ME--LESS THAN A SPECK OF DUST ON THE BACK OF AN ANT. AND YET YOU CHALLENGE ME? I WILL DESTROY YOU WITH LESS THAN A THOUGHT.
THEN STOP TALKING ABOUT IT AND DO IT!
LOOKS LIKE I'LL BE DOING THAT SAVING SOONER RATHER THAN LATER.
HEY, ADVERSARY! REMEMBER ME?
ZZZ-KK

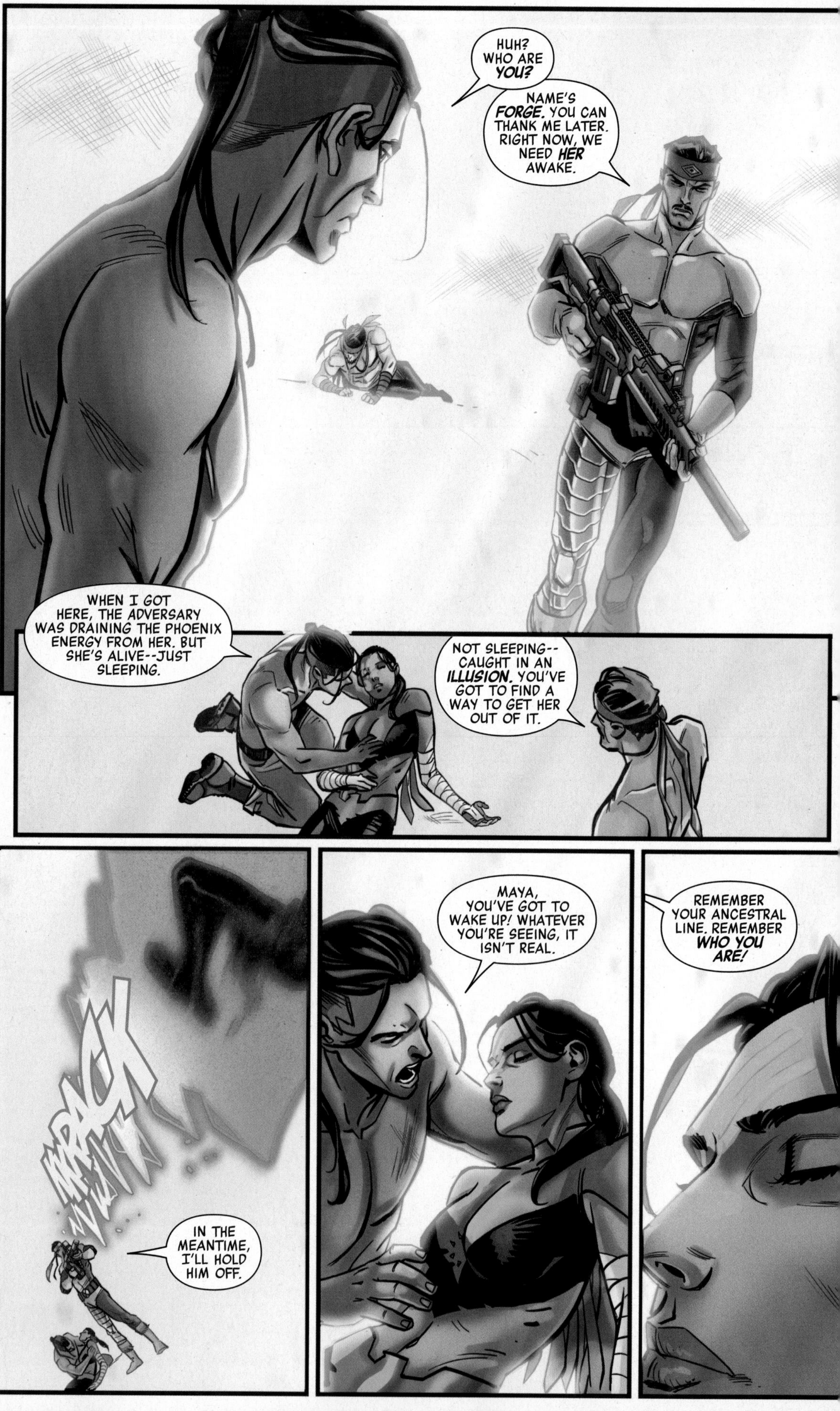
HUH? WHO ARE YOU?
NAME'S FORGE. YOU CAN THANK ME LATER. RIGHT NOW, WE NEED HER AWAKE.
WHEN I GOT HERE, THE ADVERSARY WAS DRAINING THE PHOENIX ENERGY FROM HER. BUT SHE'S ALIVE--JUST SLEEPING.
NOT SLEEPING--CAUGHT IN AN ILLUSION. YOU'VE GOT TO FIND A WAY TO GET HER OUT OF IT.
IN THE MEANTIME, I'LL HOLD HIM OFF.
MAYA, YOU'VE GOT TO WAKE UP! WHATEVER YOU'RE SEEING, IT ISN'T REAL.
REMEMBER YOUR ANCESTRAL LINE. REMEMBER WHO YOU ARE!

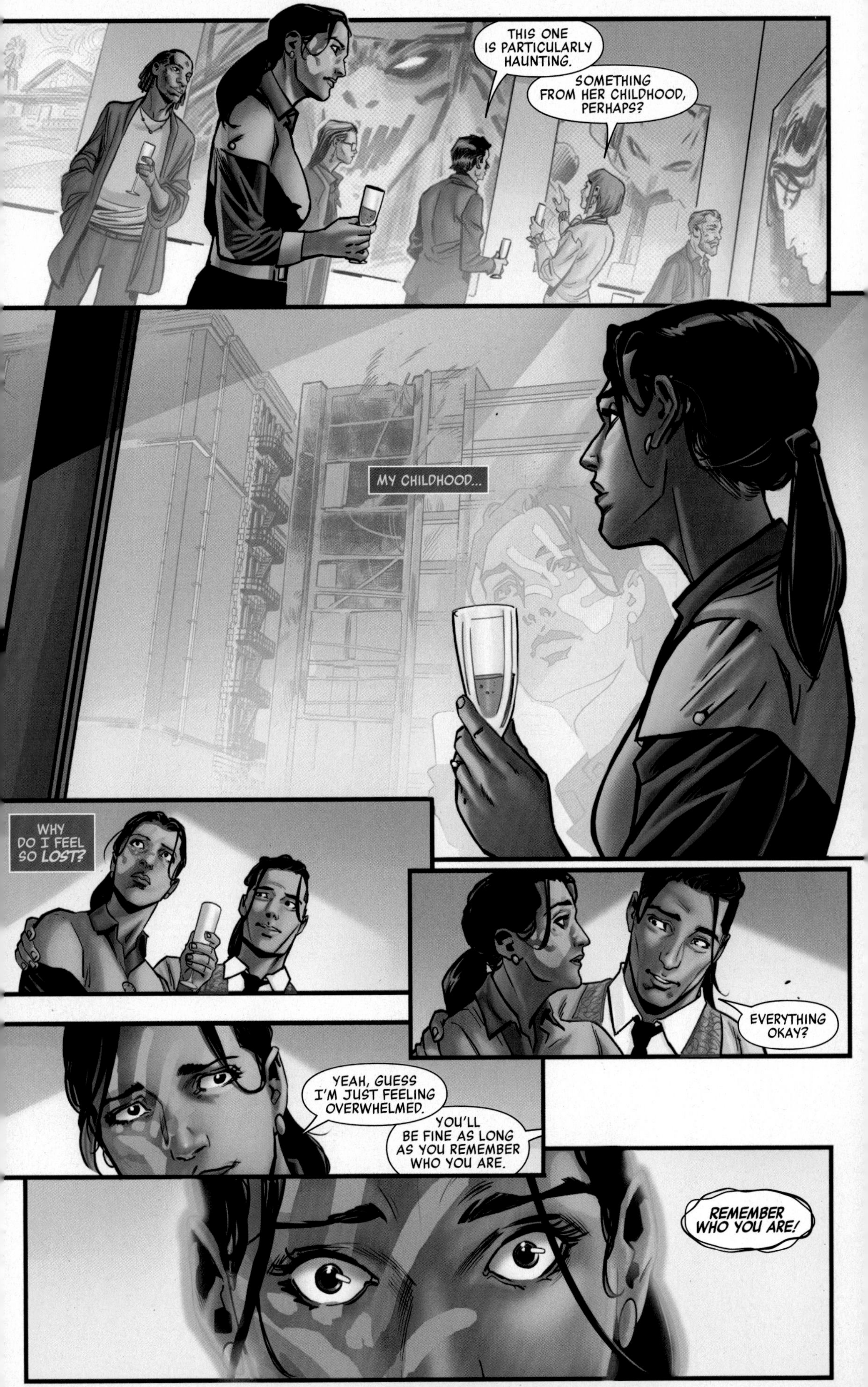

THIS ONE IS PARTICULARLY HAUNTING.
SOMETHING FROM HER CHILDHOOD, PERHAPS?
MY CHILDHOOD...
WHY DO I FEEL SO LOST?
EVERYTHING OKAY?
YEAH, GUESS I'M JUST FEELING OVERWHELMED.
YOU'LL BE FINE AS LONG AS YOU REMEMBER WHO YOU ARE.
REMEMBER WHO YOU ARE!

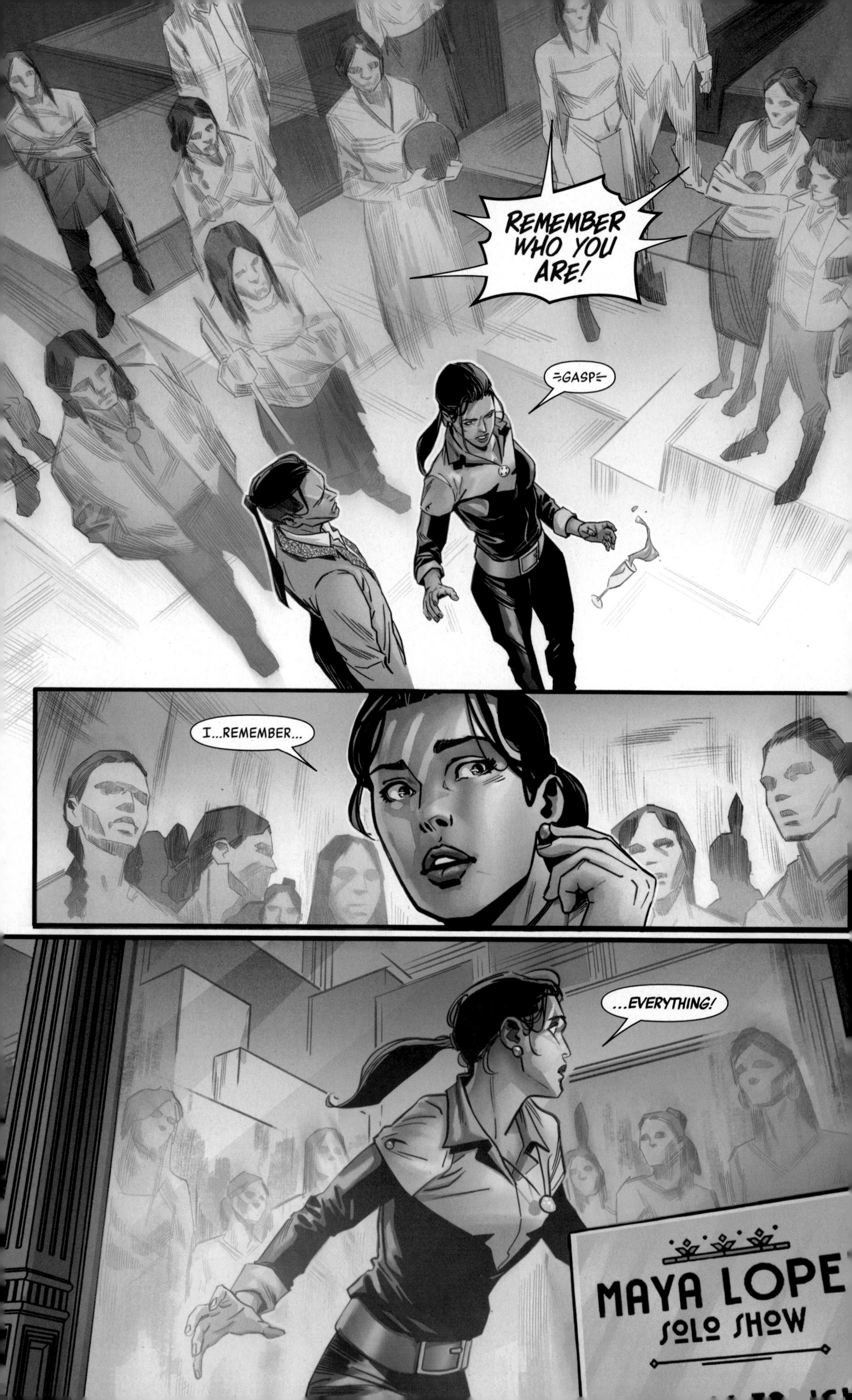
REMEMBER WHO YOU ARE!
=GASP=
I...REMEMBER...
...EVERYTHING!
MAYA LOPE
SOLO SHOW

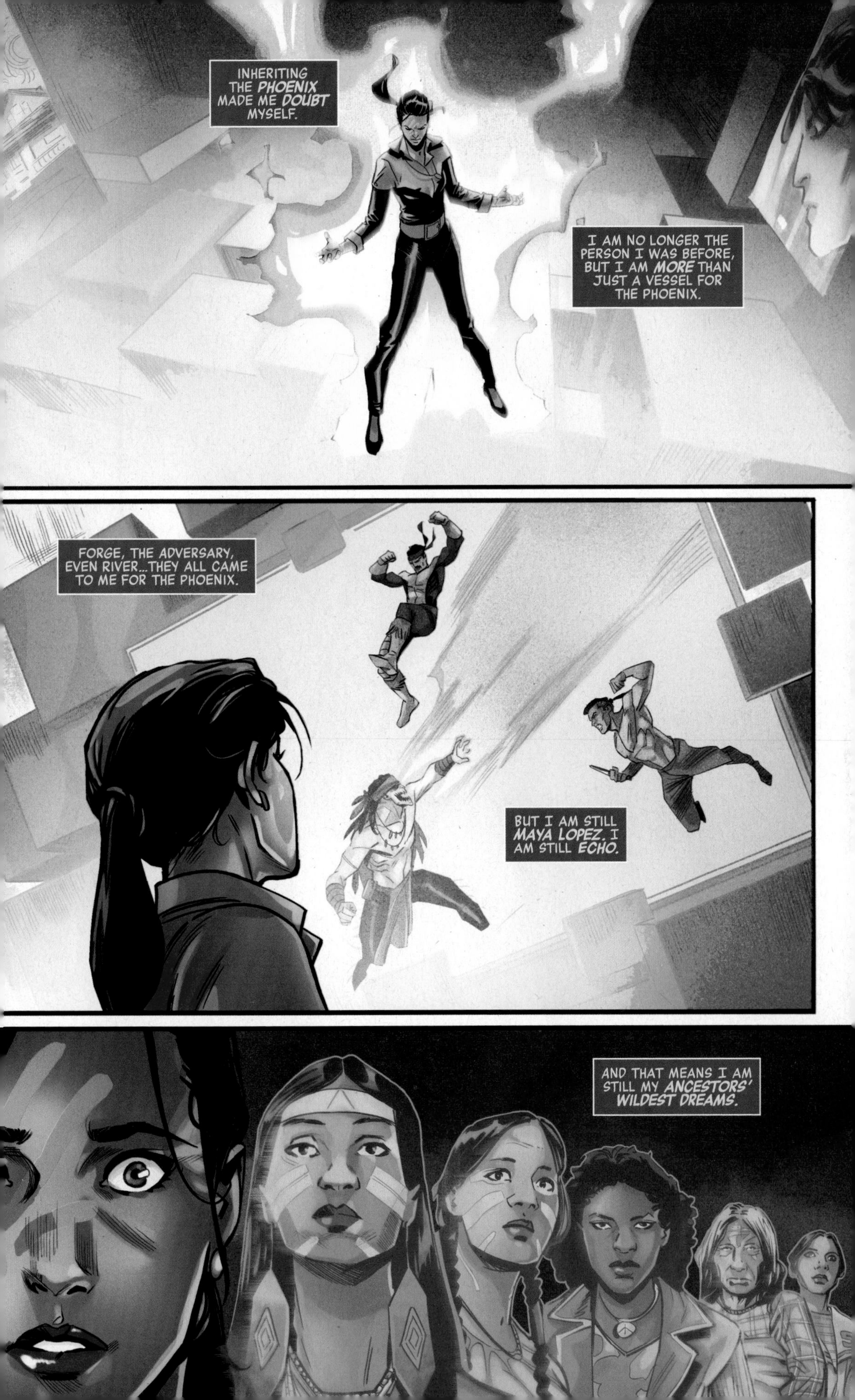
INHERITING THE PHOENIX MADE ME DOUBT MYSELF.
I AM NO LONGER THE PERSON I WAS BEFORE, BUT I AM MORE THAN JUST A VESSEL FOR THE PHOENIX.
FORGE, THE ADVERSARY, EVEN RIVER...THEY ALL CAME TO ME FOR THE PHOENIX.
BUT I AM STILL MAYA LOPEZ. I AM STILL ECHO.
AND THAT MEANS I AM STILL MY ANCESTORS' WILDEST DREAMS.

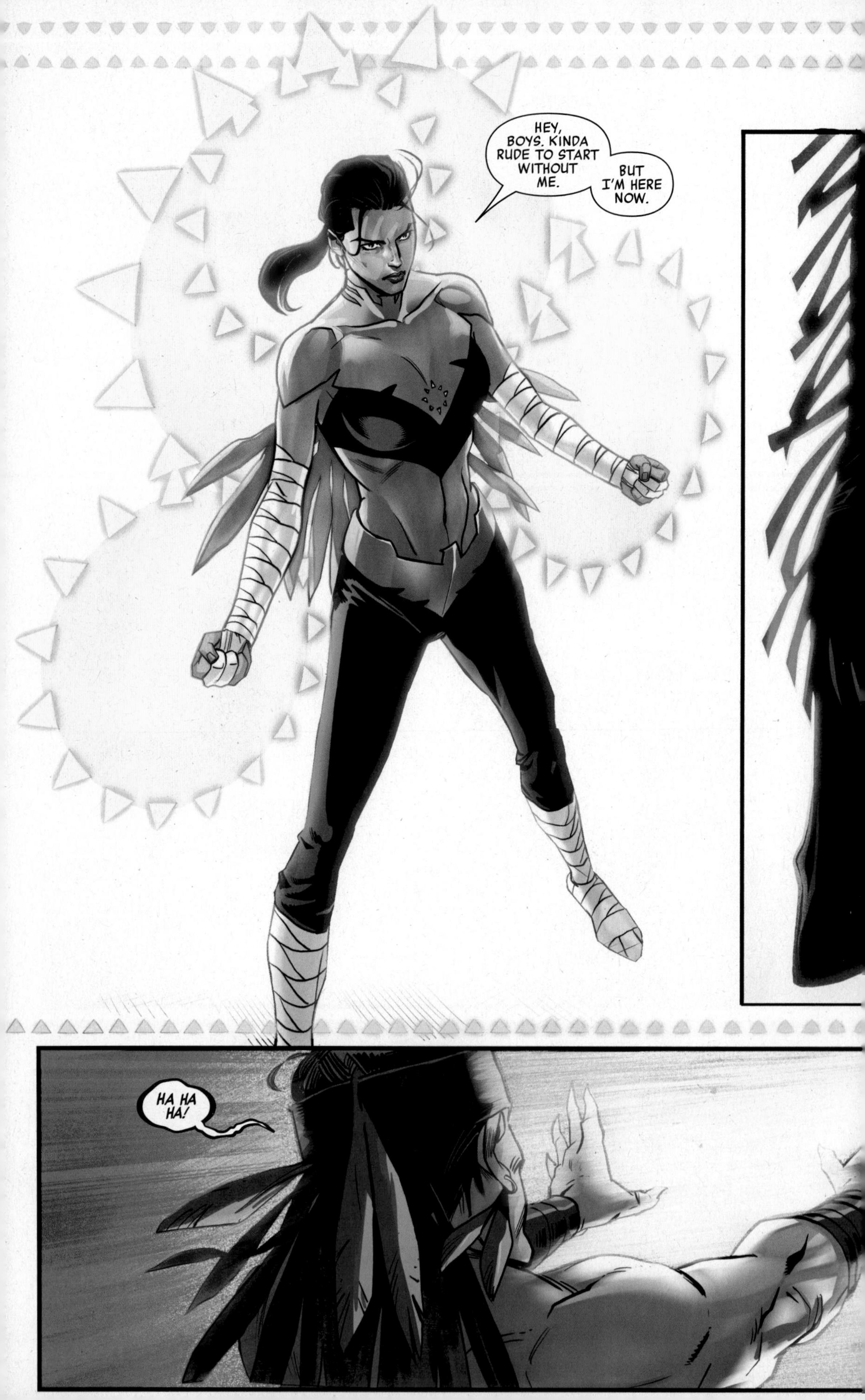
HEY, BOYS. KINDA RUDE TO START WITHOUT ME.
BUT I'M HERE NOW.
HA HA HA!

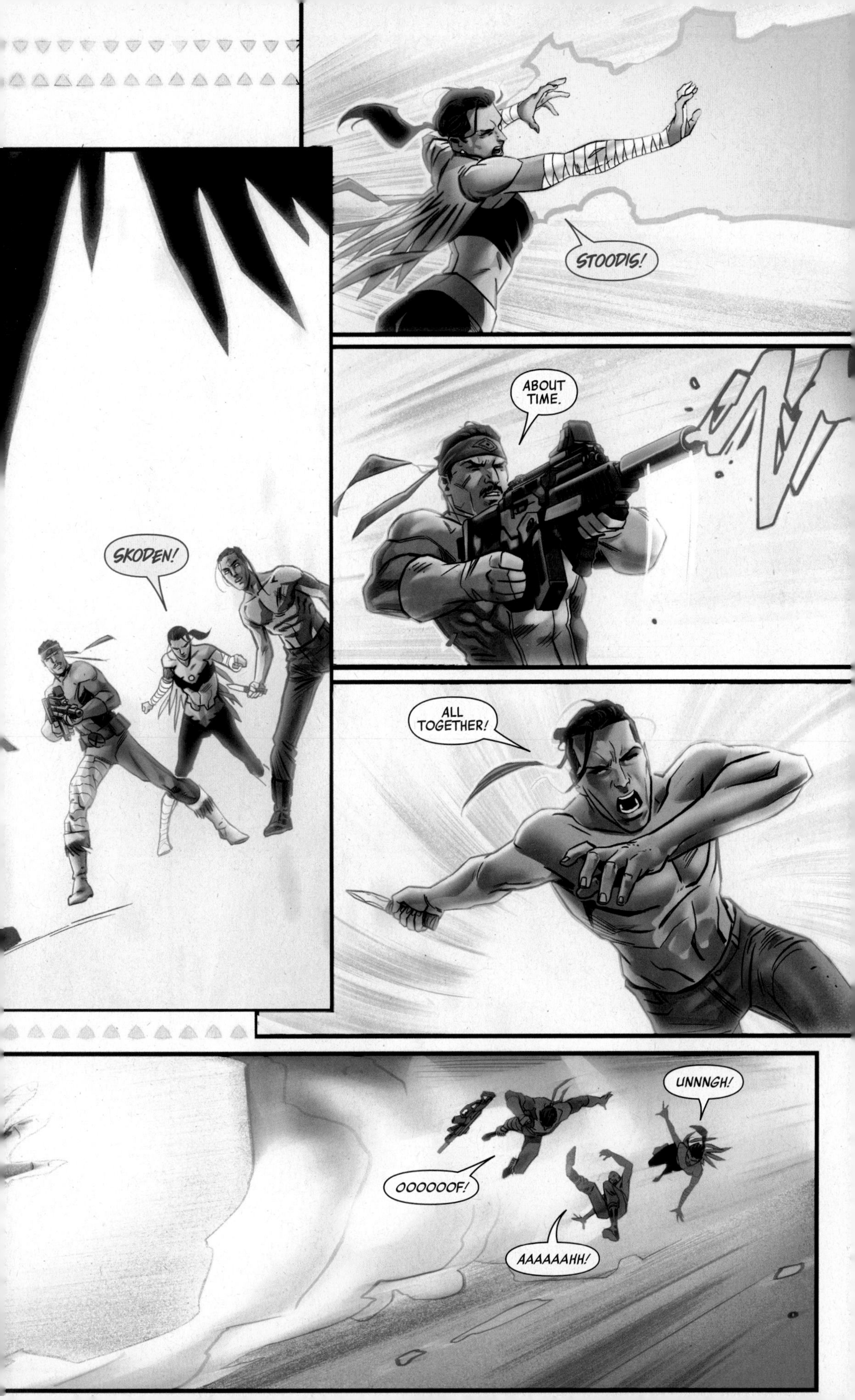
STOODIS!
SKODEN!
ABOUT TIME.
ALL TOGETHER!
UNNNGH!
OOOOOOF!
AAAAAAHH!

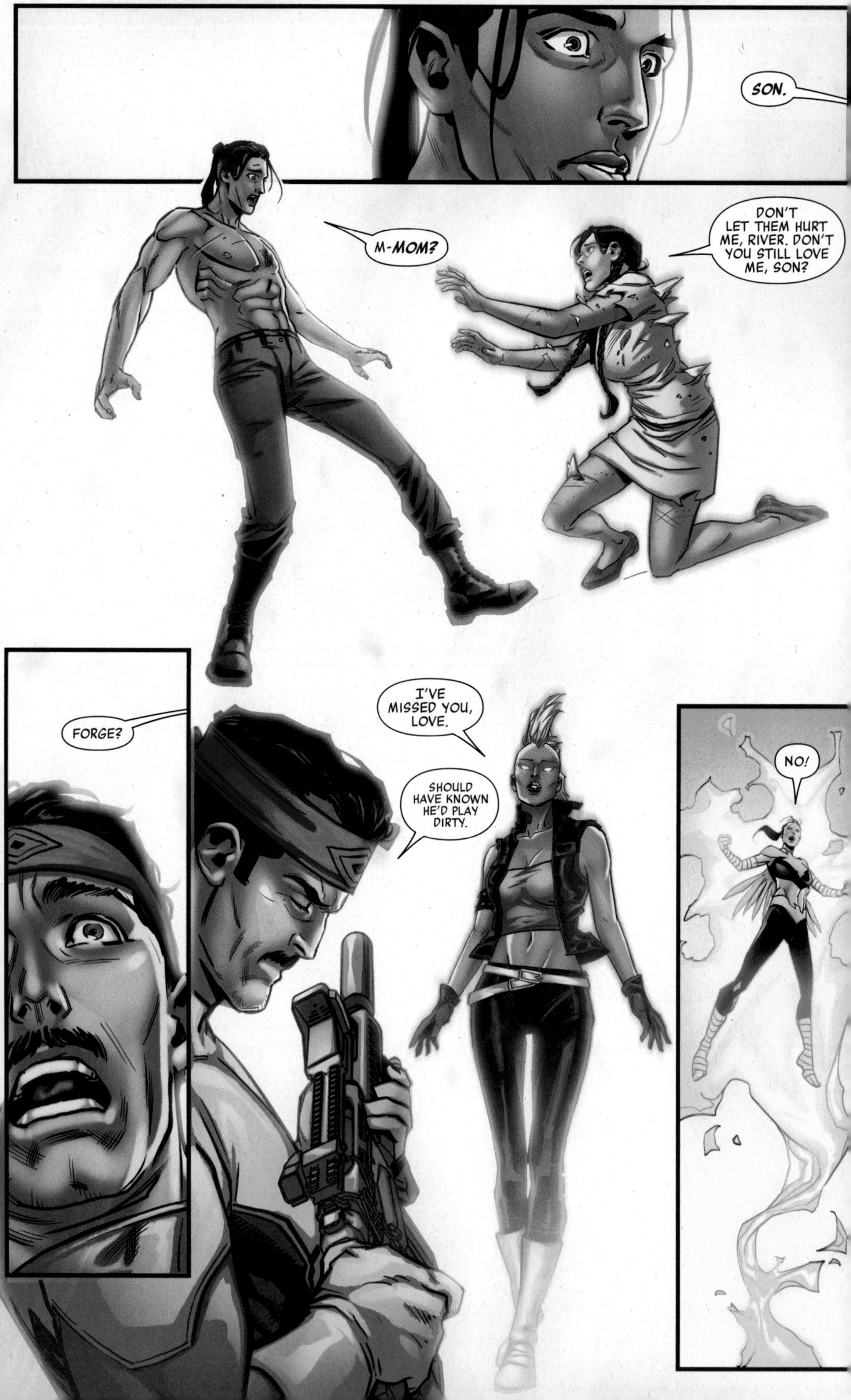
SON.
M-MOM?
DON'T LET THEM HURT ME, RIVER. DON'T YOU STILL LOVE ME, SON?
FORGE?
I'VE MISSED YOU, LOVE.
SHOULD HAVE KNOWN HE'D PLAY DIRTY.
NO!

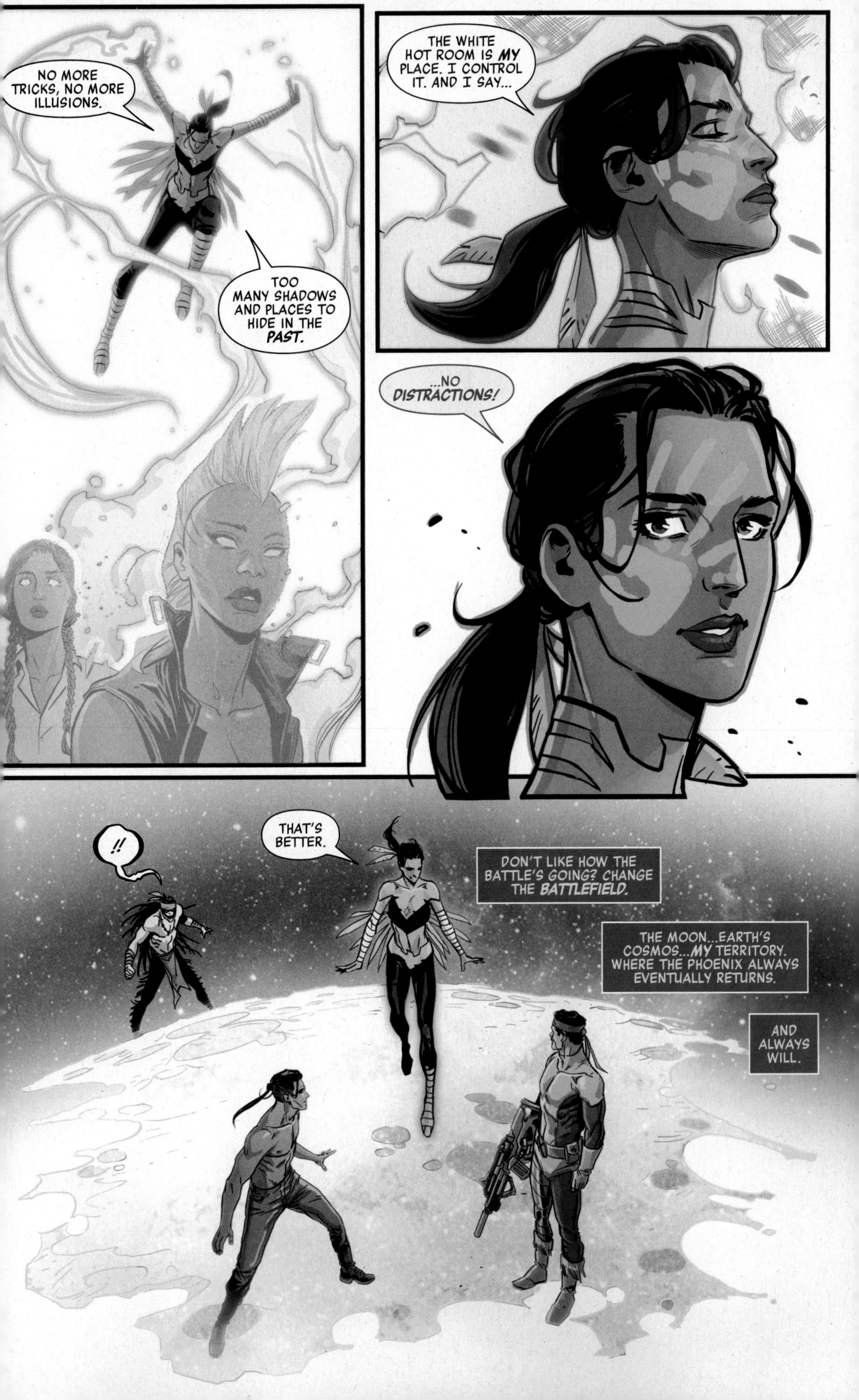

NO MORE TRICKS, NO MORE ILLUSIONS.
TOO MANY SHADOWS AND PLACES TO HIDE IN THE PAST.
THE WHITE HOT ROOM IS MY PLACE. I CONTROL IT. AND I SAY...
...NO DISTRACTIONS!
!!
THAT'S BETTER.
DON'T LIKE HOW THE BATTLE'S GOING? CHANGE THE BATTLEFIELD.
THE MOON...EARTH'S COSMOS...MY TERRITORY. WHERE THE PHOENIX ALWAYS EVENTUALLY RETURNS.
AND ALWAYS WILL.

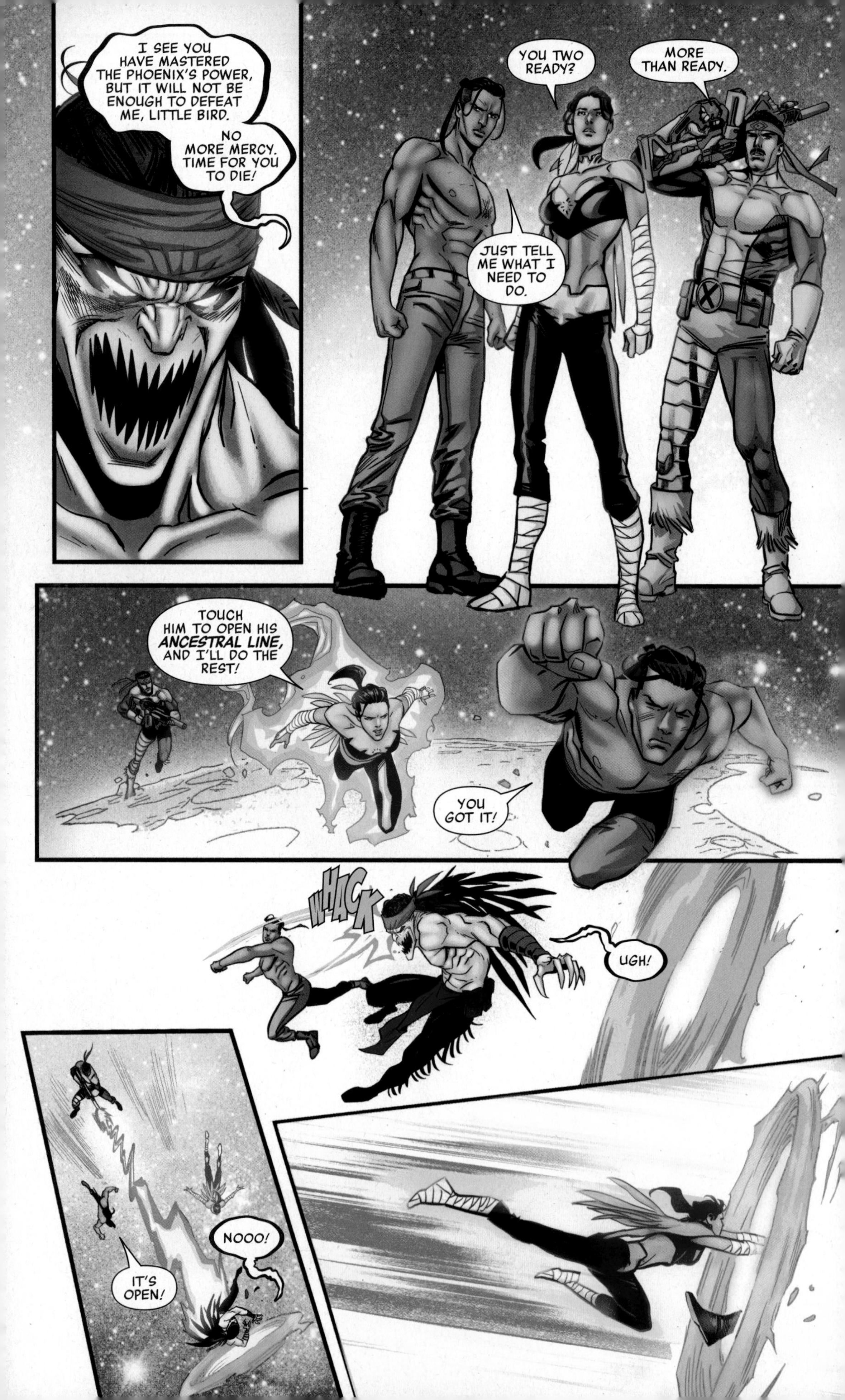
I SEE YOU HAVE MASTERED THE PHOENIX'S POWER, BUT IT WILL NOT BE ENOUGH TO DEFEAT ME, LITTLE BIRD.
NO MORE MERCY. TIME FOR YOU TO DIE!
YOU TWO READY?
MORE THAN READY.
JUST TELL ME WHAT I NEED TO DO.
TOUCH HIM TO OPEN HIS ANCESTRAL LINE, AND I'LL DO THE REST!
YOU GOT IT!
WHACK
UGH!
NOOO!
IT'S OPEN!

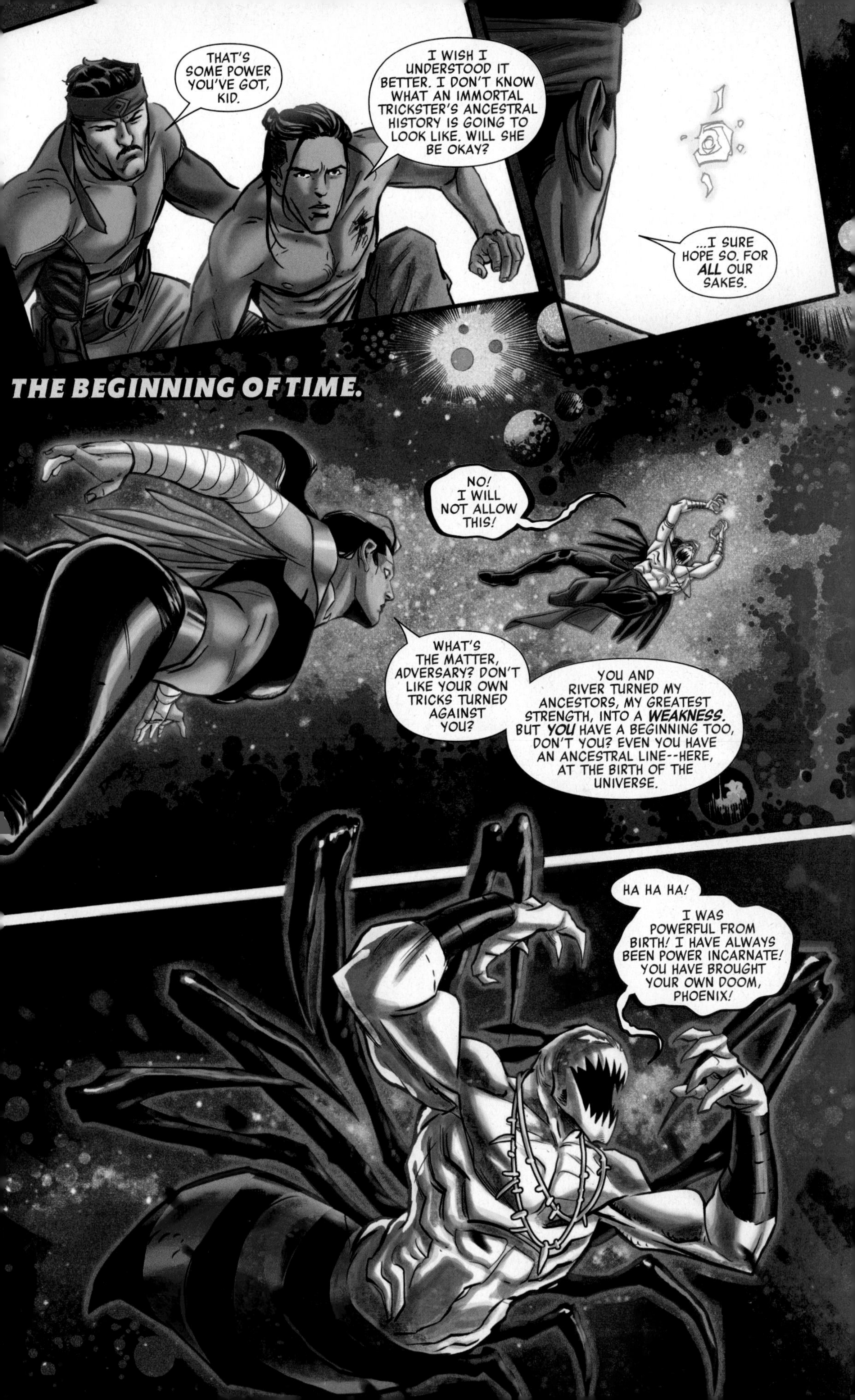
THAT'S SOME POWER YOU'VE GOT, KID.
I WISH I UNDERSTOOD IT BETTER. I DON'T KNOW WHAT AN IMMORTAL TRICKSTER'S ANCESTRAL HISTORY IS GOING TO LOOK LIKE. WILL SHE BE OKAY?
...I SURE HOPE SO. FOR ALL OUR SAKES.
THE BEGINNING OF TIME.
NO! I WILL NOT ALLOW THIS!
WHAT'S THE MATTER, ADVERSARY? DON'T LIKE YOUR OWN TRICKS TURNED AGAINST YOU?
YOU AND RIVER TURNED MY ANCESTORS, MY GREATEST STRENGTH, INTO A WEAKNESS. BUT YOU HAVE A BEGINNING TOO, DON'T YOU? EVEN YOU HAVE AN ANCESTRAL LINE--HERE, AT THE BIRTH OF THE UNIVERSE.
HA HA HA!
I WAS POWERFUL FROM BIRTH! I HAVE ALWAYS BEEN POWER INCARNATE! YOU HAVE BROUGHT YOUR OWN DOOM, PHOENIX!

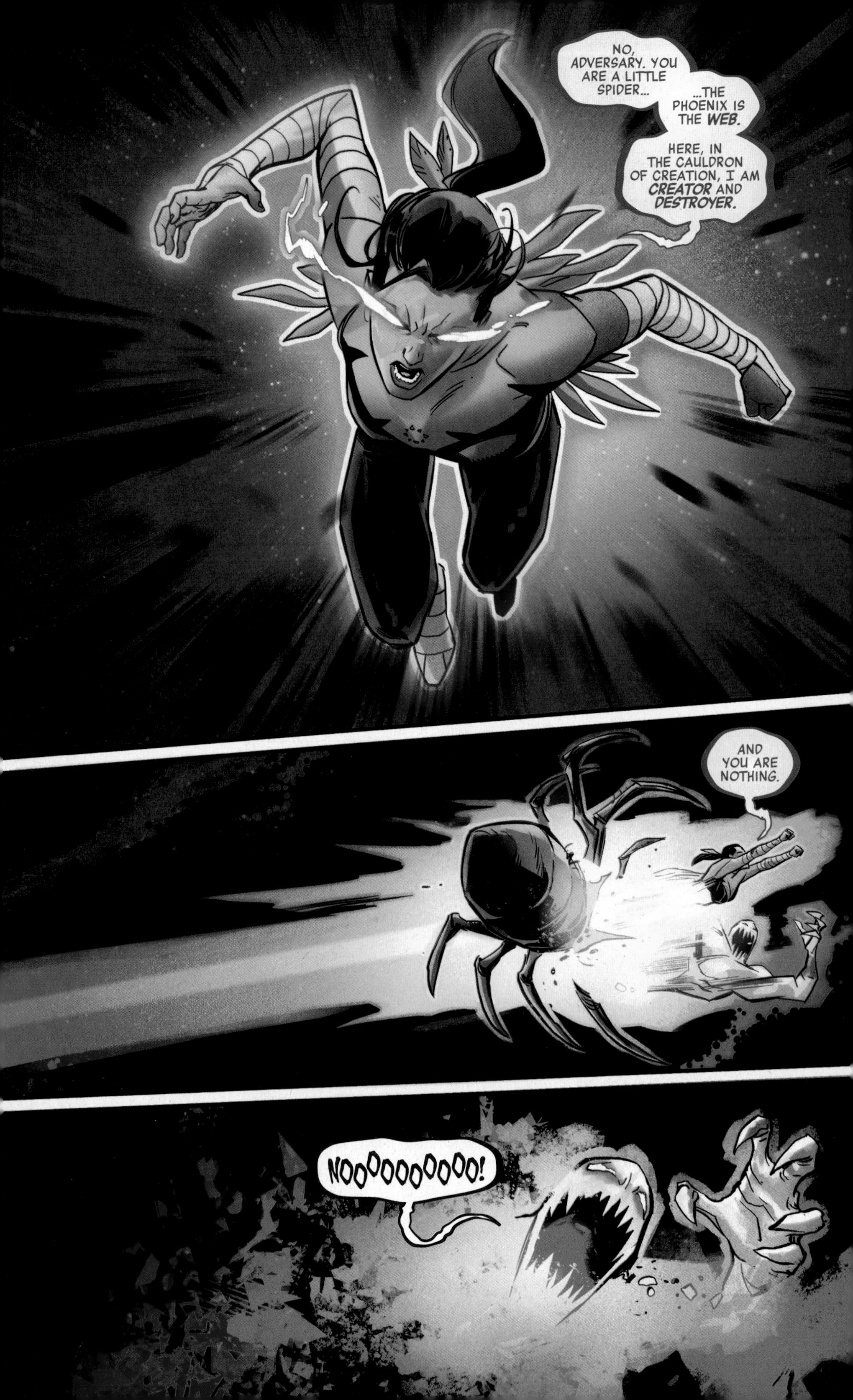
NO, ADVERSARY. YOU ARE A LITTLE SPIDER...
...THE PHOENIX IS THE WEB.
HERE, IN THE CAULDRON OF CREATION, I AM CREATOR AND DESTROYER.
AND YOU ARE NOTHING.
NOOOOOOOOOO!

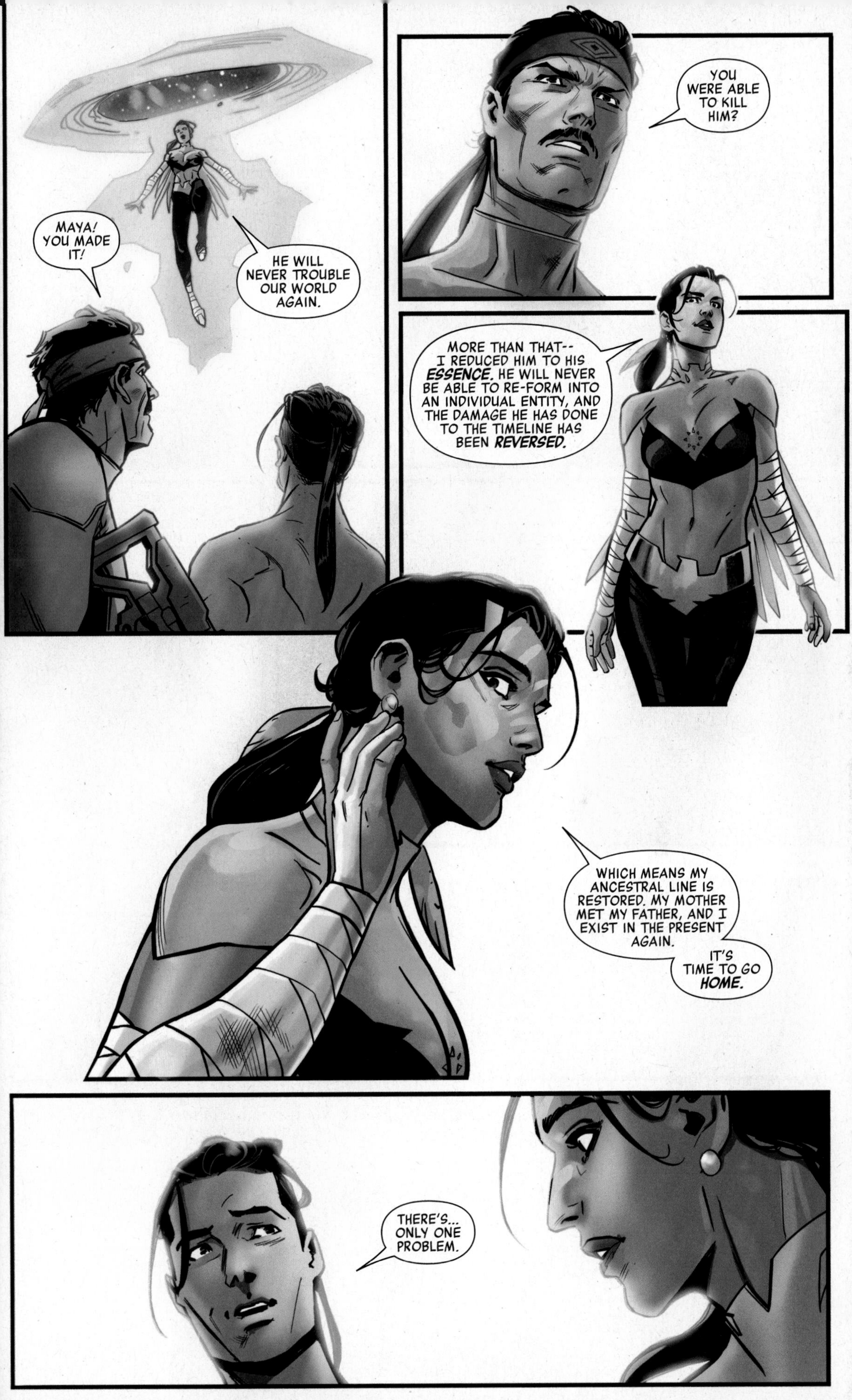
MAYA! YOU MADE IT!
HE WILL NEVER TROUBLE OUR WORLD AGAIN.
YOU WERE ABLE TO KILL HIM?
MORE THAN THAT-- I REDUCED HIM TO HIS ESSENCE. HE WILL NEVER BE ABLE TO RE-FORM INTO AN INDIVIDUAL ENTITY, AND THE DAMAGE HE HAS DONE TO THE TIMELINE HAS BEEN REVERSED.
WHICH MEANS MY ANCESTRAL LINE IS RESTORED. MY MOTHER MET MY FATHER, AND I EXIST IN THE PRESENT AGAIN.
IT'S TIME TO GO HOME.
THERE'S... ONLY ONE PROBLEM.

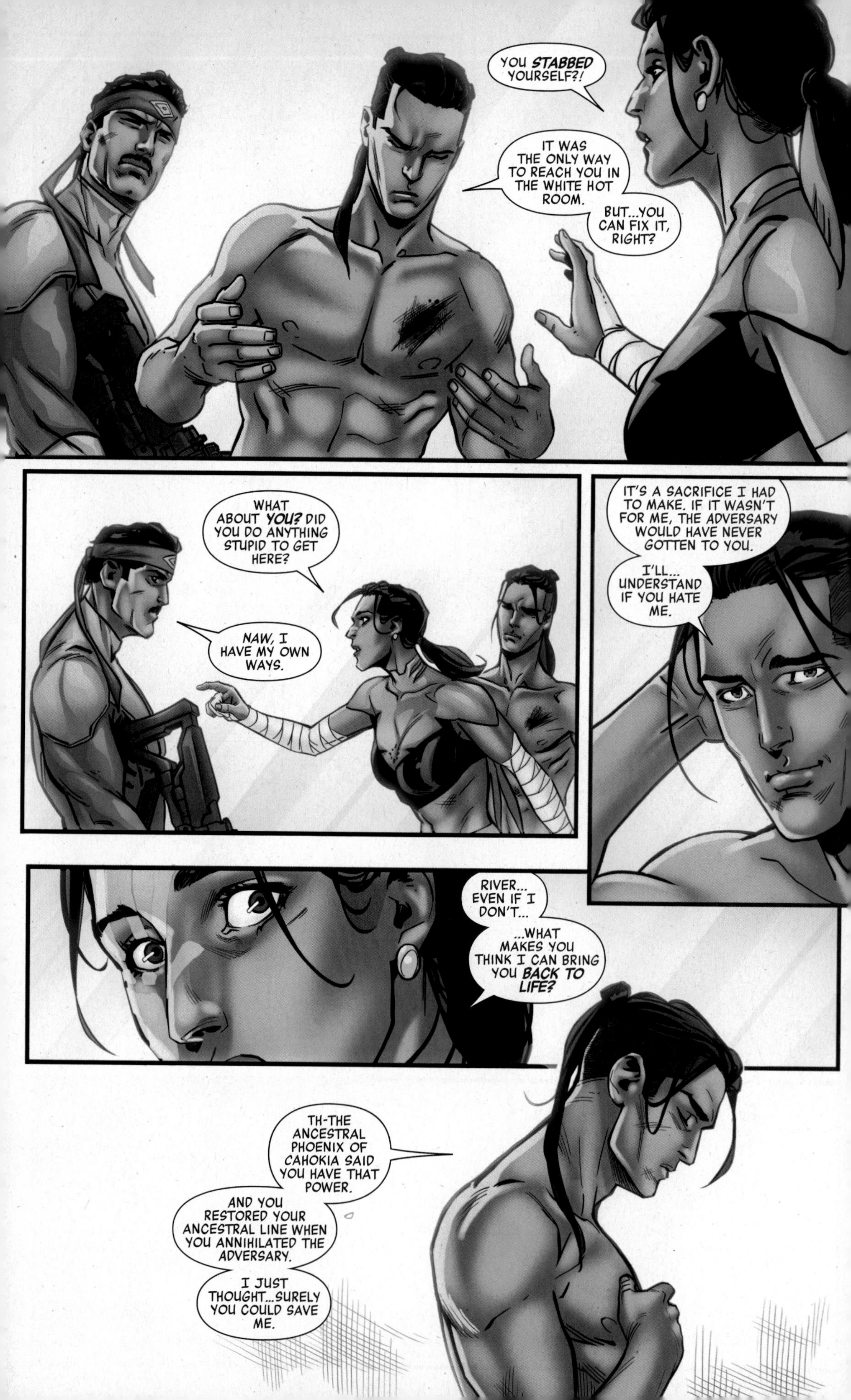
YOU STABBED YOURSELF?!
IT WAS THE ONLY WAY TO REACH YOU IN THE WHITE HOT ROOM.
BUT...YOU CAN FIX IT, RIGHT?
WHAT ABOUT YOU? DID YOU DO ANYTHING STUPID TO GET HERE?
NAW, I HAVE MY OWN WAYS.
IT'S A SACRIFICE I HAD TO MAKE. IF IT WASN'T FOR ME, THE ADVERSARY WOULD HAVE NEVER GOTTEN TO YOU.
I'LL... UNDERSTAND IF YOU HATE ME.
RIVER... EVEN IF I DON'T...
...WHAT MAKES YOU THINK I CAN BRING YOU BACK TO LIFE?
TH-THE ANCESTRAL PHOENIX OF CAHOKIA SAID YOU HAVE THAT POWER.
AND YOU RESTORED YOUR ANCESTRAL LINE WHEN YOU ANNIHILATED THE ADVERSARY.
I JUST THOUGHT...SURELY YOU COULD SAVE ME.

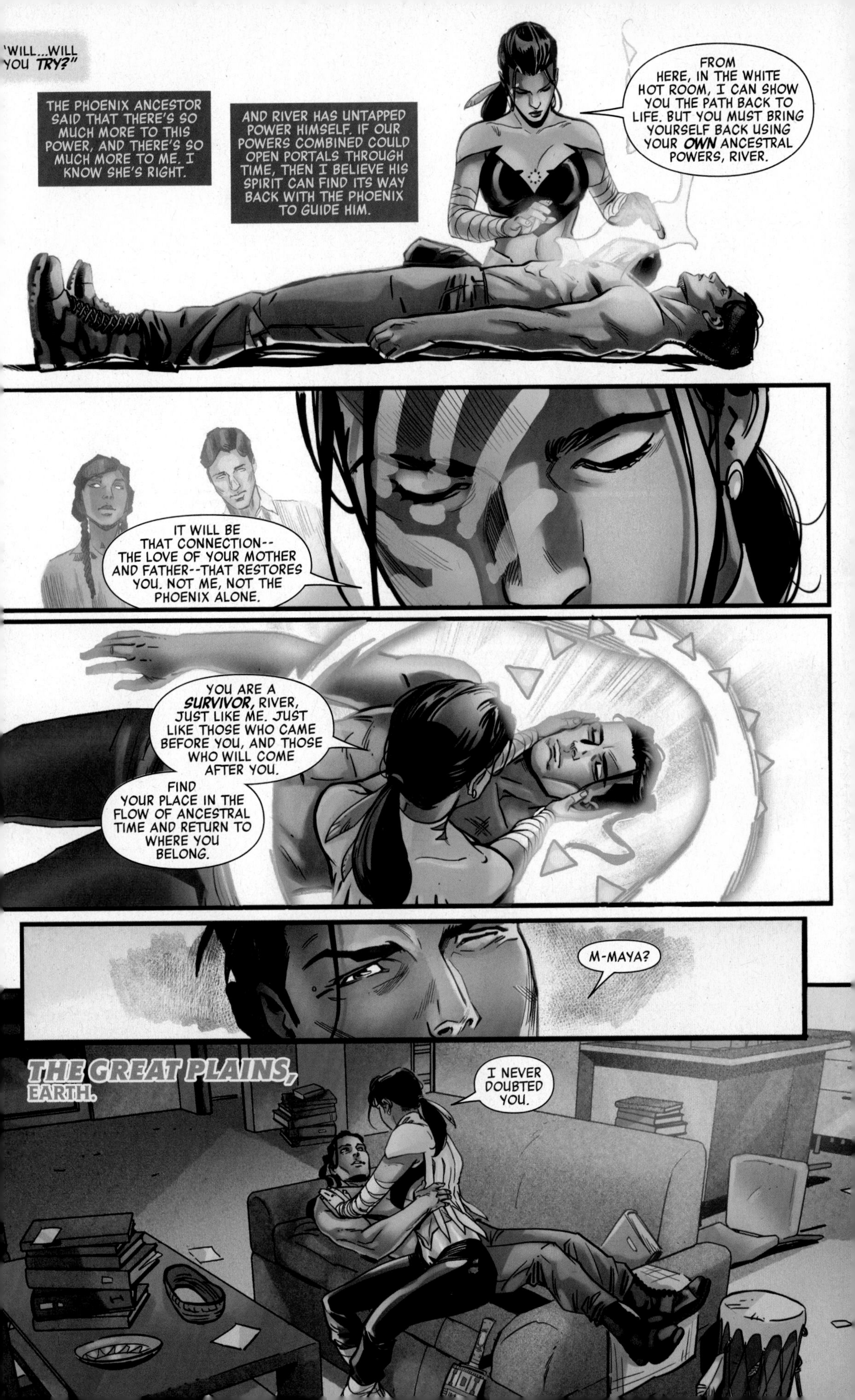
'WILL...WILL YOU TRY?"
THE PHOENIX ANCESTOR SAID THAT THERE'S SO MUCH MORE TO THIS POWER, AND THERE'S SO MUCH MORE TO ME. I KNOW SHE'S RIGHT.
AND RIVER HAS UNTAPPED POWER HIMSELF. IF OUR POWERS COMBINED COULD OPEN PORTALS THROUGH TIME, THEN I BELIEVE HIS SPIRIT CAN FIND ITS WAY BACK WITH THE PHOENIX TO GUIDE HIM.
FROM HERE, IN THE WHITE HOT ROOM, I CAN SHOW YOU THE PATH BACK TO LIFE. BUT YOU MUST BRING YOURSELF BACK USING YOUR OWN ANCESTRAL POWERS, RIVER.
IT WILL BE THAT CONNECTION-- THE LOVE OF YOUR MOTHER AND FATHER--THAT RESTORES YOU. NOT ME, NOT THE PHOENIX ALONE.
YOU ARE A SURVIVOR, RIVER, JUST LIKE ME. JUST LIKE THOSE WHO CAME BEFORE YOU, AND THOSE WHO WILL COME AFTER YOU.
FIND YOUR PLACE IN THE FLOW OF ANCESTRAL TIME AND RETURN TO WHERE YOU BELONG.
M-MAYA?
THE GREAT PLAINS, EARTH.
I NEVER DOUBTED YOU.

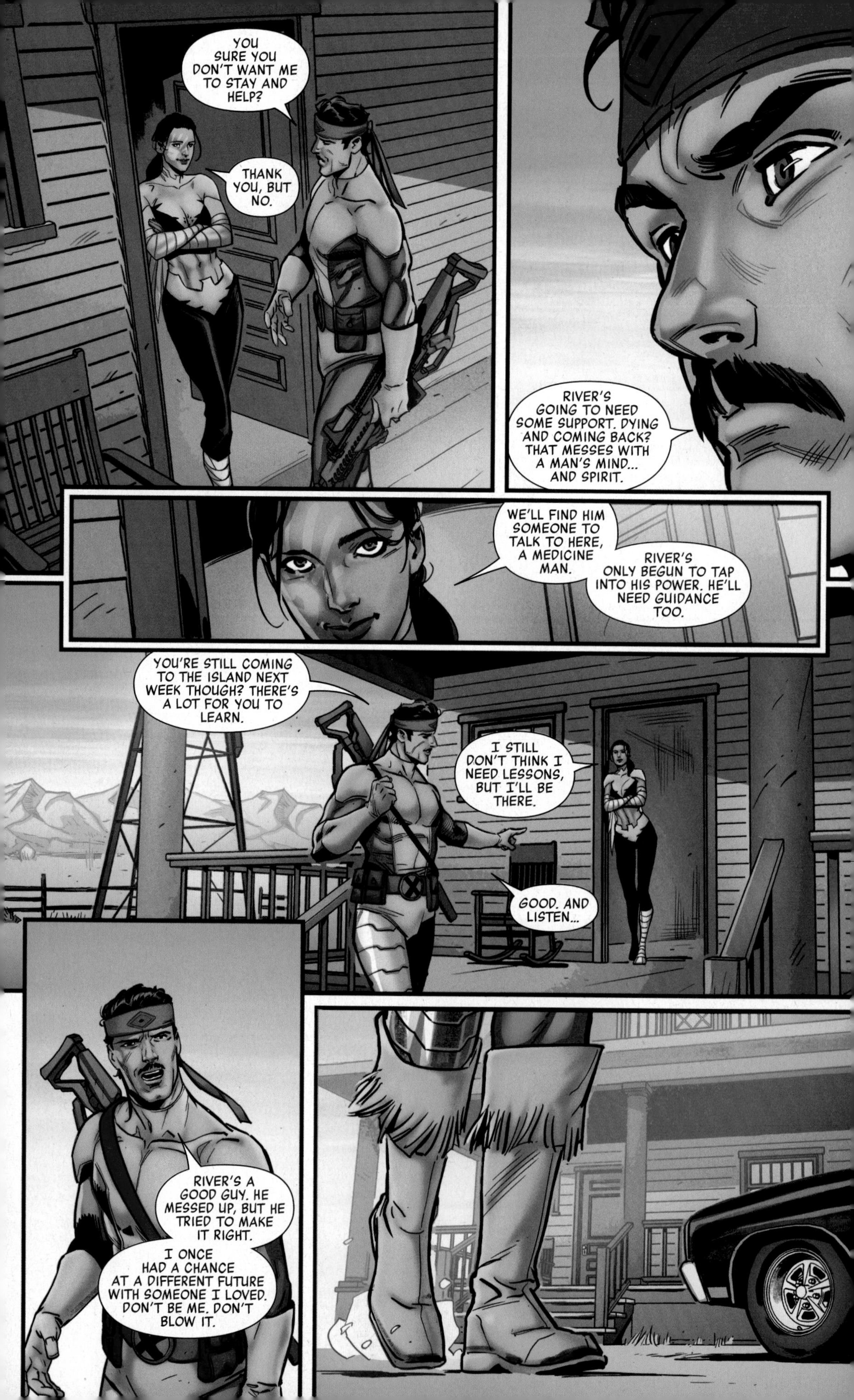

YOU SURE YOU DON'T WANT ME TO STAY AND HELP?
THANK YOU, BUT NO.
RIVER'S GOING TO NEED SOME SUPPORT. DYING AND COMING BACK? THAT MESSES WITH A MAN'S MIND... AND SPIRIT.
WE'LL FIND HIM SOMEONE TO TALK TO HERE, A MEDICINE MAN.
RIVER'S ONLY BEGUN TO TAP INTO HIS POWER. HE'LL NEED GUIDANCE TOO.
YOU'RE STILL COMING TO THE ISLAND NEXT WEEK THOUGH? THERE'S A LOT FOR YOU TO LEARN.
I STILL DON'T THINK I NEED LESSONS, BUT I'LL BE THERE.
GOOD. AND LISTEN...
RIVER'S A GOOD GUY. HE MESSED UP, BUT HE TRIED TO MAKE IT RIGHT.
I ONCE HAD A CHANCE AT A DIFFERENT FUTURE WITH SOMEONE I LOVED. DON'T BE ME. DON'T BLOW IT.

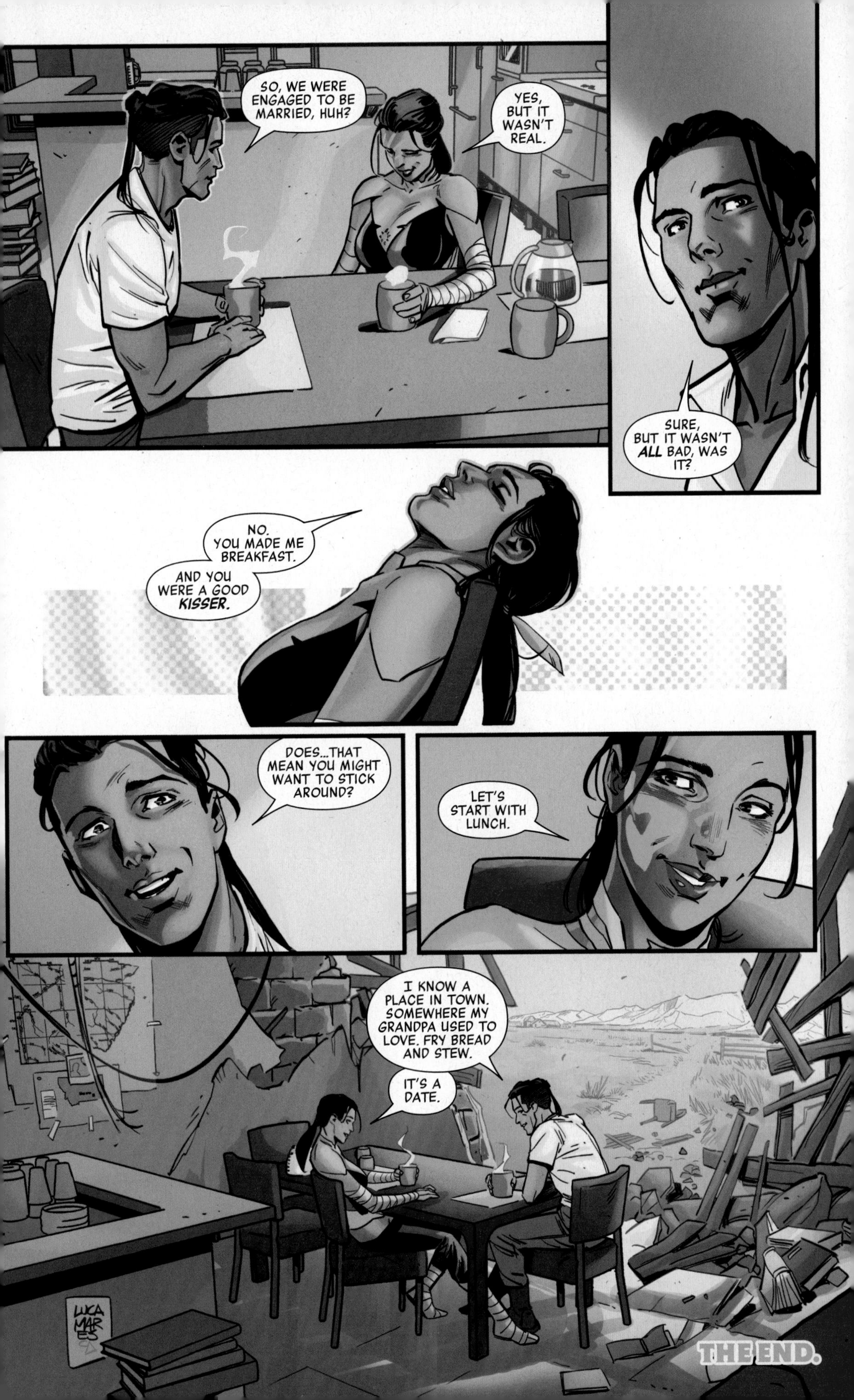
SO, WE WERE ENGAGED TO BE MARRIED, HUH?
YES, BUT IT WASN'T REAL.
SURE, BUT IT WASN'T ALL BAD, WAS IT?
NO. YOU MADE ME BREAKFAST.
AND YOU WERE A GOOD KISSER.
DOES...THAT MEAN YOU MIGHT WANT TO STICK AROUND?
LET'S START WITH LUNCH.
I KNOW A PLACE IN TOWN. SOMEWHERE MY GRANDPA USED TO LOVE. FRY BREAD AND STEW.
IT'S A DATE.
LUCA MARES
THE END.

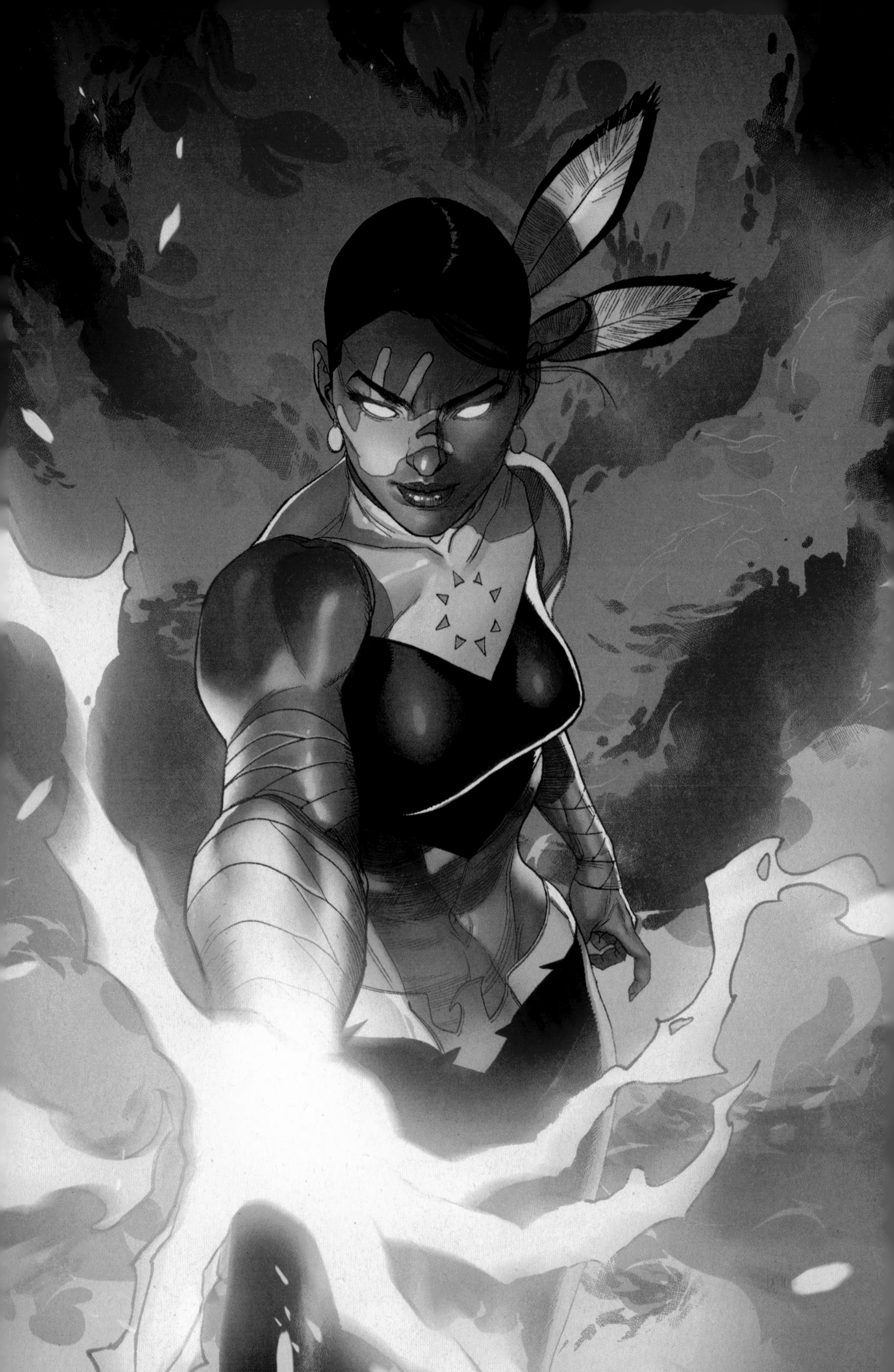

#1 VARI

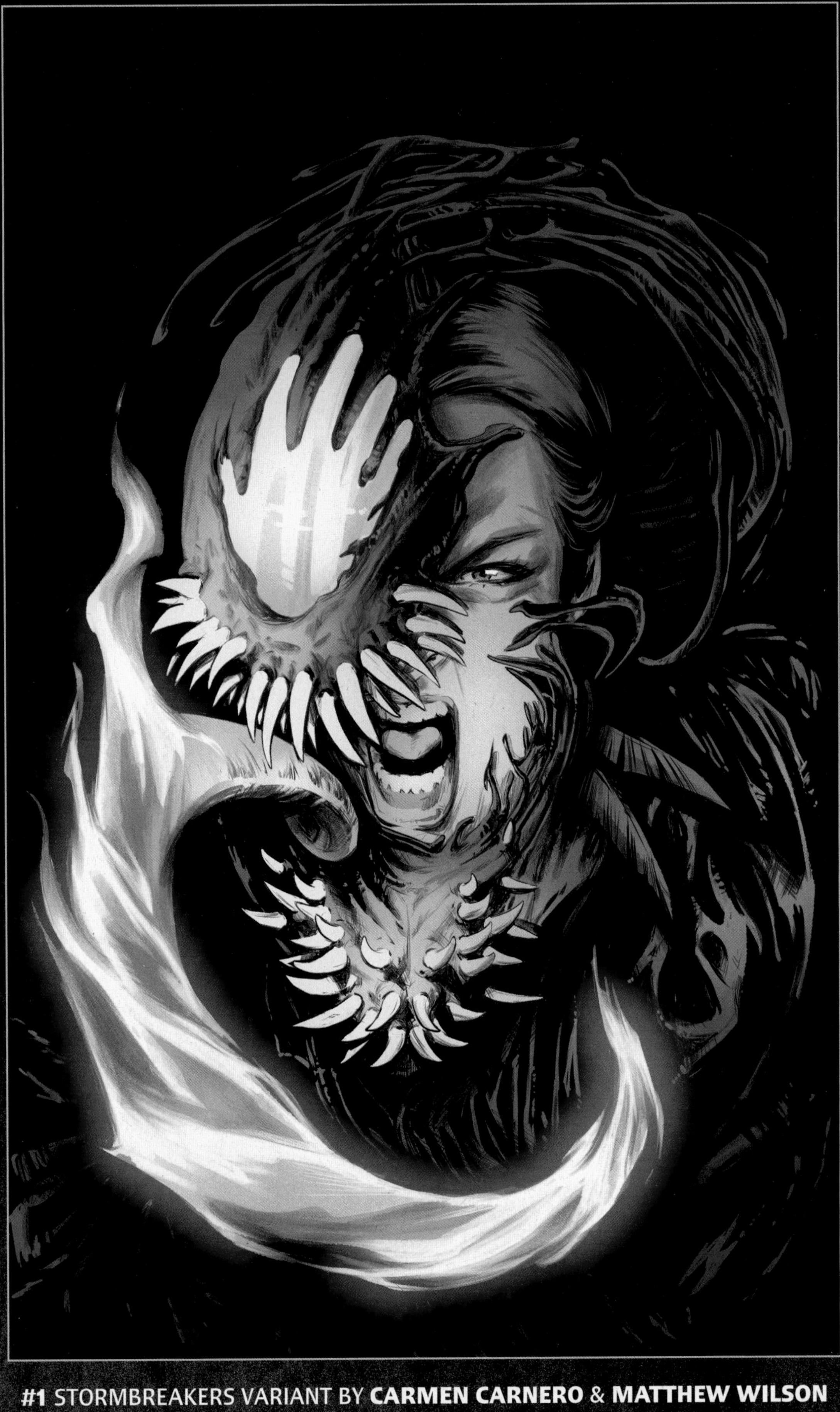

#1 STORMBREAKERS VARIANT BY **CARMEN CARNERO** & **MATTHEW WILSON**

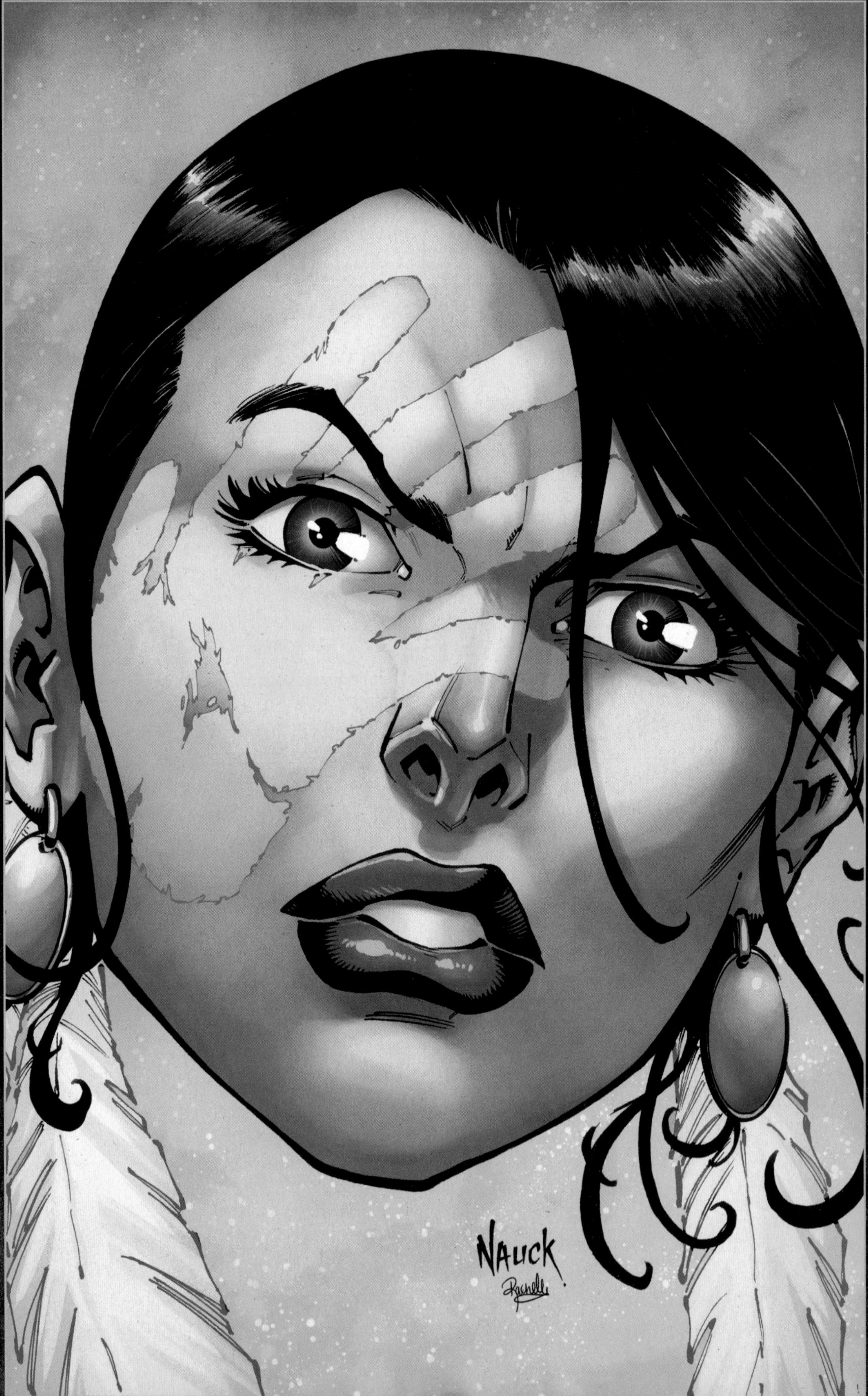
NAUCK
Rachelle

#1 HEADSHOT VARIANT BY **TODD NAUCK** & **RACHELLE ROSENBERG**

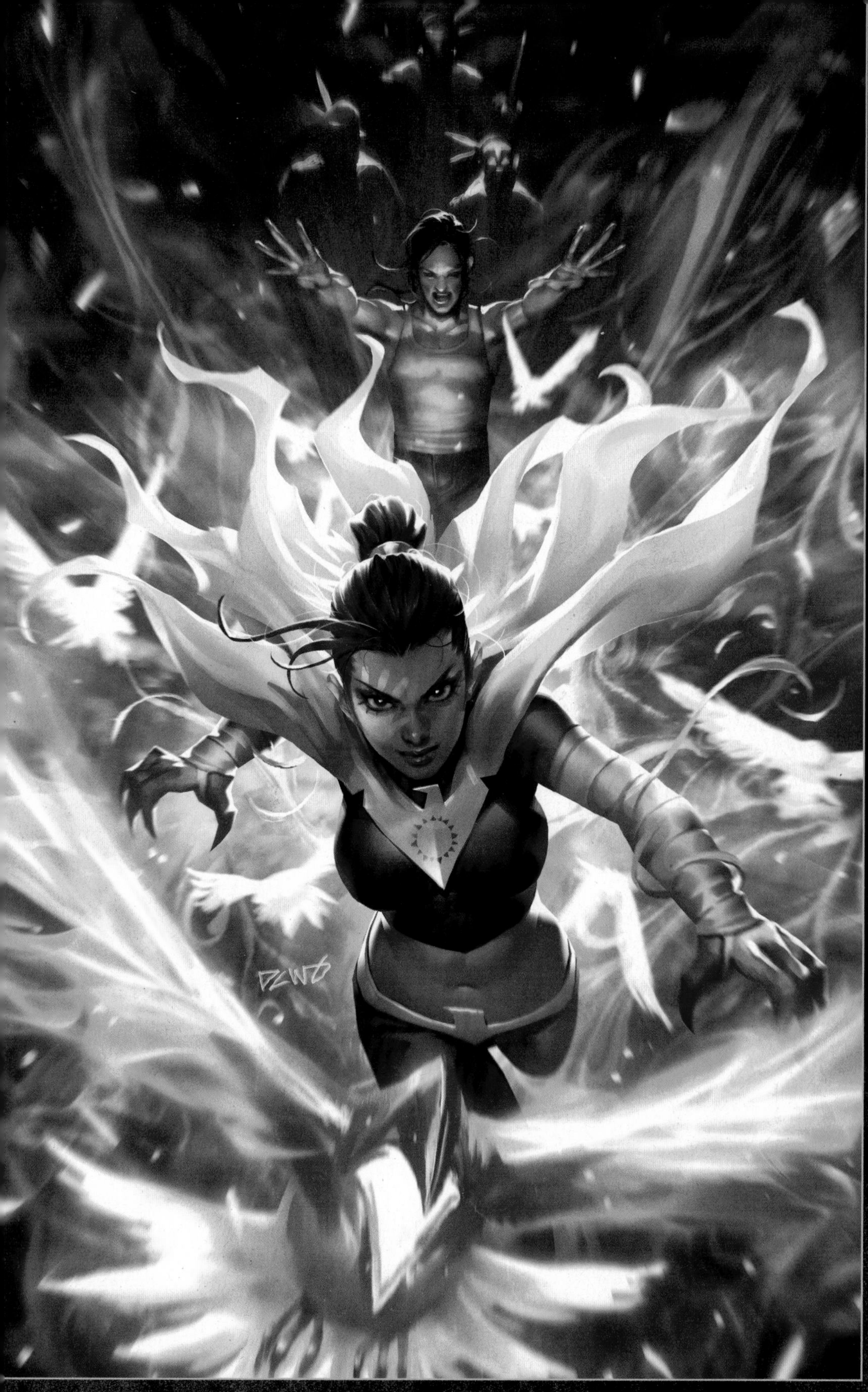

#2 VARIANT BY **DERRICK CHEW**

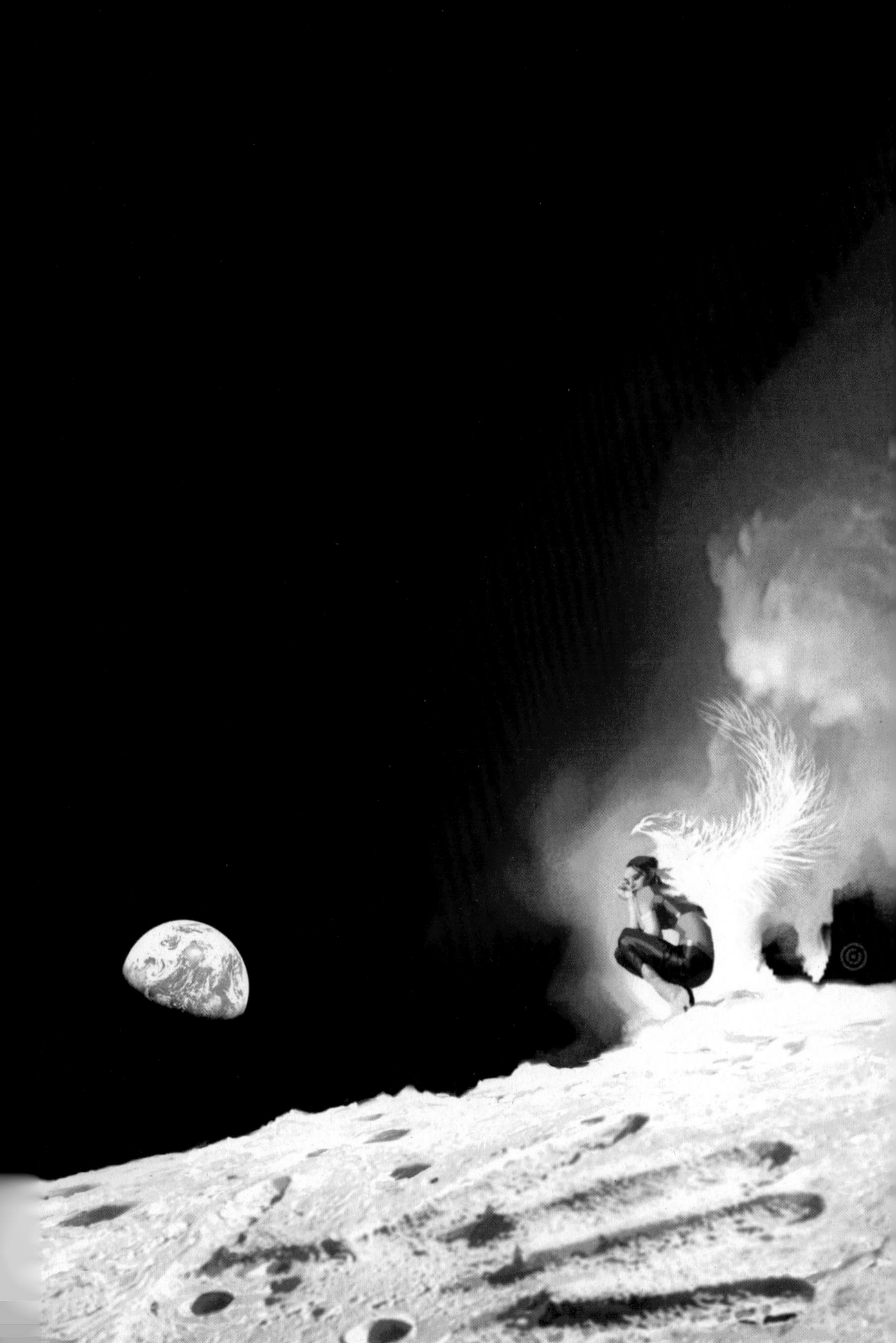

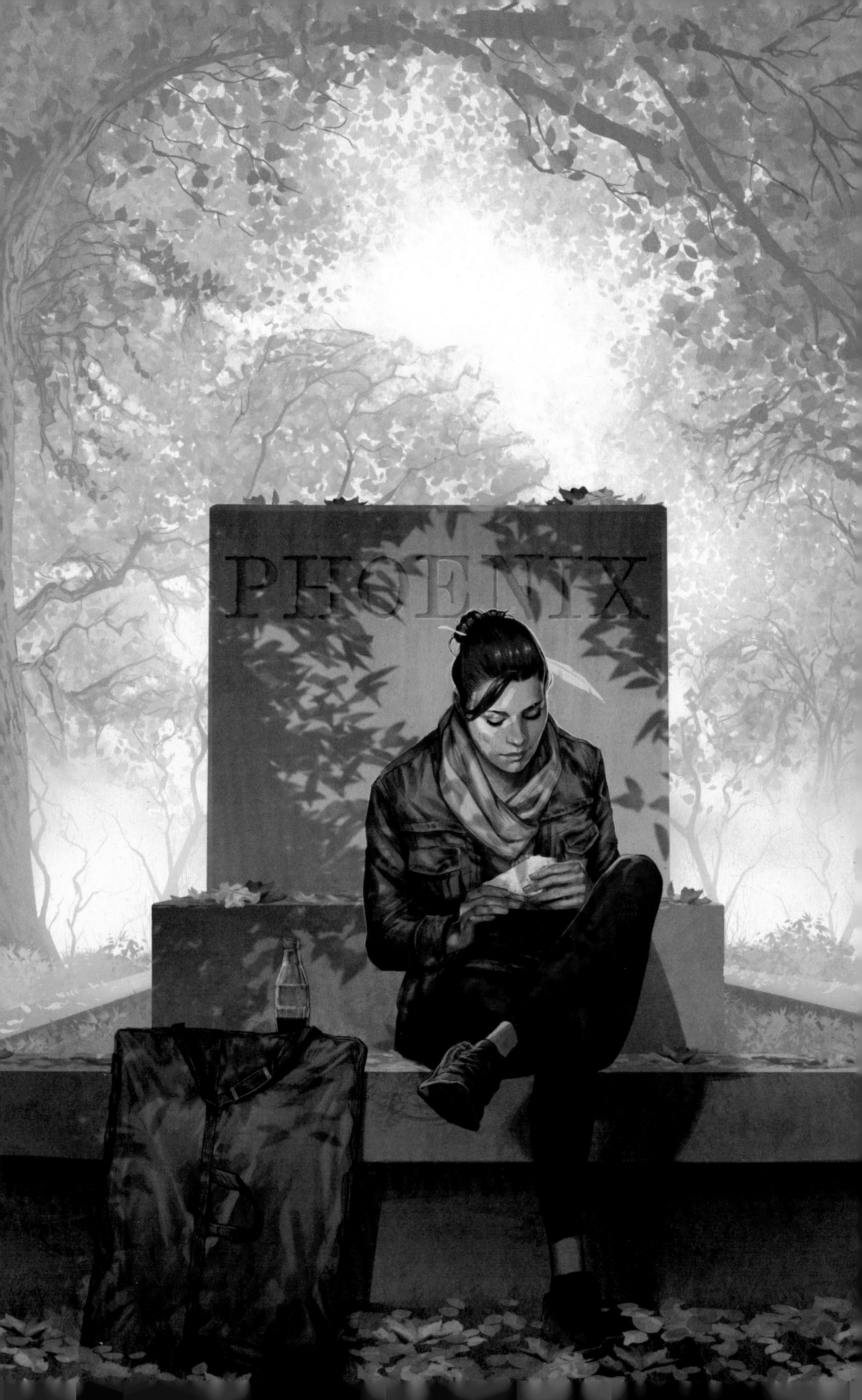
PHOENIX

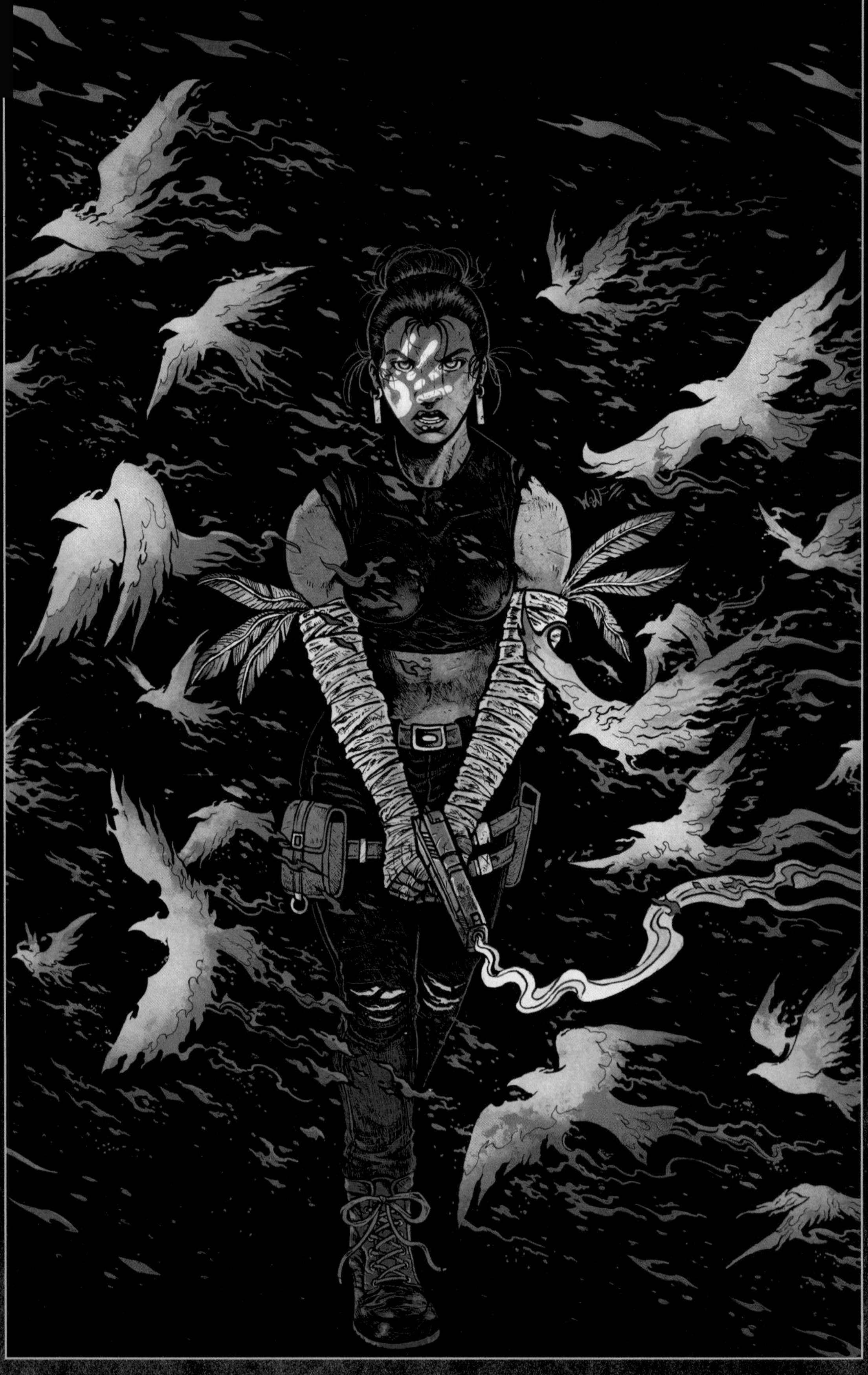

#5 HEADSHOT VARIANT BY MARIA WOLF & MIKE SPICER